Contents

PAGE 5

PAGE 51

PAGE 117

First published in 1998 by Motorbooks International Publishers & Wholesalers, 729 Prospect Avenue, PO Box 1, Osceola, WI 54020-0001

© IMS Corporation, 1998

Edited by: Anne T. McKenna
Designed by: Amy T. Huberty
Editorial Contributors: Jan Shaffer, Bruce Martin, Jonathan Ingram, Dave Argabright, Mark Robinson, and Donald Davidson
Printed in Hong Kong through World Print, Ltd.   ISBN 0-7603-0531-5

Thank You

The 81st running of the Indianapolis 500 carried as much drama and action as any of its predecessors, including the challenges of a race postponed, interrupted and restarted over a three-day period.

When the skies cooperated on Tuesday, Arie Luyendyk raced his teammate Scott Goodyear to the finish and beat him by the second closest margin in Indy history. It was Arie's second 500 win, and the first for team owner Fred Treadway. With his win, Arie became the leading money winner in Indianapolis history, and he established himself as a legend of the 500. It was the first Indianapolis 500 for the new cars and new engines of the Indy Racing League, and it was an exciting debut.

This edition of the Indy Review covers all of the excitement and drama of the month of May, as well as the highlights of the Indy Racing League's expanded season. Thank you for reading it, and thank you for your support of the Indianapolis 500 and of the Indy Racing League. I would also like to extend the sincere thanks of all the members of our family and of the employees of the Indianapolis Motor Speedway to all of the drivers, team members, car owners and sponsors who made this exciting year possible.

Sincerely,

Tony George

Tony George
President

Indianapolis Motor Speedway

A Magical Moment

By Bruce Martin

New engines, new cars, new teams, new drivers, and new venues were the key ingredients for the Indy Racing League as it entered 1997 in the Indy 200 at Walt Disney World. Although the Indy 200 was the third race of the 1996–97 season, it really marked the beginning of a new era for the IRL.

The IRL also featured new leadership, with Leo Mehl, the former director of worldwide racing for Goodyear, becoming the executive director of the series. Mehl has been called the most powerful man in racing, and his insight into the sport could help the IRL reach a new level as the series continues its development.

"It's really the beginning of the true IRL concept, which means new cars designed primarily for ovals and new stock block engines, which will return the sport to the era when mechanics worked on their own engines," Mehl said. "This is the launch of that concept.

"The engines sound great, the car handles well right out of the box, and they are pretty exciting cars. Somebody asked me what they sounded like. I said if a stock car is a bass and a Formula One car is a soprano and the old type Indy cars were tenors, these are a beautiful alto. They really do have a unique sound."

It took the creation of the Indy Racing League for a concerted effort to be made to address the speed issue. Although the series had to run with the formula of 1995 chassis with

Eddie Cheever, Jr. is congratulated by Mickey Mouse after his first career victory.

5

2.65-liter, purpose-built, turbocharged engines to launch the series in 1996, the IRL forged ahead with its desire to implement a new rules package for the 1997 season.

After months of planning and development, the first IRL car—a 1997 G Force chassis powered by an Oldsmobile Aurora engine—made its debut in a test at Phoenix International Raceway November 12–13. Arie Luyendyk, the 1990 Indianapolis 500 winner, and Treadway Racing participated in the history test which made the IRL's future a reality.

"I really can't describe it," said Tony George, president of the Indianapolis Motor Speedway and founder of the Indy Racing League. "It was a very exciting moment, something I've been looking forward to as has everybody else. To finally see it on the track and hear that engine fire and hear it pull out of the pits and work its way up to speed; it was really gratifying, just the way everybody worked to pull the thing together. The new sound is unique to open wheel racing."

That concept includes 4.0-liter, 32-valve, normally-aspirated, production-based V-8 engines—the Oldsmobile Aurora and Nissan Infiniti Indy. Those engines replaced the 2.65-liter, turbocharged, purpose-built race engines of the past. The engines are designed to cut the costs of racing, lower speeds, and make racing closer and more competitive.

The new chassis are built by G Force of England and Dallara of Italy. Riley & Scott of Indianapolis will enter as a chassis manufacturer after the 1997 Indianapolis 500. The new cars have less downforce, putting more control of the performance in the drivers' hands. With standardized parts, such as front and rear wings and spec gearboxes, the price of the chassis are $264,000, down from the $450,000 price of previous chassis.

Although the Indianapolis 500 is the cornerstone event of the Indy Racing League, the Indy 200 at Walt Disney World has already established itself as a marquee event in the sport of Indy car racing. And it has gained this plateau in just one year.

"That race has some sort of mystique to it already," said Arie Luyendyk, the 1990 winner of the Indianapolis 500. "That first Walt Disney race was one you really wanted to put your name into the record books as the winner. Unfortunately, we broke down."

Tony Stewart has started on the pole before in an IRL event, but when he won the pole for the Indy 200, it was the first time the driver from Rushville, Indiana, earned the position.

Stewart won the pole at Walt Disney World Speedway with a lap of 166.013 miles per hour around the 1.1-mile tri-oval located near the entrance to the Magic Kingdom.

The 25-year-old driver started on the pole at the Indianapolis 500 in 1996, but it came under tragic circumstances. His teammate Scott Brayton had won the pole in dramatic fashion but lost his life when he crashed in practice at the Indianapolis Motor Speedway on May 17.

Danny Ongais replaced Brayton in the starting lineup but started the race in the back of the field. That moved Stewart, who had qualified second, into the pole position for the biggest race in the world.

But at Disney World, it was the first time the young driver was the fastest in the field for an IRL event.

"I didn't earn the pole for the Indianapolis 500, I inherited it," Stewart said. "It's nice to finally earn my first pole."

Stewart started his G Force/Oldsmobile on the inside of the front row alongside Arie Luyendyk who ran a lap at 164.964 miles per hour.

"The biggest difference I've noticed about this year's cars is they seem to be a little more forgiving than last year's," Stewart said. "When these cars get a push, you can turn the steering wheel a little bit further to stay in the groove. Last year's cars, you were out of the groove, scrambling to stay off the wall. I think it will be good for the new drivers in the Indy Racing League to get into a car like this. They wanted to put the car back in the driver's hands and I think you will see that with the new cars."

Eddie Cheever has lost races the most bitter way possible. So when the two cars in front of him dropped out of the rain-shortened Indy 200 at Walt Disney World, Cheever had no regrets about inheriting the victory in the Indy Racing League event.

The race was stopped 50 laps short of the scheduled 200-lap distance. Cheever was running third on Lap 145 when Buzz Calkins' second-place car suffered an engine problem. At the same time, Stewart lost his lead when an oil line broke sending Stewart's car into a spin out of the third turn.

ABOVE
Eddie Cheever Jr. (center) celebrated his first victory with second and third place finishers Mike Groff (left) and Scott Goodyear (right).

LEFT
The track was filled with anticipation for the start of the second annual Indy 200 at Walt Disney World.

Stewart's car slid sideways down the frontstretch before coming to rest at the start/finish line.

That put Cheever, an owner/driver, in the lead under caution before a torrential downpour followed washing out the rest of the race.

It was Cheever's first victory in a major racing series in his career. Cheever previously won races in Formula Three and Formula Two and drove a Porsche to victory in a World Endurance Race in 1986. Before switching to Indy cars in 1990, Cheever competed in Formula One from 1980–89 but never won a race.

That changed in the Indy 200, thanks to some bizarre circumstances.

"I saw Tony Stewart coming out of the pits, and when I saw him out of Turn 2, there was smoke coming off his tires," Cheever recalled. "Then I saw him sideways and went on by."

Cheever has lost races in the same unfortunate manner. At Nazareth, Pennsylvania, in April 1995, Cheever was in the lead with less than two laps remaining when his car ran out of fuel. Emerson Fittipaldi went on to win the race. Now that he has won a race because of another driver's misfortunes, does Cheever feel redeemed?

"I stopped those additions a long time ago because you can drive yourself crazy thinking about that," Cheever said. "Winning that race was very important because A.J. Foyt [his team owner] hadn't won in so long. There are races I didn't win that I count as wins. I live in an imaginary world."

Cheever drove a G Force/Oldsmobile Aurora to victory at an average speed of 133.995 miles per hour. Mike Groff was second in a G Force/Nissan Infiniti Indy. Canada's Scott Goodyear was third followed by Scott Sharp and Buddy Lazier.

"I'm not only pleased, I'm ecstatic," George said of the performance of the new equipment.

"The cars held together very well and the field was able to put on a good race. We had some problems with oil lines breaking and other non-engine related parts, but the engines seemed to hold together, especially when the first part of the race went green for so long.

"We would have liked to have seen the race go the distance to see if the cars and engines would have made it to the end. But with the rain stopping it at Lap 150, I guess we'll never know what would have happened, will we?"

It was a script that has become all too familiar to Stewart.

Throughout his IRL career, Stewart has dominated races only to have an engine problem keep him from Victory Lane. It happened in the 1996 Indianapolis 500 when he set a record for most laps led by a rookie with 44 before an engine problem knocked him out of the race after 82 laps.

In the next race at Loudon, New Hampshire, he led 165 laps before an electronic trigger in the engine malfunctioned knocking Stewart out of the race 18 laps from a sure victory. Stewart had a two-lap lead on the field at the time.

So during the Indy 200 at Walt Disney World, Stewart appeared to have broken his jinx. He started on the pole and led two times for 131 of the 150 laps. But on the 145th lap, Stewart was out.

Cheever went on to win the race as Stewart's crew was left to ask, "Why us? Why again?"

"We saw some spikes in the oil pressure, but he had an oil leak," said Larry Curry, team manager at Team Menard. "I don't know what the hell it is going to take for us to ever get a break."

What made matters worse for Team Menard is a few laps after Stewart's oil line broke, the rest of the race was washed out by a vicious rain storm. If Stewart's car could have lasted four more laps, he would have been the winner.

"Standing here in the pouring rain is adding insult to injury," said team owner John Menard. "That is how it goes. It's racing and it is raining on everybody. We will get them in Phoenix."

Stewart tried to take the bitter turn of events in stride.

"We had the fastest race car all day; the crew has given me the fastest race car in testing and practice; it is unfortunate it happened," Stewart said. "There is nothing we can do about it. We led the whole race."

Stewart vowed he would not let his latest setback shake his confidence for the rest of the season.

"I am very confident," Stewart said. "I'm very confident from the standpoint I have one of the best teams in the IRL, if not the best team. The preparation they go through on these cars before the race and before practice and testing is unmatched right now. I have no doubts in my mind when I get in the race car everything is safe and nothing is going to fall off the car, and they have prepared the best car they can prepare for me."

The cars were louder than the Indy cars of the past, and nearly 15 miles an hour slower, but they were still race cars.

And the crowd of 54,000 fans at Walt Disney World Speedway appeared entertained by the race, despite the torrential downpour that washed out the final 50 laps.

So the IRL has weathered another storm and will continue to chart its own course.

In its brief history, the Indy Racing League has been met with one obstacle after another but has found a way to overcome adversity. The IRL has shown tremendous resiliency in its effort to take control of open wheel racing in the United States.

"I think you will see this series get better and better. There are some extremely talented drivers in this series," Cheever said. "I think this series will give a lot of drivers the opportunity."

Arie Luyendyk was bumped to the outside of row one after Tony Stewart captured the pole position with a lap of 166.013 miles per hour.

The Heat of the Desert

By Bruce Martin

D uring pole qualifications for the Phoenix 200, the focus was on the David versus Goliath story of drivers Jim Guthrie and Tony Stewart. David, played by Guthrie, nearly slew the Goliath operation of Team Menard by qualifying second to the pole-winning Stewart.

On Race Day, David's stone connected with its target as Guthrie beat Stewart in one of the greatest upsets in modern auto racing history.

Put Guthrie's victory in the same category as Greg Sacks beating Bill Elliott in the 1985 Firecracker 400, Derrike Cope beating Dale Earnhardt in the 1990 Daytona 500, and George Follmer—a sports car racer with a stock block engine—beating the biggest names in Indy car racing by two laps at Phoenix in 1969.

What made Guthrie's victory so special and so improbable was that his Blueprint Racing team had a very low budget, and Team Menard probably had the most money to spend of any team in the IRL.

In auto racing, it's been said, "Money buys speed," but at the end of Sunday's 200-mile race at Phoenix International Raceway, Menard's money didn't buy enough speed.

The new formula of Indy machines of 4.0-liter, normally-aspirated, production-based engines were designed so the engine shop mechanic had just as much chance at victory as high-dollar racing operations.

The Phoenix 200 at Phoenix International Raceway, in keeping with the IRL's philosophy, drew racers from varying grassroots backgrounds, including midget and sprint car racing.

11

For the first time in the history of the Indy Racing League, the top three drivers were all American oval track racers—Jim Guthrie (center) in 1st Place, Tony Stewart (right) in 2nd Place, and Davey Hamilton (left) in 3rd Place.

Guthrie and Blueprint Racing not only underlined that point, they added a huge exclamation point to that philosophy.

This victory was worth $170,100 to the team whose driver has taken out a second mortgage on his home and had his father cash in an IRA to pay the insurance on his loan to purchase his IRL car.

"I'm going to be able to pay off some bills, give my crew a little bonus and who knows what will happen after that—I might buy an engine if I have some left over," Guthrie said. "I wouldn't say I killed the giant. It's nice to win, but this is practice for Indy. That is the big one. I guess if I won Indy, then I would consider we slayed the giant."

Guthrie has had to overcome a tremendous amount of financial adversity, just to compete in the IRL with the new equipment.

"It was a real struggle just to get the funds for the car," Guthrie said. "Once we got the car, the next big hurdle was getting the necessary pieces. We begged, borrowed, and stole from everybody to get the car together. This is a big relief, obviously."

Guthrie's team had just one Oldsmobile Aurora engine for the entire race weekend for practice, qualifying, and the 200 miles of battle under the hot, Arizona sun. In fact, Guthrie had also used the same engine in the Indy 200 at Walt Disney World in Orlando in January and for a week of testing at Phoenix in the last week of February. The race-winning engine had run 860 miles without blowing up.

For the first time in the history of the Indy Racing League, the top three drivers were all American oval track racers—Guthrie, Stewart, and Davey Hamilton.

"If we have to get beat, it's neat to see the low buck guys get a win," said Stewart after finishing second to Guthrie by .854 seconds. "Nobody has worked harder than those guys. Talk about people keeping their fingers crossed with just one motor for the whole weekend. You have to applaud those guys; they did their homework. He was fast all day.

"Every time I looked in my mirror, I'd see that yellow car and say, `Man, I wish he would just go away.' He was like the black plague."

Guthrie took Stewart's advice, by taking the lead on the 154th lap and driving to as much as a half-lap lead over Stewart. Guthrie gambled on his fuel mileage by making just two pit stops. He drove the final 83 laps on the 1.0-mile mile oval without a pit stop.

"I pretty much put my head down and went to work," Guthrie said. "I knew that if I could run with Tony and not let him out of sight and not use up my car, we would be fine. That is what we planned to do and stayed right with him. The race played out in our favor."

While many teams in the IRL have Roush Racing, Katech, Rocketsports, and other established shops build their engines, Guthrie's was built by NAC out of Chicago. The company specializes in aviation applications.

"The yellow flags were a little frustrating because you want to go, but it was good for the engine to give it a break, give the tires a chance to cool off, and communicate with the team," Guthrie said.

There were numerous engine failures, several crashes, and some questionable strategy by both the drivers and USAC officials, but in the end, this race will be remembered for Guthrie's victory that proved the little guy can still knock off the giant.

"It hasn't sunk in yet," Guthrie said of the victory. "I haven't gotten any sponsorship calls yet, but I will accept any and all calls . . . collect."

Stewart won the pole for Sunday's race when he drove his Team Menard G Force/ Oldsmobile Aurora to a fast lap of 170.012 miles per hour Saturday. But Stewart was nearly knocked off the pole when Guthrie, who has literally had to beg, borrow and all but steal to make the IRL races, ran a lap at 169.484 miles per hour at the 1.0-mile desert oval. To put it in better perspective, Stewart's lap time was 21.175 seconds compared to Guthrie's 21.241.

IRL officials, Johnny Rutherford (top) and Al Unser Sr. (bottom) at the Phoenix 200.

What made Jim Guthrie's victory so special and so improbable was that his Blueprint Racing team was on a limited budget. He had one Aurora engine for practice, qualifying and race day.

(USAC) midget, sprint, and Silver Crown star has yet to win in the Indy car series.

"I'm primed for a win everywhere I go," Stewart said. "We want to win every time we go on the track. This pole and at Orlando, I got to earn the pole. The one at Indy, I inherited."

Stewart started on the pole at the Indianapolis 500 last May because his teammate, pole-winner Scott Brayton, lost his life in practice at the Indianapolis Motor Speedway on May 17.

"It really feels good to come out with a new car, a new motor package, and a fresh start this season," Stewart said. "The last time we went out after that practice session, we ran about 11 laps, and the car started coming around. We made some changes late that really made the car comfortable and drive well. I was really surprised we gained three-tenths of a second on that lap."

Although Stewart won the pole, it was obvious Guthrie was in the spotlight with his front-row qualification effort for a low budget team that is not sponsored.

"What this does is prove that Tony George's formula about the IRL is right on target," Guthrie said, referring to the IRL founder. "If you think about it, the IRL was founded to give oval racers, particularly American oval racers, a chance at the Indianapolis Motor Speedway and a chance in Indy cars. It has definitely worked for me. I think I'm living proof of his formula."

Stewart is fortunate that he is on a team that doesn't have to worry about spare parts or engines. Reportedly, team owner John Menard has a $1 million budget for wind tunnel testing

Guthrie's run put fear into the heart of Team Menard. It also impressed Stewart that the underfunded team could still compete with the elite of the IRL.

"You have to quit scaring me like that," Stewart told Guthrie after his qualification run.

It was Stewart's third pole in seven IRL races, but the former United States Auto Club

alone. Guthrie's team has hardly any testing budget, and the driver has had to borrow money from banks and personal friends to make the races this season.

"I would love to run every lap we possibly could just to fine-tune and try different things and different scenarios," Guthrie said. "At this point, we just don't have the budget or the engines to do that. We run a limited number of laps and try to get the job done quick."

Stewart's finish in the race equaled his career-best when he finished second in the first-ever IRL event, the 1996 Indy 200 at Walt Disney World.

"At least we finished a race, and that is something we haven't done in over a year now, since the first race at Orlando last year," Stewart said. "In all reality, the guys on the team feel good about it. I feel good about it. I think it is a boost to our team. We didn't have any major problems today. If we had to lose it, I couldn't have lost it to a nicer guy, I think."

Stewart's Oldsmobile Aurora engine ran flawlessly, but he was unable to catch Guthrie, who was also running an Aurora engine. Stewart attempted to win the race by pitting during the final caution for new tires while Guthrie stretched his fuel mileage to 83 laps on one tank after his last pit stop. Guthrie estimated there were 3 gallons of methanol left in his tank at the end of the race.

"It means we were lucky in the last 15 laps of the race with the caution coming out before," Guthrie said.

Stewart led the race five times for 85 laps but in the end could not catch Guthrie's car.

"I think the IRL should be happy," John Menard said. "We had some close racing at the end. That means this series is starting to come of age, and that is very gratifying to me.

"To have three American oval track racers finish 1-2-3 is really gratifying. We are very happy about that.

"There were a bunch of midget and sprint car drivers out there going for it. That is great. This is what the series was founded for; this is what it is all about, and we couldn't be happier."

At the end of the race, Stewart was able to close dramatically to the rear of Guthrie's car. But passing him was a different story.

"I needed some help," Stewart said. "Starting as far back as we did, with 10 laps to go we needed some help getting to the front. Catching the guy is one thing, but getting around him is another. Once we got there, the freshness of the tires went away, and the understeer came back to it, and there was no way we could get around him.

"When the guy qualified as well as he did on Saturday, we knew he was a threat. After the second

lap, we knew he was a threat. You knew the guy was good, and when he didn't fall off, you knew he would be a contender all day.

"You can't take anything away from Jim, because he just flat beat us today. The guy didn't luck into it; he didn't fall into it; he just flat beat us. We didn't like it, but he just flat beat us."

"We were a little lucky in the last 15 laps," Guthrie said. "Tony is still a great driver on an awesome team. I'm sure he will still set the standard at Indy. We still don't have the money behind us. We are still playing catch-up."

But at Phoenix, nobody could catch Guthrie, who helped illustrate that the playing field in the IRL is as level as any in racing. It's a victory for the grass-roots race drivers that a Jim Guthrie can win an Indy car race.

"Hope," Guthrie said. "I hope this gives them hope, to know that anybody can do it if they persevere."

Front row drivers Tony Stewart (#2) and Jim Guthrie (#27) paced the field to the start of the Phoenix 200.

Car	Gar	YR	Driver	Hometown	Car Name	C / E / T	Entrant	Chief Mechanic
1	A-1	1	Paul Durant	Manteca, CA	Conseco AJ Foyt Racing	G / A / G	AJ Foyt Enterprises	Craig Baranouski
1T	A-2	3	Scott Sharp	Danville, CA	Conseco AJ Foyt Racing	D / A / G	AJ Foyt Enterprises	Craig Baranouski
2	C-14	1	Tony Stewart	Indianapolis, IN	Glidden/Menards/Special	G / A / F	Team Menard, Inc.	Bill Martin
2T	C-15	1	Tony Stewart	Indianapolis, IN	Glidden/Menards/Special	G / A / F	Team Menard, Inc.	Bill Martin
3	C-12	1	Robbie Buhl	Grosse Pointe, MI	Quaker State/Special	G / A / F	Team Menard, Inc.	John O'Gara
3T	C-13	1	Robbie Buhl	Grosse Pointe, MI	Quaker State/Special	G / A / F	Team Menard, Inc.	John O'Gara
4	A-14	R	Kenny Brack	Karlstad, Sweden	Monsoon Galles Racing	G / A / G	Galles Racing International	Gary Armentrout
4T	A-15	R	Kenny Brack	Karlstad, Sweden	Monsoon Galles Racing	G / A / G	Galles Racing International	Gary Armentrout
5	B-10	12	Arie Luyendyk	Scottsdale, AZ	Wavephore/Sprint PCS/Miller Lite	G / A / F	Treadway Racing, LLC	Skip Faul
5T	B-11		TBA		Treadway Racing	G / A / F	Treadway Racing, LLC	TBA
6	B-12	6	Scott Goodyear	Toronto, ONT, Canada	Nortel/Sprint PCS/Quebecor Printing	G / A / F	Treadway Racing, LLC	Kevin Blanch
7	C-25	2	Eliseo Salazar	Santiago, Chile	Copec/Cristal/Scandia	D / A / G	Team Scandia	Dane Harte
7T	C-26	2	Eliseo Salazar	Santiago, Chile	Copec/Cristal/Scandia	D / A / G	Team Scandia	Dane Harte
8	C-23	R	Vincenzo Sospiri	Monte Carlo, Monaco	Old Navy Scandia Alta Xcel	D / A / G	Team Scandia	Luke Wethington
9	C-22	5	Johnny Unser	Sun Valley, ID	Lifetime TV-Cinergy	D / I / F	Hemelgarn Racing, Inc.	Mike Colliver
10	B-19	3	Mike Groff	Pasadena, CA	Jonathan Byrd's Cafeteria/Visionaire/Bryant	G / I / F	Jonathan Byrd-Cunningham Racing LLC	Mark Olson
10T	B-20	3	Mike Groff	Pasadena, CA	Jonathan Byrd's Cafeteria/Visionaire/Bryant	G / I / F	Jonathan Byrd-Cunningham Racing LLC	Mark Olson
11	A-6	R	Billy Boat	Phoenix, AZ	AJ Foyt Enterprises	D / A / G	AJ Foyt Enterprises	Craig Baranouski
12	B-31	1	Buzz Calkins	Denver, CO	Bradley Food Marts	G / A / G	Bradley Motorsports	Steve Ritenour
12T	B-32	1	Buzz Calkins	Denver, CO	Bradley Food Marts	G / A / G	Bradley Motorsports	Steve Ritenour
14	A-3	1	Davey Hamilton	Boise, ID	AJ Foyt PowerTeam Racing	G / A / G	AJ Foyt Enterprises	John King
14T	A-4	1	Davey Hamilton	Boise, ID	AJ Foyt PowerTeam Racing	D / A / G	AJ Foyt Enterprises	John King
15			TBA		Tempero-Giuffre Racing	G / I / G	Tempero-Giuffre	Tom Campbell
16	C-6	R	Sam Schmidt	Las Vegas, NV	HOPE Prepaid Fuel Card	D / A / F	Blueprint Racing, Inc.	Tommy O'Brien
17	B-21	R	Affonso Giaffone	Sao Paulo, Brazil	General Motors of Brazil Chitwood Dallara	D / A / G	Chitwood Motorsports, Inc.	Mark Stainbrook
17T	B-22	R	Affonso Giaffone	Sao Paulo, Brazil	General Motors of Brazil Chitwood Dallara	D / A / G	Chitwood Motorsports, Inc.	Mark Stainbrook
18	A-32	R	Tyce Carlson	Indianapolis, IN	Klipsch Tnemec Overhead Door Pyle V-Line Earl's	D / A / G	PDM Racing, Inc.	John Pearson
20	C-9		TBA		Menards/Special	G / A / F	Team Menard, Inc.	TBA
20T	C-10		TBA		Menards/Special	G / A / F	Team Menard, Inc.	TBA
21	A-17	12	Roberto Guerrero	San Juan Capistrano, CA	Pennzoil-Pagan Racing Dallara Infiniti	D / I / G	Pagan Racing	John Barnes
21T	A-18	12	Roberto Guerrero	San Juan Capistrano, CA	Pennzoil-Pagan Racing Dallara Infiniti	D / I / G	Pagan Racing	John Barnes
22	C-29	2	Marco Greco	Sao Paulo, Brazil	Side Play Int'l Scandia Alta Xcel	D / A / G	Team Scandia	Tim Wilson
27	B-7	1	Jim Guthrie	Albuquerque, NM	Jacuzzi/Blueprint Racing Dallara	D / A / F	Blueprint Racing, Inc.	Randy Ruyle

LEGEND: R- Indianapolis 500 Rookie   **CHASSIS:** D- Dallara; G- G Force
ENGINE: A- Oldsmobile Aurora V-8; I- Nissan Infiniti Indy V-8   **TIRES:** F- Firestone; G- Goodyear

Car	Gar	YR	Driver	Hometown	Car Name	C / E / T	Entrant	Chief Mechanic
28	A-30	1	Mark Dismore	Greenfield, IN	Kelley Automotive Group	D / A / G	PDM Racing, Inc.	Paul Murphy
30	A-23	R	Robbie Groff	Atlanta, GA	Alfa-Laval/Team Losi/McCormack Motorsports	G / A / G	McCormack Motorsports, Inc.	Phil McRobert
30T	A-24	R	Robbie Groff	Atlanta, GA	Alfa Laval/McCormack Motorsports	G / A / G	McCormack Motorsports, Inc.	Phil McRobert
33	C-23	1	Fermin Velez	Barcelona, Spain	Old Navy Scandia Alta Xcel	D / A / G	Team Scandia	Brad McCanless
34	C-27	2	Alessandro Zampedri	Monte Carlo, Monaco	Mi-Jack Scandia	D / A / G	Team Scandia	Jack Pegues
34T	C-28	2	Alessandro Zampedri	Monte Carlo, Monaco	Mi-Jack Scandia	D / A / G	Team Scandia	Jack Pegues
36	A-21	1	Scott Harrington	Indianapolis, IN	Johansson/Immke Motorsports	G / A / G	Johansson Motorsports, Inc.	Steve Melson
40	A-25	R	Dr. Jack Miller	Carmel, IN	AMS/Crest Racing	D / I / F	Arizona Motorsports	Joe Kennedy
40T	A-26	R	Dr. Jack Miller	Carmel, IN	AMS/Crest Racing	TBA/TBA/F	Arizona Motorsports	Joe Kennedy
41	A-7		TBA		AJ Foyt Enterprises	TBA / A / G	AJ Foyt Enterprises	TBA
42	A-1	3	Robby Gordon	Cornelius, NC	Coors Light	G / A / G	Team Sabco	Dave Forbes
42T	A-11	3	Robby Gordon	Cornelius, NC	Coors Light	G / A / G	Team Sabco	Dave Forbes
43	C-30		TBA		Scandia Royal Purple Alta Xcel	TBA/TBA/G	Team Scandia	TBA
44	A-28	R	Steve Kinser	Bloomington, IN	One Call/Menards/Quaker State	D / A / G	Sinden Racing	Owen Snyder
50	B-15	R	Billy Roe	Gilbert, AZ	Sega/Progressive Electronics/Eurointernational	D / A / F	Eurointernational Inc.	Billy Bignotti
50T	B-16	R	Billy Roe	Gilbert, AZ	Italy at Indy/Keco/U.J.T.Eurointernational Dallara	D / A / F	Eurointernational Inc.	Billy Bignotti
51	B-1	7	Eddie Cheever, Jr.	Tampa, FL	FirstPlus Team Cheever	G / A / G	FirstPlus Team Cheever	Mitch Davis
51T	B-2	7	Eddie Cheever, Jr.	Tampa, FL	FirstPlus Team Cheever	G / A / G	FirstPlus Team Cheever	Mitch Davis
52	B-3	R	Jeff Ward	San Juan Capistrano, CA	FirstPlus Team Cheever	G / A / G	FirstPlus Team Cheever	Norm Johnson
52T	B-4	R	Jeff Ward	San Juan Capistrano, CA	FirstPlus Team Cheever	G / A / G	FirstPlus Team Cheever	Norm Johnson
54	B-27	1	Dennis Vitolo	Ft. Lauderdale, FL	SmithKline Beecham/Kroeger/Beck Motorsports	D / I / F	Beck Motorsports	Greg Beck
54T	B-28	1	Dennis Vitolo	Ft. Lauderdale, FL	SmithKline Beecham/Kroeger/Beck Motorsports	D / I / F	Beck Motorsports	Greg Beck
72	B-8	R	Claude Bourbonnais	Ile Perrot, Quebec, Canada	Blueprint Racing	D / A / F	Blueprint Racing, Inc.	Dale Wise
77	B-25	2	Stephan Gregoire	Vittel, France	Chastain Motorsports	G / A / G	Chastain Motorsports	Darrell Soppe
81	B-24		TBA		Terhune-Barnets Racing	D / A / G	Terhune-Barnets Racing	TBA
90	C-22	5	Lyn St. James	Daytona Beach, FL	Lifetime-TV-Cinergy	D / I / F	LSJ Racing/Hemelgarn Racing, Inc.	TBA
91	C-20	4	Buddy Lazier	Vail, CO	Delta Faucet-Montana-Hemelgarn Racing	D / I / F	Hemelgarn Racing, Inc.	Dennis LaCava
91T	C-19	4	Buddy Lazier	Vail, CO	Delta Faucet-Montana-Hemelgarn Racing	D / I / F	Hemelgarn Racing, Inc.	Dennis LaCava
97	B-6	R	Greg Ray	Plano, TX	Tobacco Free Kids	D / A / F	Thomas Knapp Motorsport	TBA
98	B-29		TBA		Beck Motorsports	D / I / F	Beck Motorsports	TBA
98T	B-29		TBA		Beck Motorsports	D / I / F	Beck Motorsports	TBA

LEGEND: R- Indianapolis 500 Rookie   **CHASSIS:** D- Dallara; G- G Force

ENGINE: A- Oldsmobile Aurora V-8; I- Nissan Infiniti Indy V-8   **TIRES:** F- Firestone; G- Goodyear

The following chronology of the month of May 1997 was written by Jan Shaffer, Trackside Report editor for the Speedway. The information was compiled under the direction of Fred Nation, IMS vice president of corporate communications and public relations, and Mai Lindstrom, director of public relations.

Contributing to this chronicle as the month of May unfolded were Lisa Sommers, IMS public relations manager; Nancy Doan, IMS media operations manager; Kris Callfas, IMS statistics coordinator; Tony Troiano, IRL public relations manager; Speedway Press Room Manager Bill York and staffers Bob Clidinst, Roger Deppe, Josh Laycock, Tim Sullivan, Jack Marsh, and Bob Wilson; the Trackside Report team of assistants Debbie Atkerson, Becky Lenhard, and Vern Morseman and staffers Niki Allen, Ty Cheatum, Ruth Ann Cadou Hofmann, Tony Hofmann, Dave Lecklitner, Sylvia Moore, Suzanne Robinson, Debbie Shaffer, and Starre Szelag, and historian Bob Watson; and Speedway Manager of Racing Information Services Lee Driggers and computer resources assistants Joe Berkemeier, Richard Smith, and Sue Watson.

The 1997 Trackside Report was dedicated to the memory of Bob Laycock (1914–1995), the longtime Indianapolis Motor Speedway historian. Bob's unparalleled knowledge of the Indianapolis 500, his contributions to the information system, the Speedway family, the racing community, and the history of the sport are greatly missed.

Rain dampened the chance to fire up the engines on Opening Day, but the ceremonies went on, and the track was officially opened.

Opening Day in recent years seems to be synonymous with rain, and May 1997 was no different.

For the third time in four years, Opening Day was rained out. USAC Chief Steward Keith Ward called it quits at 2:30 P.M.

Opening ceremonies went on, however, under the Tower Terrace Suites as the rain fell, with the same traditions of the past.

Darwin Clark, general manager of the Oldsmobile division and vice president of General Motors, presented the keys of the 1997 Oldsmobile Aurora pace car to Tony George, president of the Speedway. George passed them along to USAC Chief Steward Keith Ward, signifying the opening of the track.

With USAC's Rookie Orientation Program opening the track for the second straight year, 11 cars were on hand many of the bidders for their first "500" starting berth.

Kenny Brack, Vincenzo Sospiri, Sam Schmidt, Affonso Giaffone, Tyce Carlson, Robbie Groff, Jack Miller, Billy Roe, Russ Wicks, Greg Ray, and Jeff Ward all attended a preliminary meeting the previous day.

Carlson and Ward would be required to take 20-lap, two-phase refresher tests because of previous appearances at Indy, although they had not yet made a "500" field.

A total of 22 drivers got driver physicals out of the way and were cleared to drive by Dr. Henry Bock, Speedway medical director. Those completing that mission were Brack, Buzz Calkins, Carlson, Eddie Cheever Jr., Giaffone, Scott Goodyear, Stephan Gregoire, Groff, Roberto Guerrero, Jim Guthrie, Steve Kinser, Miller, Ray, Roe, Eliseo Salazar, Schmidt, Sospiri, Tony Stewart, Fermin Velez, Ward, Wicks and Alessandro Zampedri.

Passing the physical was especially important to Zampedri. It was the first step on his comeback trail from leg injuries suffered in the 1996 Indianapolis 500. It had been a long road, and he was ready to go.

But fans and racers alike would have to wait for another day before engines would be fired and the battle would begin.

Date:	Saturday, May 3
Weather:	Rain, High 47°
Drivers On Track:	0
Cars On Track:	0
Total Laps:	0

QUOTE OF THE DAY
"Too bad I'm not a better basketball player."
Roberto Guerrero

While activities on Day 1 were limited to ceremonies, Day 2 started fast.

Dr. Jack Miller, The "Racing Dentist" from nearby Carmel, Indiana, who was fulfilling a dream, was first away after AMS/Crest crewman Terry Taylor fired the engine on the #40 AMS/Crest Racing entry at 11:30 A.M.

Robbie Groff and Vincenzo Sospiri were next, and Jeff Ward, Kenny Brack, and Sam Schmidt would follow to start work on drivers' tests.

Within 35 minutes, Miller was first to complete a phase of his driver's test. In just a little more than 2 hours, Sospiri completed four phases in the #8 Scandia Royal Purple Alta Xcel machine. By the end of the day, Brack had also finished his fourth phase in the #4 Monsoon Galles Racing entry.

For Sospiri, it was his first time on an oval. He had the most laps (78) of the day and the fastest lap at 211.964 miles per hour. He and Brack had talked extensively during the Opening Day rain since Brack had run—and led—at Phoenix and tested at Texas.

Sospiri had started the season in the Formula One ranks before shifting his racing adventure to the United States.

"Little scary, really, but I like it," Sospiri said. "Luckily, we had the fastest lap, and I'm happy about that. There's a lot more speed to catch out there. Since I was 14 1/2 and I started to watch Formula One, I've dreamed of being world champion in Formula One and winning an Indy 500."

Brack also was embarking on a new element of his racing career. "It's my first day on the track," he said. "The surface was fantastic—huge long straights, wide, quick corners. My only problem was with my helmet buffeting, but they [the Galles crew] fixed that with the windscreen.

"I've always known about Indianapolis, I guess, since I was 7 or 10 years old," he added. "I never knew how big it was until I got here."

Robbie Buhl, Mark Dismore, and Marco Greco passed driver physicals, boosting the list to 25.

At a news conference, Team Menard announced it was switching from Firestone to Goodyear tires and that Tony Stewart would re-main with the team through the 1996–97 season and continue in 1998.

"We were waiting for Tony's NASCAR negotiations to finalize his Indy Racing League deal," said

team owner John Menard. "Tony has the best of both worlds."

"In any scheduling conflicts, the IRL will take top priority over NASCAR," said Stewart. "Any scheduling conflicts we'll work out. Any additional events that I will run will need the permission of both John and Joe Gibbs [NASCAR owner]. To be a driver in heavy demand is flattering. It's nice to know your services are wanted by quality teams and owners."

Meanwhile, 21 drivers joined Special Olympians for a basketball shootout and barbecue, the 17th annual "Save Arnold" gathering founded by Speedway Chairman Mari Hulman George. The fundraiser, the largest annually for Special Olympics of Indiana, has raised $1,388,000 over its duration.

And it also gives a special meaning to drivers and Special Olympians alike at the beginning of the month of May.

"I'm pleased to participate in the Special Olympics event every year," said Scott Goodyear. "I also support Special Olympics here and in Toronto. They (the athletes) have the same dreams and aspirations and goals as we do. It's an event I really enjoy."

"It's a nice cause that Mari does for the kids, and it's fun for all," said Roberto Guerrero. "Too bad I'm not a better basketball player."

The 17th Annual "Save Arnold" Barbecue for Special Olympics of Indiana has raised $1,388,033 in its history. IMS Chairperson of the Board, Mari Hulman George presented the check.

Date:	Sunday, May 4
Weather:	Windy, High 63°
Drivers On Track:	6
Cars On Track:	6
Total Laps:	256

Top Five Drivers of the Day

Car	Driver	Speed
8	Vincenzo Sospiri	211.964
51T	Jeff Ward	205.780
4	Kenny Brack	204.997
40	Dr. Jack Miller	194.246
30	Robbie Groff	191.759

Trackside workers took advantage of the rain delay to grab a bite to eat.

A pit crew member checks the tire pressure before mounting the tire.

An early track closing, again because of rain, led USAC Chief Steward Keith Ward to schedule continued drivers' tests from 9–11 A.M. each day "as necessary."

Eighty laps were turned by four drivers in the abbreviated activity, and rookie Sam Schmidt completed the first two phases of his driver's test in the #16 Blueprint Racing entry before running over a piece of debris on the front straightaway.

"I've done three laps in the third stage at 197 miles an hour," Schmidt said. "That's where I'm at. Things are going fine except for the suspicious weather. This is an exciting experience."

Meanwhile, USAC technical director Mike Devin said that an oil-absorbent device had been mandated to the undertrays of the new Indy Racing League machines to contain oil from leaks.

"It's not a new technology, but it's the first time it's been adapted to these cars," Devin said. "It's a material spawned out of the environmental world. It's a real, real thirsty chemical fabric."

The number of cars in Gasoline Alley swelled to 33.

Off the track, the 200,000 square-foot area next to the Speedway's Hall of Fame Museum had almost completely been transformed into Indy FanFest, the free, family-oriented racing theme park, in preparation for opening four days later.

Robby Gordon, Mike Groff, Davey Hamilton, Scott Sharp, Lyn St. James, and Johnny Unser passed their physicals. For St. James, it was also a first step toward a comeback from the wrist injury she suffered late in the 1996 Indianapolis 500.

Even though action was scarce, at least one track record was believed to be set.

When Kenny Brack and the #4 Monsoon Galles Racing entry stopped in the north short chute, Brack needed a tow. As the tow truck approached pit road, Brack continued holding the tow line. After holding it as the truck towed him past the Galles pit, Brack was forced to take another complete lap around the 2 1/2-mile oval.

It was roughly a 3 1/2-mile tow-in.

"I was sort of wondering what the guy was doing," Brack said with a laugh. "Normally, they tow you to the pit [in Europe]. I didn't realize I was supposed to let go. No one told me. A record? That's good to know, but I want to set other records."

Date:	Monday, May 5
Weather:	Rain, High Winds, High 66°
Drivers On Track:	4
Cars On Track:	4
Total Laps:	80

Top Drivers of the Day		
Car	Driver	Speed
4	Kenny Brack	205.597
16	Sam Schmidt	198.325
97	Greg Ray	185.494

As veterans took the track for the first time, Arie Luyendyk showed everyone the short way around the 2 1/2-mile Speedway oval.

Luyendyk hadn't tested in the weeks leading up to the month of May. But as a former winner, he knew his way around and put together a lap at 218.707 miles per hour in the #5 Treadway Racing WavePhore Miller Lite entry.

That was more than 3 miles an hour faster than Robby Gordon, the second driver on the daily speed chart who reached 215.569 in the #42 Coors Light machine.

"I think when you have a good team and a good engineer like Tim Wardrop—I get around this place pretty good," Luyendyk said. "I don't think we're that far behind. I'm glad we didn't test for 20 days. It's too cold.

"The corners have less grip than the cars [had] last year," he went on. "They move around a little more, and the wind affects them more. The straightaways are much slower. We're going top speed for this type of car."

For Gordon, who did extensive pre-May testing, the day was a new start.

"Today I didn't run a flat-out lap," he said. "I think this car might be a little easier to save than the old ones. We're trying to run a lot less downforce because we don't have the horsepower. When we get the balance right, we'll be back up to 218. I have no doubt."

Twenty-five cars took the track, running a total of 929 laps. USAC's Rookie Orientation Program reached several milestones, with five drivers completing the final observation phase of their tests and the total lap count for the 17-year history of ROP reaching 20,017.

Kenny Bräck was the first to pass, followed by Robbie Groff, Greg Ray, Vincenzo Sospiri, and Affonso Giaffone.

It was also a day when another "rookie" entered the picture. Fourteen-time World of Outlaws champion Steve Kinser got the nod in a Dallara fielded by Sinden Racing Services. Kinser passed the driver's test at the Speedway in 1981 but hadn't made a "500" field.

"I've lived in Indiana my whole life and have never seen an Indianapolis 500," Kinser said. "I got started racing, and every [Race Day for the] Indianapolis 500, I'm racing some place else. Growing up, I told everybody at school that I was going to race at the Indianapolis 500 some day.

"I think with all the success we had with the sprint car I got to making a fairly good living and

QUOTE OF THE DAY
"I have no doubt."
Robby Gordon

Davey Hamilton, Scott Sharp, and IRL official, Brian Barnhart watched some of the veterans who took the track for the first time today.

those dreams, I lost them a little bit."

Jeff Ward became the first casualty of the Speedway walls, spinning and tagging the concrete in Turn 3.

"[I'm] fine," Ward said. "I just pulled out, and the oil line blew. Nothing I could do."

Off the track, doors to the Hall of Fame Library in the Speedway's museum building opened for the first time, honoring the donation of 500 books and boxes of clippings and other literature by Charles Saylor of Columbus, Ohio.

Earlier, Luyendyk and five other drivers passed their physicals, bringing the total to 37. The others were John Andretti, Paul Durant, Buddy Lazier, Danny Ongais, and John Paul Jr.

But the race for speed had started, with drivers and teams searching for the end of the envelope that would lead to the pole position.

Date:	Tuesday, May 6	
Weather:	Cloudy, High 64°	
Drivers On Track:	24	
Cars On Track:	25	
Total Laps:	929	

Top Ten Drivers of the Day

Car	Driver	Speed
5	Arie Luyendyk	218.707
42	Robby Gordon	215.569
2	Tony Stewart	214.337
91	Buddy Lazier	214.128
1	Scott Sharp	214.041
3	Robbie Buhl	213.843
18	John Paul Jr.	212.555
12	Buzz Calkins	212.339
6	Scott Goodyear	211.282
33	Fermin Velez	210.280

IMS Staff Photographer Walt Kuhn was on hand to catch that perfect shot.

Fire and safety crews cleaned up after Scott Sharp's accident.

Arie Luyendyk served notice that his Day 4 speed wasn't a fluke by turning the first 220-mile-per-hour lap at the Speedway with the Indy Racing League's new car-engine combination.

Although the 1990 winner was clearly "best of show," others made their moves behind his standard of 220.297 miles per hour in the #5 Treadway Racing WavePhore Miller Lite machine.

Scott Sharp was next at 217.402 in the #1 Conseco AJ Foyt Racing entry, Jim Guthrie reached 216.076 in the #27 Jacuzzi/Blueprint Racing Dallara, and Robby Gordon hit 215.993 in the #42 Coors Light car.

"It's always fun to be fast and the one that people are targeting," Luyendyk said. "Last year in Las Vegas, we didn't test in the summer because I said it was too hot to test, and we were fast right out of the box."

For Sharp, however, the fast lap was close to his last of the day. Just 3 minutes after turning it, Sharp hit the wall in Turn 4, the car sustaining heavy left-side damage. Sharp was examined and released from Hanna Medical Center with a bruised right knee and was cleared to drive.

"I felt it tighten up, a loud noise, and it turned in," said Sharp. "When it turned in, the car turned right around. We'll pick up where we left off. We're getting there and did make progress today."

Guthrie felt the focus was clearly on Luyendyk to set the pace.

"We have the speed, and there's a lot more left in the car . . . and myself," he said. "I predict Luyendyk will probably reach 220–222 come pole weekend. I only have a few laps here where he's the expert, and you can tell he's got the laps in."

Off the track, Buddy Lazier was presented a personalized replica of the Borg-Warner Trophy in the Speedway's Hall of Fame Museum for his 1996 victory.

"It's going to be a fascinating month with the new cars and engines," Lazier said. "You can see the enthusiasm with all the drivers and everybody in the pits."

Ron Hemelgarn, the owner of the car that Lazier drove to victory, recalled his longtime interest in the "500"—and the Borg-Warner Trophy.

"In 1964, when I came to this race, I just wanted to get close to it [the trophy]," he said. "When I came here as a sponsor in 1978, I wanted to touch it. Last year, I actually got to touch it without the yellow shirts yelling at me."

Racin Gardner, Joe Gosek, Andy Michner, and Dennis Vitolo passed driver physicals, bringing the total to 41. The cast was mounting for shots at a starting berth.

Date:	Wednesday, May 7	
Weather:	Light Rain, High 67°	
Drivers On Track:	19	
Cars On Track:	20	
Total Laps:	611	

Top Ten Drivers of the Day

Car	Driver	Speed
5	Arie Luyendyk	220.297
1	Scott Sharp	217.402
27	Jim Guthrie	216.076
42	Robby Gordon	215.993
2	Tony Stewart	215.750
33	Fermin Velez	214.174
6	Scott Goodyear	214.123
12	Buzz Calkins	213.792
4	Kenny Brack	212.821
7	Eliseo Salazar	212.465

Arie Luyendyk continued to reign atop the speed chart despite a near brush with disaster, Team Menard went back to Firestone tires, and Steve Kinser turned his first lap at the Speedway since 1981 in an abbreviated session.

Rain and wet conditions delayed the track opening until 3:01 P.M. Luyendyk was out with the early runners and put up the top number at 217.318 miles per hour in the #5 Treadway Racing WavePhore Miller Lite entry.

But at 3:17 P.M., the Flying Dutchman got loose in the south short chute, spun twice, and just barely hit the outside wall in Turn 2.

"It was probably cold tires, or the wind could've played a factor," Luyendyk said. "There could've been a little spot of moisture on the track also, but they'll probably check that. When it came around, I slammed on the brakes hard, and when it came down into the grass, that's probably where it picked up speed. But all I'm missing is a nose cone. I should be back out in a few minutes."

Later, after being assured of the top practice speed for the third consecutive day, there was little left to say.

"Like I said, same as yesterday, we tried to do what we were doing before," Luyendyk said. "To tell you the truth, yesterday's setup was better."

Meanwhile, Team Menard returned to the Firestone camp after four days on Goodyears. Tony Stewart was second fastest of the day at 215.822 in the Glidden/Menards/Special.

"We weren't able to get the cars to the confidence level we'd like to have for our drivers," said Larry Curry, the team's director of racing.

For the record, Kinser first took out the #44 One Call/Menards/Quaker State entry at 3:35 P.M. and passed the first phase of his driver's test at 5:03 P.M.

Later, Alessandro Zampedri brought out the caution when the #34 Mi-Jack Scandia Royal Purple entry caught fire, and he stopped on the front straightaway just past the scoring pylon. Zampedri was frustrated.

"It just blew out of [Turn] 4," he said. "All day we've been waiting for this rain to stop, and then this happens. We've been struggling. I think I only have a total of 16 laps and not even up to speed. I was lucky it blew coming out of the turn and not in the entrance."

Off the track, Blueprint Racing announced sponsorship from High Opportunity Petroleum Enterprises for Sam Schmidt and Cruisin' America for Jim Guthrie.

QUOTE OF THE DAY
"... right where I'd hoped we would be ..."
Tony George

And Speedway President Tony George and Leo Mehl, Speedway vice president and executive director of the Indy Racing League, met with the media for a "state-of-the-sport" session.

"We really want anybody that wants to compete in the Indy Racing League or the Indianapolis 500 to feel that they have an opportunity to do that," George said. "I think we're right where I thought we would be or right where I'd hoped we would be. We're very fortunate to have him [Mehl] on board and so, based on where we started, maybe we're a little bit ahead of where we'd like to be."

"I figured it out when I was quietly retired one day," Mehl said. "There's nearly a billion dollars in investment in the last several years and planned for the future ... a billion dollars in investment in racing tracks in the United States, and every penny of it has been in ovals. So it's my opinion that there is a place in that billion-dollar investment for a very closely competitive, reasonably-priced, open-wheel series that can concentrate just on that."

One day of practice remained before the pole would be decided.

Date:	Thursday, May 8
Weather:	Rain, High 70°
Drivers On Track:	21
Cars On Track:	22
Total Laps:	489

Top Ten Drivers of the Day

Car	Driver	Speed
5	Arie Luyendyk	217.318
2T	Tony Stewart	215.822
3T	Robbie Buhl	215.708
90	Lyn St. James	212.565
42	Robby Gordon	212.229
18	John Paul Jr.	211.640
12	Buzz Calkins	211.248
21T	Roberto Guerrero	210.664
6	Scott Goodyear	209.966
16	Sam Schmidt	209.864

The official track tow truck moved Scott Sharp's car off the track. Sharp hit the Turn 4 wall and was transported to Methodist Hospital with a concussion.

QUOTE OF THE DAY
"That still doesn't mean anything."
—Arie Luyendyk.

Four rookies finished drivers' tests, Arie Luyendyk was fastest again, accidents diminished the hopes of a pair of veterans, and a special award was announced while 31 cars ran 1,195 laps on the Speedway as the race for pole speed wound down.

Dr. Jack Miller, Steve Kinser, and Sam Schmidt finished off rookie tests, the final observation phase, in front of veterans Johnny Rutherford, Paul Durant, Tyce Carlson, and Lyn St. James. And Jeff Ward finished his 20-lap refresher.

"Now we need to get out, there and run for speed and hopefully qualify tomorrow," said Miller.

"Now we want to get this thing smoothed out and get some speed," echoed Kinser.

"Today, we went out and we were running 203, 204, and the car didn't feel real comfortable," Schmidt said. "We put wickers on both front and rear wings, and the car ran like a dream."

Luyendyk took the #5 Treadway Racing WavePhore Miller Lite machine to its customary spot at the top of the speed chart with a lap at 218.325. Tony Stewart was second fastest in the #2 Glidden/Menards/Special at 217.355.

"We've been the fastest here for four days in a row," Luyendyk said. "That still doesn't mean anything on Pole Day."

John Paul Jr. and Scott Sharp, a pair of veterans with high hopes, went to the sidelines in separate incidents.

At 12:42 P.M., Paul Jr. spun and hit the outside wall in Turn 4 in the #18 Klipsch Tnemec Overhead Door Pyle V-Line Earl's entry. Paul was admitted to Methodist Hospital with a broken lower right leg and a broken left heel. The car was heavily damaged.

At 5:17 P.M., Sharp also spun and hit the Turn 4 wall in the #1 Conseco AJ Foyt Racing entry.

Sharp was transported to Methodist Hospital with signs of a concussion, and the car sustained extensive right-side damage. The accident closed the track for the day.

Earlier, Stephan Gregoire spun in the Turn 2 warmup lane and barely touched the inside guard rail in the #77 Chastain Motorsports entry, the car sustaining minor nose-cone damage.

Off the track, the creation of the Scott Brayton Driver's Trophy was announced to honor a past or present entrant that best exemplifies the character and racing spirit of the late two-time "500" pole winner.

The announcement of the annual trophy and $25,000 award was made by Andrew Evans, the chairman of the award's presenting sponsor, Royal Purple Motor Oil. The selection was to be made by Evans, Speedway President Tony George, and Lee Brayton, Scott's father.

"My wife [Jean] and I think that this is just a great tribute," said Brayton. "I think that the trophy itself would be a great honor to receive and that the financial award is a great incentive for somebody to program their life after my son."

Pole Day awaited.

Date:	Friday, May 9
Weather:	High Winds, High 51°
Drivers On Track:	28
Cars On Track:	31
Total Laps:	1,195

Top Ten Drivers of the Day

Car	Driver	Speed
5	Arie Luyendyk	218.325
2	Tony Stewart	217.355
3	Robbie Buhl	216.899
14	Davey Hamilton	215.853
33	Fermin Velez	215.760
42	Robby Gordon	215.326
17	Affonso Giaffone	215.162
7	Eliseo Salazar	214.690
1T	Scott Sharp	214.148
8	Vincenzo Sospiri	213.498

It was time.

The labors of an entire year came down to this day, when the fastest of the fast would be determined.

With the new Indy Racing League cars and engines, a different degree of wonder spread through Gasoline Alley. The competition was closer, the development uncertain. Who showed their cards? Who didn't?

One move had been made. The Hemelgarn team acquired an Aurora engine for defending "500" winner Buddy Lazier, and car owner Ron Hemelgarn announced that Lyn St. James and Johnny Unser would use Infiniti power.

"It was a hard decision," Hemelgarn said. "It is a very mixed decision, but it is not a wrong decision. I promised Nissan that I would be running two cars at Indy. Lyn will be [in] one, and Johnny Unser will be [in] one. We have to thank Stan Wattles for the Aurora engine. Stan [has] a new team, but he won't be starting up until a little later."

When qualifying opened, Mike Groff was first away and registered a four-lap run of 208.537 miles per hour with the first G Force and first Infiniti ever to qualify at Indianapolis, the #10 Jonathan Byrd's Cafeteria/VisionAire/Bryant entry. His fourth lap of 208.943 was the 2,500th qualifying lap at more than 200 miles per hour ever recorded at Indianapolis. It had been 20 years since Tom Sneva had recorded the first in excess of 200 at 200.401 in 1977.

"We had a little trouble with the car bottoming out, but we ran for all it's worth," Groff said. "We ran comparable to what we ran in practice, and we were qualifying with an engine that had 400 miles on it. To us, that's a good sign for engine reliability."

Groff made history.

It was the first completion of a qualification run with a normally aspirated engine since Sammy Swindell qualified a March/Pontiac at 201.840 in 1987 and wound up first alternate for the race.

Groff, with his locked-in status, was also the first driver to make the field with normally-aspirated power since Kevin Cogan qualified with a Pontiac engine in 1984.

Groff also broke the qualifying record for normally-aspirated engines of 204.224 miles per hour set by Steve Chassey in 1985.

When Groff qualified, the track temperature was 91 degrees, according to Firestone tire engineers. Heat and weather would play an important part in the way the day played out.

Next was Jeff Ward, who put together a solid

QUOTE OF THE DAY
"I'm not the world's biggest optimist . . . "
Arie Luyendyk

run at 214.517 in the #52 FirstPlus Team Cheever car, the second machine in the Eddie Cheever stable. The first Aurora engine had qualified.

"Eddie's great every day," Ward said. "He sits me down and talks with me. It feels great. I was here in '95 and was close. It was very emotional. [Danny] Sullivan came over and gave me a hug."

Dr. Jack Miller then put the #40 AMS/Crest Racing entry in the field at 209.250, the first Dallara to make the field at Indy.

"I can probably go quicker than that," Miller said. "On my third lap, I turned a little too soon and had to let up on the throttle, but I still ran 209."

Rookie Affonso Giaffone was next and put the #17 General Motors of Brazil Chitwood Dallara in the field at 212.974.

"The starting position doesn't really matter because it's a long, long race," Giaffone said. "Now that we've qualified, we're just looking for consistency. We'll cool down. You don't want to rush here."

After Giaffone's run, the first waveoff occurred, as Robbie Buhl went to the pits after three laps in the 214–215 bracket. Clearly, Team Menard backed off for a shot at the pole.

Eliseo Salazar did the same after hitting a bird in the third turn.

Lyn St. James was next and put the #90 Lifetime TV-Cinergy machine in the show at 210.145. She, too, considered a waveoff.

Arie Luyendyk in the #5 WavePhore/Sprint PCS/Miller Lite entry was the one to beat on Pole Day.

Arie Luyendyk won the $100,000 PPG Pole Award with a qualifying speed of 218.263 miles per hour.

"The track has changed considerably [since the repaving]," she said. "[Turns] 3 and 4 have gotten better and [Turns] 1 and 2 have gotten worse. This is a real weird game. I don't know how to play those strategy games. I looked for the yellow; if we were going as bad as I thought we might be, it occurred to me [that the run would be waved off].

"God didn't teach me to walk on water like Scott Pruett, and he didn't give me the wherewithal of Tony Stewart, but he did teach me to paddle real hard."

After Roberto Guerrero and Robbie Groff waved off, the latter because of brushing the wall in the south short chute, the qualifying line broke. The track had changed. For most, the pole would remain a waiting game.

For more than 3 hours, no one pushed a car into line. It was a war of nerves among teams vying for the pole. Finally, the Treadway team, with a determined Arie Luyendyk, played leader.

Luyendyk rolled away in the #5 WavePhore/Sprint PCS/Miller Lite entry at 3:21 P.M., with a long line of potential qualifiers frantically jockeying for spots in line in his wake.

He recorded a steady, fast run of 218.263 miles per hour, giving those behind him an impressive mark as a headliner.

"The call was up to me, coming out of Turn 4, whether we wanted to keep the run, and I had my mind made up that if it was over 218, we'd take it," Luyendyk said. "I'm not the world's biggest optimist because the Menard guys have run quick. You

can only run so many laps around this place before you get it right, and I think we're pretty close."

Kenny Brack followed and put the #4 Monsoon Galles Racing entry in the field at 211.221.

"It could be better, but for the time we've had I'm pretty comfortable," Brack said. "The first stage is completed."

Jim Guthrie, fresh off a win in the Phoenix 200, put the #27 Jacuzzi/Blueprint Racing Dallara in the field at 215.207.

"In Turn 4 yesterday, the motor just quit," Guthrie said. "The guys flew up to Chicago to work on the motor. Then today, USAC noticed we had some fluid leaking. We fixed that and decided to go ahead and put it in the show."

Davey Hamilton was next and put the #14 AJ Foyt Power team Racing machine in the field at 214.484.

"In the third lap, we picked up a little push, came a little close to the wall," said Hamilton. "It caught me off guard. I like this year's cars better than last year's cars. You've really got to drive them."

After Fermin Velez waved off with engine trouble after one lap, Scott Goodyear posted the day's second fastest four-lap average at 215.811 in the #6 Nortel/Sprint PCS/Quebecor Printing car.

"I'm pretty happy to get through the day without motor problems," Goodyear said. "I thought we'd be quite good but it was quite slow. We borrowed information from Arie's setup yesterday. Every time we went out, something happened. . . electrical, weird things. We couldn't get quality time until yesterday."

Rookie Vincenzo Sospiri was next. He surprised railbirds with the day's second fastest run, 216.822 in the #8 Scandia Royal Purple Alta Xcel entry.

"[The] feeling is like [a] bullet in a gun," Sospiri said. "You go so close to the wall and you go so fast, you are like a bullet. Jacques Villeneuve and I talked, and he said yes to do IRL and Indy 500 because it is the best in the world. I think being here longer is better for me. I have [had] one basic week testing before I qualified."

Sospiri's run raised hopes for those in line. If a rookie could post such an impressive run, track conditions could be right for others. Tony Stewart was next up and was considered the top challenger for Luyendyk.

Stewart's run in the #2 Glidden/Menards/ Special was 218.021, just short of Luyendyk's speed. Over four laps, the difference in time was just .183 of a second. He had missed but still looked like a good candidate for the front row.

Mike Groff made history in the #10 Jonathan Byrd's Cafeteria/ Visionaire/ Bryant entry. His fourth lap of 208.943 was the 2,500th qualifying lap at more than 200 miles per hour recorded at Indianapolis.

"If you would have given me two more days, I guarantee we would have been on the pole," said Stewart. "The car actually stuck too good to the track and was not free enough. That actually cost us the pole, by sticking too good."

After Alessandro Zampedri waved off, Eliseo Salazar took a second attempt and became the month's 13th qualifier at 214.320 in the #7 Copec/Cristal/Scandia Dallara.

"We ran 300 miles in total, nowhere near enough to be on the front row," Salazar said. "The package is obviously new, and we will make improvements. In three or four years, they will be back up to 230 again, and they will need to slow up the cars again."

Robbie Buhl was next and waved off after a lap at 217.082. Clearly, the Menard team wanted to take one final shot at Luyendyk for the pole.

After Buzz Calkins waved off after three laps in the 208–209 bracket, Stephan Gregoire, in the #77 Chastain Motorsports entry, qualified at 213.126.

"I wanted to be in the first three rows," Gregoire said. "At the end of yesterday, we made some changes in spring settings. We went the wrong way. It had a big push, especially in Turns 1 and 2 because of the wind. The car was a bit tweaky."

Just 48 minutes were left in Pole Day qualifying when Eddie Cheever Jr. rolled away in the #51 FirstPlus Team Cheever machine and chalked up a run of 214.073.

"The last two laps, I was sliding all he way around the track," Cheever said. "Unfortunately, we didn't run in the beginning of the week, and that hurt us."

After Cheever, Buddy Lazier warmed up but did not take the green. Sam Schmidt went out next and spun in the warmup lane in the south short chute and hit the inside guard rail.

Schmidt's spin left track activity dormant until 5:30 P.M. when Robby Gordon took the #42 Coors Light entry out and recorded a run of 213.211. It was a disappointment because Gordon had tested extensively and was looking for a front-row spot.

"We've got a lot of work to do," Gordon said. "There are gonna be a lot of late nights. We've got two weeks to get it all sorted out."

Alessandro Zampedri was next, and he made a comeback run of 209.094 in the #34 Mi-Jack Scandia Royal Purple entry.

"Unfortunately, I didn't have many chances to test the new car," Zampedri said. "I got to test in April. We lost two engines. We ran here this week,

and we had some troubles, and then my gearbox got stuck this morning. They fixed it during practice."

Calkins tried again. On his second attempt, he soldiered to a four-lap average of 209.564 in the #12 Bradley Food Marts G Force.

"We had no horsepower and didn't get any practice," said the 1996 Indy Racing League co-champ. "But we got in the field. This is anyone's race. We've had pretty good luck with engines until today, so I think we'll be all right."

With 10 minutes left, Robbie Buhl went out, determined to get a third straight pole for Team Menard. However, he fell short with a run of 216.102 in the #3 Quaker State Special. He had taken two earlier shots.

"Actually, I was waiting for them to pull me [on the first qualifying attempt]," Buhl said. "I was waiting for a waveoff. We knew there was more in the car. [It's] not actually the way you want to do things, qualifying on your third attempt. The final run was to get the car in the show. Obviously, we wanted to be on the front row, but we're not disappointed."

Buddy Lazier, the defending champion, rolled away with 10 minutes remaining. His run in the #91T Delta Faucet-Montana-Hemelgarn Racing entry was 214.286.

"The car is capable of 215s," Lazier said. "There were things we had to guess on. I've got the right race car and the right crew. We can win this thing. We went out after a massive change, and we didn't have a chance to test that change. If we don't win the race, hopefully we'll make it tough on the one who does."

As the six o'clock gun went off, Roberto Guerrero was on the track in the #21 Pennzoil-Pagan Racing Dallara. He was allowed to complete his run and checked in at 207.371, slower than he wished and the slowest speed posted, but it was a locked-in spot.

"It seems the second week around this place lots of race cars appear," Guerrero said. "We have another car ready if it's needed, and hopefully we'll have more engines."

Twenty-one cars had qualified, and Luyendyk, Stewart, and Sospiri were entrenched on the front row. Others would have to wait.

Competition for the pole had been fierce. Luyendyk's pole run was 15.455 miles an hour slower than the late Scott Brayton's run of a year earlier. The new Indy Racing League cars, designed to be slower for safety reasons, had been right where visionaries wanted them to be.

The initial search for speed had concluded.

"I just kept saying, 'It's not over till it's over,'" Luyendyk said. "Team Menard had the pole two years in a row. You never know . . . they could have done like they did last year and withdraw a car and try again. The great surprise today was Sospiri. You just never know when somebody's going to come out of the blue like that and take you by surprise."

The drivers had the support of many race fans all throughout the month of May.

Date:	Saturday, May 10
Weather:	Sunny, 74°
Qualification Attempts:	29
Qualifiers:	21

Pole Day Qualifiers

Car	Driver	Speed
5	Arie Luyendyk	218.263
2	Tony Stewart	218.021
8	Vincenzo Sospiri	216.822
3	Robbie Buhl	216.102
6	Scott Goodyear	215.811
27	Jim Guthrie	215.207
52	Jeff Ward	214.517
14	Davey Hamilton	214.484
7	Eliseo Salazar	214.320
91T	Buddy Lazier	214.286
51	Eddie Cheever, Jr.	214.073
42	Robby Gordon	213.211
77	Stephan Gregoire	213.126
17	Affonso Giaffone	212.974
4	Kenny Brack	211.221
90	Lyn St. James	210.145
12	Buzz Calkins	209.564
40	Dr. Jack Miller	209.250
34	Alessandro Zampedri	209.094
10	Mike Groff	208.537
21T	Roberto Guerrero	207.371

An official IRL truck made a lap around the track with spotters, who were looking for debris.

Car owner A.J. Foyt and Chief Mechanic Craig Baranouski were pleased to have Billy Boat driving for the injured Scott Sharp.

Robbie Groff was persistent, Steve Kinser made the show, and Greg Ray had a misfortune as not-yet-qualified drivers scrambled to get in the field without waiting for a week to do so.

Groff practiced the #30 Alfa-Laval/Team Losi/McCormack Motorsports entry at 207.646 in the morning practice and was first up when qualifying opened.

He took one warmup lap, but the engine misfired, and he pulled to the pits without taking the green. One hour and three minutes later, he ran laps of 202.156 and 201.505 before waving off.

With 10 minutes left in qualifying, on the car's third and final strike, Groff put together a run of 207.792 miles per hour to gain a "locked in" spot in the field. With the effort, he and his brother Mike became the first pair of brothers to start a "500" since Gary and Tony Bettenhausen were in the 1993 field.

"We didn't want to get it down that far, but I had to get a Mother's Day gift for my mom," Groff said. 'It's a terrible thing when you're down to your last attempt. I just put my head down and bit my teeth together."

After Groff pulled in after an initial warmup lap to start qualifying, Kinser rolled away in the #44 One Call/Menards/Quaker State machine.

He posted a four-lap run of 210.793 miles an hour, and the 14-time World of Outlaws champion was in his first "500" field.

"This is the most relaxed since I've been here, knowing I could get the car over 210," Kinser said. "We weren't expecting to qualify today. We went

out this morning, saw the speeds we were running, and decided to get this thing in the race and keep the miles down.

"We planned to get sprint-car stuff all done and concentrate on qualifying in the second weekend," he added. "In fact, I'm going to be in trouble with my father tonight. I told him I had no intention to qualify today, and he's not here, and he's bigger than me."

No other qualifiers pushed into line until Greg Ray's #97 Tobacco Free Kids entry went through inspection and pulled out just 13 minutes from the close of track action for the day.

Ray put together laps of 214.813, 215.332, and 215.595 before he ran out of fuel in Turn 2 of the last lap, negating what could have been the day's fastest run.

But others started preparing for the second weekend. Billy Boat warmed up the #1T Conseco AJ Foyt Racing entry. Dennis Vitolo was named to the #54 SmithKline Beecham/Kroger/Beck Motorsports Dallara/ Infiniti. And others were trying to put together the right combinations.

Date:	Sunday, May 11
Weather:	Windy, High 70°
Qualification Attempts:	4
Qualifiers:	2

Car	Second Day Qualifiers Driver	Speed
44	Steve Kinser	210.793
30	Robbie Groff	207.792

QUOTE OF THE DAY
"I wouldn't consider doing it
for anybody else but A.J."
Cale Yarborough

Some gained, some planned, and some changed during a busy day off and on the Speedway.

The gainers were Billy Boat, who passed his 10-lap refresher test, and Billy Roe, who smoothly went through all five phases of his driver's test.

The planners were led by Stefan Johansson Motorsports, which announced that its entry assigned to veteran Scott Harrington would run with Infiniti power and Firestone tires.

The changes were in the A.J. Foyt camp. With veteran Scott Sharp out for the month because of his head injury, Foyt targeted John Andretti as a possible replacement in the #1 Conseco AJ Foyt Racing entry . . . but all hands said it would be difficult because of schedules.

And Monsoon Galles Racing, SABCO Racing, and FirstPlus Team Cheever fielded cars which advanced to the quarterfinal round of the $70,000 Coors Pit Stop Challenge.

Arie Luyendyk continued his fast ways, posting the day's fastest lap at 217.103 in the #5 WavePhore/Sprint PCS/Miller Lite pole machine. Treadway Racing teammate Scott Goodyear was second quick at 216.092 in the Nortel/Sprint/PCS/Quebecor Printing entry.

Of the 18 cars on the track, only 2—the #11 AJ Foyt Enterprises car driven by Boat and the #50 Sega/Progressive Electronics/Eurointernational machine driven by Roe—had not-yet-qualified drivers in the cockpits.

The program for Harrington with the #36 Johansson/Immke Motorsports entry took shape.

"We are delighted to be associated with the Nissan Infiniti Group, and we have Ron Hemelgarn and Lee Kunzman to thank for making it happen since they were instrumental in providing a Nissan Infiniti engine to us," said Vern Schuppan, managing director of the team and a "500" veteran.

Meanwhile, Andretti, Foyt, and "500" veteran Cale Yarborough were pondering the possibilities. Andretti had a heavy schedule in Charlotte driving Yarborough's Winston Cup car.

"Cale and I have discussed it, and it's going to be hard getting him back and forth," Foyt said. "We're good friends, and I've asked him for a big favor."

"If they can work out how all sides benefit, not just me, I can be at the Speedway," said Andretti.

"At this late date, the probability is less than if [arrangements were made] earlier in the year]."

"Certainly I wouldn't want to stand in the way of John having a chance to win the Indianapolis 500," Yarborough said. "If it wasn't such an important two weekends for us, it might be a little different. I haven't told John 'No.' Like A.J. said, we've been friends a long time. I wouldn't consider doing it for anybody else but A.J."

The decisions would continue.

Of the 18 cars
on the track,
Billy Roe (#50)
was one of only
two drivers
who had not
yet qualified.

Date:	Monday, May 12
Weather:	Windy, High 62°
Drivers On Track:	18
Cars On Track:	18
Total Laps:	737

Top Non-Qualified Drivers of the Day

Car	Driver	Speed
11	Billy Boat	212.334
50	Billy Roe	206.096

A member of the track fire crew was on hand in case of an emergency.

Buddy Lazier and others went fast, and two drivers emerged with rides as teams geared up for the final weekend of time trials.

Lazier was fastest of the day with a lap at 217.040 miles per hour in the #91 Delta Faucet-Montana-Hemelgarn Racing entry, and nine other drivers—a combination of qualified and not-yet-qualified pilots—also turned their fastest laps of the month.

"This is just our third day in the car," Lazier said, referring to the Hemelgarn team's switch to an Aurora powerplant. [Team manager] Lee Kunzman and [engineer] Ronnie Dawes are really working hard. I think it's definitely getting to be a better race car. We ran full tanks today and worked on better setups. I think we are really catching up."

Eddie Cheever Jr., Steve Kinser, Billy Boat, Lyn St. James, Roberto Guerrero, Marco Greco, Mike Groff, Billy Roe, and Dennis Vitolo also turned their fastest laps of the month.

Boat was the fastest of those still seeking to qualify with a lap at 214.133 in the #11 AJ Foyt Enterprises machine.

"I just wanted to settle down, get focused on my job," Boat said. "A.J.'s really been fantastic, letting me work with the race car at my own pace. I know we're not going to sit on the pole. That's already done. I'm just trying to get a good seat-of-the-pants feel for it."

Elsewhere in the Foyt camp, Foyt named Johnny O'Connell to step into the #1 Conseco AJ Foyt Racing entry for the injured Scott Sharp. PDM Racing named Tyce Carlson to replace the injured John Paul Jr. in the #18 Klipsch Tnemec Overhead Door Pyle V-Line Earl's Dallara.

The naming of O'Connell happened after details could not be worked out on John Andretti's schedule.

"It was such a hardship on Cale Yarborough, also myself and John Andretti, that I just didn't feel it would be fair for him, us, or Cale," said Foyt. "So we've come to the conclusion this morning that John would not be in the car."

"Basically, this is a huge opportunity for any guy to drive for A.J.," O'Connell said. "I'm going to approach the next couple of days and weeks here not looking at A.J. so much as an owner [but] as a coach."

"It's tough," Sharp said. "This is the race that means everything for the year, particularly with Conseco as our sponsor from Indianapolis. Johnny did a really good job last year. I'm sure once A.J. figures out a little bit about his style, he'll do just fine."

Carlson was named as Paul returned to the track, and a steady stream of well-wishers visited him at the PDM garage.

"I've been part of PDM for a year now," Carlson said. "I never wanted to get in the seat with the circumstances that have happened, but I'm going to do my best to win this race not for myself but for the guys that have tried so hard to put this car in the field."

"I'm here to support Tyce," said Paul. "Hopefully, there are some things I can help him with about these IRL cars as far as different conditions with the wind and whatever."

"They [Carlson and Paul] are probably two of the most unselfish people that I've ever had the pleasure of doing business with in this industry," said PDM co-owner Paul Diatlovich. "I have to commend John for wanting to do this and helping us out [when] we need him. Rest assured we will help him out."

Date:	Tuesday, May 13	
Weather:	Windy, High 61°	
Drivers On Track:	17	
Cars On Track:	17	
Total Laps:	849	

Top Non-Qualified Drivers of the Day

Car	Driver	Speed
11	Billy Boat	214.133
22	Marco Greco	210.079
50	Billy Roe	209.888
54	Dennis Vitolo	196.002

QUOTE OF THE DAY
"We had to put a lot of Band-Aids on the car for qualifying"
Buddy Lazier

Buddy Lazier and Billy Boat led the way for a second straight day for qualified and not-yet-qualified drivers, respectively, as the talk turned to increased speeds.

Lazier reeled off a lap at 216.570 miles per hour in the #91T Delta Faucet-Montana-Hemelgarn Racing machine. Boat reached 215.151 in the #11 AJ Foyt Enterprises entry.

Fifteen cars were on the track, and some drivers ran laps faster than they qualified on the previous weekend. There seemed to be a variety of reasons.

"We had to cram a month's worth of work into one qualifying morning," said Lazier. "We had to put a lot of Band-Aids on the car for qualifying. Now we've had time to go back, and that's why we're going faster. Every time we run we get a whole catalog of new things to review. We're working on it all.

"We're five positions back from where you'd like to be," he added about his starting spot. "We're going to have to take our time, and I'm going to have to use my head. Just when you think you're going to have to run 203, guys will run 216 and finish. Just when you think it's going to take 216, guys will run 203 and finish. It's a long race. Certainly we're feeling better and better about it."

Buzz Calkins said his gains came from the engine compartment.

"[We] blew up the engine in the morning [of pole qualifying]," Calkins said. "The first time we got out with the new engine was when we qualified. We're trying to get more downforce. We're running with more fuel. We're just trying to get comfortable."

"I don't feel like we're going faster," said Stephan Gregoire. "We aren't trying to get the fastest lap. We're trying to know the car. We're trying to concentrate on setup for the race."

Meanwhile, the conversion from an Aurora to an Infiniti engine for the #36 Johansson/Immke Motorsports entry was completed after four days of work.

"The change really put us behind, and there have been a lot of obstacles we didn't think we'd have to deal with," said Vern Schuppan, managing director of the team.

Two days remained before the final qualifying weekend would unfold.

Buddy Lazier qualified on Pole Day at 214.286 miles per hour.

Date:	Wednesday, May 14
Weather:	Windy, High 67°
Drivers On Track:	15
Cars On Track:	15
Total Laps:	533

Top Non-Qualified Drivers of the Day

Car	Driver	Speed
11	Billy Boat	215.151
50	Billy Roe	210.669

Tyce Carlson, Mark Dismore, Claude Bourbonnais, Johnny O'Connell, and Johnny Unser took the track for the first time and got up to impressive out-of-the-box speeds, and Sam Schmidt was fastest of the day as practice wound down.

Carlson, as the replacement for John Paul Jr. in the #18 Klipsch Tnemec Overhead Door Pyle V-Line Earl's Dallara, was second fastest with a lap at 210.590 miles per hour. Dismore, in the #28 Kelley Automotive Group entry, reached 210.389.

Meanwhile Schmidt set the pace with a lap at 211.989 in the #16 HOPE Prepaid Fuel Card machine.

Bourbonnais saddled up to Schmidt and Jim Guthrie in the #72 Blueprint Racing team car. O'Connell got his first laps in the #1 Conseco AJ Foyt Racing machine. Unser was in the #91 Delta Faucet-Montana-Hemelgarn Racing backup to Buddy Lazier.

"I didn't think I would be [fastest]," Schmidt said. "I guess the wind bothered everyone else more. I haven't had much time to run behind somebody. I ran behind Robby [Gordon] today, and it was turbulent."

Carlson had been helping the PDM team prepare the car prior to being named to the cockpit. Now, his role changed.

"I bought breakfast yesterday," Carlson said when asked how much he helped on the car. "They said I'm a driver, and I don't have to work on cars any more. Every bit of the setup goes back to John Paul Jr. He did all the testing. It's all in being comfortable and trusting your crew."

Bourbonnais breezed through four phases of his driver's test after securing the Blueprint ride. The "seat time" was his first at the Speedway.

"I had to get used to the new car I'd never driven," he said. "The first time [out] was harder than the second time. I came here three weeks ago and didn't have anything. I thought if I wasn't here, I wouldn't get anything. I've been walking the garage area every day talking to everyone. I wanted to get with Blueprint and talked to them even before I got here."

Off the track, the Speedway and the American Red Cross announced a new national partnership designed to enable the two organizations to reach out to families with messages about personal and family safety, emergency response, and preparedness in communities around the country.

"It is important for all of us to realize that we are part of a larger community," said Speedway President Tony George. "Motorsports is sports,

entertainment, and business. It is also an opportunity for us to be involved in helping others."

Also, Ed Keating and Roger Allen of GM Motorsports were honored with the 31st annual Louis Schwitzer Award for their design of the Indy Aurora V-8 engine. The award was presented by Steve Roby, award committee chairman for the Indiana Section, Society of Automotive Engineers.

"They had to supply a new product for a new series," Roby said. "At GM, there's a core group, then there's a cadre of vendors. There are a lot of people involved."

Keating addressed the month-long speculation about the engines' first racing test at 500 miles.

"We have had a significant number of engines that have gone significantly over 500 miles in the week-and-a-half of testing here," he said. "There're a lot of smart people out there. Our sense from the teams which have been here for many, many years is very positive."

The racing family also expanded on this day. At 8:26 P.M., Scott and Leslie Goodyear celebrated the arrival of their third child, Hayley Alexandra, who weighed 7 pounds, 15 ounces.

Date:	Thursday, May 15
Weather:	Windy, High 65°
Drivers On Track:	18
Cars On Track:	17
Total Laps:	668

Top Non-Qualified Drivers of the Day

Car	Driver	Speed
16	Sam Schmidt	211.989
18	Tyce Carlson	210.590
28	Mark Dismore	210.389
91	Johnny Unser	208.497
1	Johnny O'Connell	207.054
72	Claude Bourbonnais	203.841
54	Dennis Vitolo	200.615

Greg Ray made the news on the track and Indy Racing League Executive Director Leo Mehl made the news off of it as 12 drivers tried to work up to speed for the final qualifying weekend.

Tony Stewart, already qualified, led the speed chase with a lap at 216.388 in the #2T Glidden Menards Special. Ray was tops among not-yet-qualified drivers with a lap at 215.069 in the #97 Tobacco Free Kids entry.

The news wasn't good for Johnny O'Connell, who was working up to speed in the #1 Conseco AJ Foyt Racing entry. O'Connell had an engine problem going into Turn 1 and hit the outside wall at the entrance to the south short chute. He was transported to Methodist Hospital with a dislocated arch in his left foot requiring surgery and minor facial cuts, ending his month and sending the Foyt team back to the drawing board.

Ray, after running out of fuel on a qualifying attempt the previous weekend, returned to the cockpit to prepare for his second bid.

"I've been out of the car for five days, and we ran the same speed as we did Sunday," he said. "The nice thing is, we've been running on full tanks. The fourth lap we did today was 215. Since I was out of the car for five days, they wanted to allow me to get comfortable. We tried a little race setup, but the focus is qualifying."

Speeds of not-yet-qualified drivers ran from Scott Harrington's first shakedown of the #36 Johansson/Immke Motorsports entry to Ray's. Mark Dismore was second fastest with a lap at 213.848 in the #28 Kelley Automotive Group entry, followed by Sam Schmidt in the #16 HOPE Prepaid Fuel Card machine at 213.564.

Claude Bourbonnais finished the final observation phase of his driver's test with veterans Joe Gosek, Paul Durant, Johnny Rutherford, and Tero Palmroth serving as observers.

"I need the rookie orientation to get back up to speed, but I'm glad to have completed it," Bourbonnais said. "I would've done exactly the same thing if I wouldn't have had rookie orientation because I would've got up to speed at the same rate."

Meanwhile, Mehl announced that the so-called "25-8" qualifying incentive was eliminated for 1998, technical specifications and manufacturer participation guidelines had been solidified, and the prices for engines and cars in 1998 will move to $80,000 and $275,000, respectively. He said the qualifying incentive had served its purpose.

"This program was necessary to provide a strong incentive to participate in the IRL and com-

QUOTE OF THE DAY
" . . . it's time to move on . . . "
Leo Mehl

pete in all League races," Mehl said. "In this regard, it has been very successful. Everybody understood it was a necessary thing to start off the League. I met with the owners this morning, and they understand it's time to move on from that."

The final qualifying weekend loomed just ahead.

Date:	Friday, May 16
Weather:	Windy, High 62°
Drivers On Track:	21
Cars On Track:	21
Total Laps:	762

Top Ten Non-Qualified Drivers of the Day

Car	Driver	Speed
97	Greg Ray	215.069
28	Mark Dismore	213.848
16	Sam Schmidt	213.564
11	Billy Boat	213.013
1	Johnny O'Connell	212.922
18	Tyce Carlson	212.846
50	Billy Roe	212.409
22	Marco Greco	211.775
33	Fermin Velez	209.844
72	Claude Bourbonnais	207.569

Claude Bourbonnais took to the track for the first time on Day 13. He qualified on the fourth qualifying day with a speed of 210.523 miles per hour.

Alessandro Zampedri and his crew members ride to the pits. After being bumped from the field by Paul Durant, Zampedri registered a run at 211.757 miles per hour, bumping Lyn St. James on the fourth qualifying day.

On the third morning of qualifications, a number of drivers soared to acceptable speeds and were instantly ready to qualify.

Mark Dismore, Billy Boat, and Dennis Vitolo turned their fastest laps of the month in the morning practice, Dismore leading the way with a lap at 217.360 miles per hour in the #28 Kelley Automotive Group entry.

Greg Ray reached 215.260 in the #97 Tobacco Free Kids machine to be third fastest and was first up in the qualifying line.

He had run out of fuel on a qualifying run the first weekend and headed the speed chart for not-yet-qualified drivers the previous day. But engine trouble struck on his warmup lap which eventually would send him to the fourth time-trial day for his bid. Later, the problem was diagnosed as a piston failure, and the team spent the rest of the day installing its race engine.

Boat was next. He had reeled off a practice lap at 216.201 in the #11 Conseco AJ Foyt Enterprises machine in the morning, then put together a four-lap run of 215.544 to handily make his first "500" field.

"The race car was wanting to go that fast," Boat said. "The harder I drove it, the better it felt. It heated up on us a little bit right in the middle of the day. The race car seemed to like the heat. We put a little bit of front wing in it to make sure it didn't push."

Next out was rookie Billy Roe, who recorded a four-lap average of 212.752 miles an hour to make his first "500" field as the month's 25th qualifier.

"This morning, I told the crew not to talk to me during qualifying unless I was under 212," Roe said. "I didn't hear from them so I knew it was good enough. I saw the speeds on the tower for the first two laps, a 212 and 213, and tried to duplicate them. A 213 is as quick as we ever went."

Fermin Velez came out and soldiered through a run of 206.512 for a "locked in" spot in the #33 Old Navy Scandia Alta Xcel entry.

"We made the race," Velez said. "I'm relieved we've made it. We had no time to set the car up since we've blown the engine last weekend. The car's not well-balanced. We didn't want to take any chances."

Tyce Carlson, who replaced John Paul Jr. in the #18 Klipsch Tnemec Overhead Door Pyle V-Line Earl's entry, rolled away and nailed down a spot with a run of 210.852, joining the field after being barely too slow to make the 1996 show.

"I've had 364 days to wait for this moment," said Carlson. "When I got out of the car and saw my family and friends who have been behind me since I started racing, this is a dream come true."

Dennis Vitolo was next in the #54 SmithKline Beecham/Kroger/Beck Motorsports entry and took a locked-in spot at 207.626.

"I was a little concerned with the engine," Vitolo said. "It was losing RPMs, and I was flat-out. It lost a lot of horsepower today. I think, come Race Day, the Infinitis will be real reliable. The goal is to finish the race incident-free and then finish as high as we can."

As the track temperature jumped 17 degrees in an hour to 120, Mark Dismore left for his run. After a 217-plus in morning practice, he posted a four-lap average of 212.423 in the #28 Kelley Automotive Group machine.

"I just snuck up on it," Dismore said. "We have no rocket scientists on this team. They just have a lot of common sense. Every change we made, we stuck with. I think that was the key—we didn't panic. Everybody kept their cool, and I think that's what made the difference."

After he qualified, Dismore went to the PDM/Kelley garage in Gasoline Alley, dragged out a Sharpie, and started to sign autographs. Two and a half hours later he was done after signing everything from T-shirts to "hero" cards to one man's bald head.

Sam Schmidt was next in the #16 HOPE Pre-paid Fuel Card entry. He became the 30th qualifier of the month with a four-lap run of 215.141, the second fastest of the day.

"Last week, we peaked at 217," Schmidt said. "We had to wait for an engine since we only have one engine. We wanted to qualify last weekend, but the water pump went. We've run the emotional spectrum this week."

Marco Greco was the last in the qualifying line for the moment. He took a locked-in spot with a run of 210.322 in the #22 Side Play International Scandia Alta Xcel entry.

"We didn't expect high speeds," Greco said. "We didn't practice much. We didn't come here because we had a guaranteed spot. I am a professional driver. It's very tough, especially for myself, sitting in the garage and waiting."

Others practiced, but Greco's attempt was to be the last of the day.

The Blueprint team was hounded by another setback just 28 minutes from the end of the day's track action. Claude Bourbonnais, in the #72 Blueprint Racing entry, brushed the wall twice in Turn 2 and drove back to the pits on two wheels with damage.

"I had a bit of a push," said Bourbonnais. "I came in and did some changes. I misjudged the changes and couldn't get into the apex. We'll be back out tomorrow."

One day remained to make the "500" field.

Last minute preparations were made in Gasoline Alley with only one day left for qualifying.

Date:	Saturday, May 17	
Weather:	Sunny, High 81°	
Qualification Attempts:	8	
Qualifiers:	8	

Third Day Qualifiers

Car	Driver	Speed
11	Billy Boat	215.544
16	Sam Schmidt	215.141
50	Billy Roe	212.752
28	Mark Dismore	212.423
18	Tyce Carlson	210.852
22	Marco Greco	210.322
54	Dennis Vitolo	207.626
33	Fermin Velez	206.512

One team had to burn the midnight oil, squirrels caused cautions, and others were ready for the final run to Indianapolis 500 starting berths as "no tomorrow" time came for the month of May.

Along with it, veteran Paul Durant made a whirlwind entry into the picture and had to change his plans—for the better.

Blueprint Racing's #72 entry driven by Claude Bourbonnais underwent a major transformation overnight. Damaged in an accident on Day 15, the team replaced the bell housing, back of the engine, transmission, right-side suspension, underwing, and rear wing.

"The team's been up all night," said Tom O'Brien, team manager and co-owner of Blueprint. "They've done a good job. The team hasn't gone to sleep yet. If we get the third car in, it'll be worth it."

In the morning practice, the caution flashed twice as a pair of pesky squirrels chose ringside seats in the south short chute.

But at noon, two cars were in the qualifying line and ready to go.

Johnny Unser took out the #9 Lifetime-Tv-Cinergy entry from Hemelgarn Racing and registered a four-lap run at 209.344 to become the month's 32nd qualifier.

"Qualifying was a bit of a gamble but it was a gamble we had to take," Unser said. "I drove the car as hard as I could. There was a voltage problem. The engine cut out but only on the back straightaway. I don't know why. I was just hoping it would come back on right away and it did."

Then rookie Greg Ray filled the field with a four-lap average of 213.760 miles per hour in the #97 Tobacco Free Kids Dallara. It was a welcome run after Ray ran out of fuel on a qualifying attempt the previous weekend.

"We were definitely running the car with a little extra methanol," Ray said. "We definitely had a conservative car. It was all the car had. Last night, we put the race engine in, which we didn't want to do until Thursday."

With the field full at 33 starters, Alessandro Zampedri was on the bubble. And A.J. Foyt rolled out the #1 Conseco AJ Foyt Racing entry with Durant ready to go, helmet in hand.

At 12:17 P.M., Durant climbed into the car for the first time, with team driver and old supermodified foe Davey Hamilton and Foyt standing by to "coach." Hamilton had shaken down the car in the morning practice.

At 12:21 P.M., Durant drove off pit road for his

first lap of the month. Eighteen minutes later, he had 12 total laps.

"We got it up to 210, and it felt pretty good," he said. "We're going to make a few adjustments and then go out and qualify."

"It's up to speed, and they're just going to let him go," said Hamilton.

Durant put together a smooth four-lap average of 209.149 to bump Zampedri from the field. From the time he had climbed into a car for the first time in May to the time he completed a qualifying run was just 52 minutes.

"It really is exciting, considering that a little over an hour and a half ago, I thought I was going home," Durant said. "The last couple of hours seemed like a whirlwind. Racing has the highest highs and lowest lows, and in a matter of two hours, I've had both of them. I feel very fortunate that A.J. gave me the opportunity.

"I had trouble relaxing in the car, really, but I've raced against Davey [Hamilton] for 15 years now, so when he told me the car was good, but it had a little push, I knew that would actually be the case."

Durant's next task was getting on a phone in the press room—to extend his stay in Indianapolis and change his flights.

Shortly after Durant's run, Sam Schmidt had an engine problem in the #16 HOPE Prepaid Fuel Card/Blueprint Racing entry and did a three-quarter spin with no contact in Turn 3.

"It just went 'boom!'" Schmidt said. It was a setback for Blueprint, but 37 minutes after Schmidt's misfortune, the team's third entry, driven by Claude Bourbonnais, went out to qualify.

Bourbonnais put together a run of 210.523 miles per hour to bump Johnny Unser from the field. Minutes later, Zampedri went out in his backup and registered a run at 211.757, bumping Lyn St. James as raindrops emerged.

"The wind picked up, and we had a half-hour window," Bourbonnais said. "I got some sleep last night, but the crew didn't. They put the car back together. The crew assured me the car would be the same. Sometimes when you put the car back together, it's not the same, but it was."

For Zampedri, bumping back into the field was another chapter in his determined comeback.

www.indyracingleague.com

"Yesterday and today, the team worked to put the backup car together," Zampedri said. "I was very confident with the car and knew if I had to take it out, we could make it. I saw the drops on my visor on the second lap, and Dick Simon started talking to me to keep me from getting distracted by the rain on my visor."

The track was yellow for rain for 56 minutes before it reopened at 3:15 P.M., with 2 hours and 45 minutes of time left before the close of qualifications.

That time would be used by one final competitor, veteran Scott Harrington, whose Johansson/Immke Motorsports crew put the number #36 on one of A.J. Foyt's machines that had previously been run by Davey Hamilton as #14T.

With 9 minutes remaining in qualifying, Harrington went out for the last qualifying run of the month. His first lap was a healthy 214.061 miles per hour, but he hit the Turn 2 wall on his second lap, ending time trials for 1997.

After qualifying, Indy Racing League Executive Director Leo Mehl went to the Trackside Conference Room and announced that the two bumped drivers who had not requalified—Johnny Unser and Lyn St. James—swould be reinstated and the field for the 1997 Indianapolis 500 would number 35.

"We must start the 33 fastest cars, so we will add the two bumped cars," Mehl told media representatives. "As you know, last Friday, we discontinued the reserved positions for the 1998 race. This is not an easy call to make. I can't tell you if this is the fairest, truest decision, but it was decided that this was what had to happen. We didn't want those who had qualified and were in the field to be bumped by those with reserved spots."

For the 35 starters, Carburetion Day was all that remained before the race.

Many fans were on hand to see the final day of qualifying.

Date:	Sunday, May 18
Weather:	Rain, High 85°
Qualification Attempts:	6
Qualifiers:	5

Fourth Day Qualifiers		
Car	Driver	Speed
97	Greg Ray	213.760
34T	Alessandro Zampedri	211.757
72	Claude Bourbonnais	210.523
9	Johnny Unser	209.344
1	Paul Durant	209.149

Johnny Unser discussed his race day strategy with his uncle, Al Unser (left) and a crew member.

QUOTE OF THE DAY
"Just truckin' around . . ."
Mike Groff

The handle "Carburetion Day" has stood the test of time well past the days of carburetors on Indy-style race cars.

It's a 2-hour final practice in which teams put the finishing touches on race setups, run with full fuel loads, and make the last preparations for the world's biggest auto race.

Sometimes, teams show their hands on what they have in store for their competitors three days later. Sometimes, they "hold 'em."

And on Carb Day 1997, no clear-cut favorite emerged. The top of the speed chart for those two hours ran like this:

11:29 A.M. — Lyn St. James, 209.795 miles per hour, fastest of session.

11:52 A.M. — Affonso Giaffone, 209.922, fastest of session.

12:14 P.M. — Alessandro Zampedri, 211.854, fastest of session.

12:15 P.M. — Scott Goodyear, 212.972, fastest of session.

12:40 P.M. — Greg Ray, 214.807, fastest of session. And also at 12:40 P.M., — Tony Stewart, 215.502, fastest of session.

So, as those two hours played out, who do you pick for Race Day?

"We changed a lot of things," Stewart said. "We changed two or three things at a time, including the helmet and the padding around my head. We changed a lot of variables, so we're not sure what made the difference. But I'll be using that helmet for Race Day, that's for sure. The car was pretty close . . . not exactly the way we want it, but it's close. I feel really good about Race Day."

"Just truckin' around, just feeling the car out," said Mike Groff.

"We only did two laps at real speed," said pole winner Arie Luyendyk. "We just wanted to check the systems to make sure there were no leaks or anything."

After being reinstated to the starting lineup the day before, Lyn St. James posted a fast lap of 209.795 on Carburetion Day.

"Getting back in the car is like getting back to reality," said Vincenzo Sospiri. "There's one thing no one's noticed: The last time a rookie won this competition was back in 1966, and that was the year I was born."

For the record, the best lap times for the top nine drivers were within a second. Curiously, the ninth driver on the speed chart, Johnny Unser, had Infiniti power, and that raised eyebrows among the Aurora contingent. Could the Infiniti emerge as a factor?

Date:	Thursday, May 22	
Weather:	Cloudy, High 64°	
Drivers On Track:	32	
Cars On Track:	32	
Total Laps:	644	

Top Five Drivers of the Day		
Car	Driver	Speed
2	Tony Stewart	215.502
97	Greg Ray	214.807
6	Scott Goodyear	212.972
4	Kenny Brack	212.741
5	Arie Luyendyk	212.054

Fermin Velez ran the most laps—34—of any driver, followed by Unser at 32.

On the pit road, Galles Racing International captured the $40,000 top prize in the $70,000 Coors Indy Pit Stop Challenge, posting a time of 14.284 seconds in the final.

The victory marked the second straight for Galles, which has won the contest five times in the past nine years. The Galles team beat FirstPlus Team Cheever, which clocked in at 15.133 seconds in the final.

"We practice a lot outside the shop in Albuquerque, New Mexico," said Galles Crew Chief, Gary Armentrout. "Sometimes we draw a crowd. It's become a tradition. We expect to win. Mitch Davis, the crew chief on Cheever, won it for Galles last year. We practice stops for the contest just carrying tires over the wall."

"It came down to lane choice," said Davis. "The outside lane had more grip, but they won the toss. It was THAT close."

Other than tweaking, polishing, and pampering, the 1997 Indianapolis 500 was all that remained.

Roberto Guerrero and his crew practiced a pit stop in preparation for race day.

41

INDY 500 MEMORIES

85 YEARS AGO
•1912•

BY DONALD DAVIDSON

The 24 starters rumble slowly through Turn 1 to begin the pace lap.

1912 winner Joe Dawson is congratulated by Speedway president and founder Carl Fisher. This is the same Carl Fisher who developed Miami Beach out of swamp lands and who later headed up the Lincoln Highway Commission which built the first trans-continental highway, linking the East Coast with the West.

Len Zengel (Stutz), Bob Burman (Cutting), Spencer Wishart (Mercedes), and Ralph Mulford (Knox) battle early in the going.

The start of the second annual Indianapolis 500 is only a few minutes away as the drivers and riding mechanics, who will man the 24 participating cars, pose for the pre-race panoramic photograph, a tradition in itself which continued until 1957. A locally-built Stutz passenger car, in only its second year of production. is ready to lead the field around on the pace lap. Note that the cars are lined up in rows of five rather than three. Four-abreast starts were used between 1913 and 1920. with the famed three-abreast start becoming established in 1921.

In perhaps the Speedway's most dramatic moment ever, Italian immigrant Ralph DePalma has just led 196 of the 200 laps, failing to lead only the first two and the last two. Undaunted by the fact that a broken connection rod forced him to stop just about a lap and a quarter from the finish, he and his Australian riding mechanic, Rupert Jeffkins, have just pushed their heavy Mercedes several hundred yards down the mainstraight from Turn 4. In spite of a thunderous ovation from the crowd, they are simply too exhausted to push around for another lap, and, besides, Joe Dawson (foreground) has already won the race. But DePalma has just become a Speedway legend.

Because there are no bleachers along the inside of the mainstraight, early arrivals who aim for north of the pits, can park their automobiles right up against the fence.

Ralph Mulford, runner-up in the 1911 500, also finished 10th in 1912 with this Knox automobile but not without considerable difficulty. Hampered by a slipping clutch and various other problems, he fell far behind the rest of the field. Prize money in 1912 was posted only to the first 12 finishers, and, in order to claim one of the prizes, a competitor was required to complete the entire distance, regardless of how long it took. One by one the cars either dropped out or else completed 500 miles until nine had finished with only Mulford still running. He never did give up and even made a late-race pit stop for coffee and sandwiches (it had been a long day) before finally finishing just before sundown in a time of 8 hours and 53 minutes, with an average speed of 56.29 miles per hour. It was also a very long day for the officials since the checkered flag was not waved for Mulford until 2 hours and 31 minutes *after* Joe Dawson had won the race.

INDY 500 MEMORIES

50 YEARS AGO
·1947·

Between 1909 and 1975, the main entrance to the Indianapolis Motor Speedway was located at the corner of West 16th Street and Georgetown Road. This is how it appeared in 1947.

A huge controversy develops in the late stages of the race when car owner Lou Moore, wishing to protect the healthy lead enjoyed by his two drivers, Bill Holland and Mauri Rose, holds out a pit board sign reading "EZY," meaning "slow down and nurse your car to the finish." Holland, a 39-year-old veteran dirt track driver, who is competing in the 500 for the first time, complies with the communication. His wily teammate does not! Rose makes up a deficit of half a minute and passes Holland with seven laps to go. Holland even waves Rose by, believing his teammate merely to be unlapping himself. *Above:* Holland (left) is not amused when Rose talks with him afterwards, but he retains his composure and stays with the team. The following year, the same two drivers in exactly the same cars will finish one-two again.

Ted Horn and Cliff Bergere lead a group of cars into Turn 2. The grandstand, which ran parallel with West 16th Street, was built in 1913. It survived, minus its roof in later years, until the mid-1960s.

Mauri Rose heads back to the garage area accompanied by Hollywood actress Carole Landis, while chatting with Rose is a very young Andy Granatelli.

Three-time 500 winner Wilbur Shaw, who by this time was the Speedway's president and general manager, poses with the 1947 Nash pace car. This would be the last four-door hardtop to pace the race until the Oldsmobile Aurora in 1997 half a century later. This shot was evidently taken in the early part of May as the windows in the landmark Japanese-style pagoda are still boarded up from the winter.

Ted Horn (right) wins the pole with Wilbur Shaw's 1939- and 1940-winning Maserati. He is joined on the front row by Cliff Bergere (center) in one of the crowd-pleasing V-8 supercharged Novi racing cars and by eventual winner Mauri Rose (left). All three cars are front drives.

Thousands of cars jam the infield.

500 Festivities

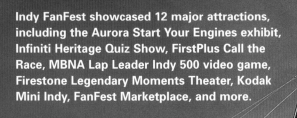

Indy FanFest showcased 12 major attractions, including the Aurora Start Your Engines exhibit, Infiniti Heritage Quiz Show, FirstPlus Call the Race, MBNA Lap Leader Indy 500 video game, Firestone Legendary Moments Theater, Kodak Mini Indy, FanFest Marketplace, and more.

Thousands of runners competed in the 500 Festival Mini-Marathon, including driver Stephan Gregoire who finished 76th overall.

Before The Roar

GASOLINE ALLEY

www.indyracingleague.com

Racing's Greatest Spectacle

By Dave Argabright

INDY RACING LEAGUE

Rookie Vincenzo Sospiri, a former Formula One driver, started from the front row and finished in 17th place.

The arrival of May in Indianapolis usually brings the roar of Indy cars to the corner of Sixteenth Street and Georgetown Road, along with the sunshine and warmth of spring.

This year racing machines were ready to fire up for the 81st running of the Indianapolis 500; unfortunately, springtime lagged behind at the onset of May and never really caught up.

The Indianapolis 500 was scheduled as the third event on the 1997 Indy Racing League schedule, but it is difficult to think of Indy as anything other than what it is: the single most important event in all of motorsports. So while the IRL teams fought for important points and momentum needed for success in their overall season, they knew that this was the most prestigious stop of the year.

They arrived at Indianapolis with more questions than answers. For the first time in many years, an entirely new chassis and engine formula was in place, affecting every entry. New chassis, designed to reduce spiraling costs in Indy car racing, were built by two manufacturers, Dallara and G Force. Engines, built to the 4.0-litre, naturally-aspirated V-8 specs set by IRL officials, were built by Oldsmobile Aurora and Nissan Infinity.

Several weeks prior at the Phoenix 200 teams struggled with engine woes, many cars

The cars were gridded and ready to go, but it began raining before the engines were fired. The race was postponed until Monday—the first time since 1986—only to be postponed once again due to rain until Tuesday, May 27.

dropping out with powerplant troubles. The 500-mile Indianapolis grind would be an important test of the technical adjustments made by various engineers as a result of Phoenix.

One of the objectives of the fledgling Indy Racing League was to allow tighter competition among more contenders. By early May, that was obviously effective, as a significant range of drivers eagerly lined up to try and place their likeness on the famed Borg-Warner trophy.

Defending champion Buddy Lazier had fought through physical challenges in 1996 that were wrought by a serious accident, and this year he would be in top physical condition for Indianapolis. Lazier, however, was struggling with the Infinity powerplant.

Nineteen-ninety Indianapolis winner Arie Luyendyk was eager to get back up front after a very brief outing at Phoenix. Always tough at Indianapolis, the Dutchman also enjoyed the advantage of team engineer Tim Wardrop, and the combination would be formidable.

Tony Stewart returned to his Hoosier homeland where just two years earlier he was a star in sprint cars and midgets. His ascent to IRL stardom had been shockingly rapid, and he was a leader in nearly every IRL event to date. But victory had eluded him, and the 1996 Indy 500 Rookie of the Year was itching to win for the Menard team.

Defending IRL co-champ Scott Sharp, driving A.J. Foyt's Conseco entry, had been fast at Phoenix but suffered from several engine problems before dropping out early. So Sharp, along with the ever-competitive Foyt, knew Indianapolis would be a fine place to regain their momentum.

Mike Groff, who carried the IRL point lead to Indianapolis, was the "steady-Eddie" of the league. Groff faced the 2.5-mile Indy oval with a calm, cool approach, hoping that a win here would give him a solid boost toward the championship.

Surprises? You like surprises? Jim Guthrie was ready to deliver, after shocking the IRL order with a thrilling win over Stewart at Phoenix. The Albuqueque, New Mexico, auto body man was still

Only 15 laps were completed on Monday before rain postponed the race again to Tuesday.

grinning from ear-to-ear when he arrived at Indy, ready to prove that he, along with Team Blueprint Racing, were not flukes.

But rain washed out or shortened three of the first five days, and the cool temperatures added to the misery. On Friday, May 9, the chill brought great havoc to the Speedway as several drivers experienced trouble due to the cool track temperature.

Scott Sharp, who had crashed lightly two days earlier, was knocked unconscious when he hit the wall in the fourth turn, with the car grinding along the outside wall down the frontstretch.

Fermin Velez worked his way from 29th starting position to finish 10th.

Marco Greco reached as high as 7th place before a gearbox problem ended his day in 16th place.

Sharp's head injury was serious enough to sideline him for several weeks.

John Paul Jr. lost control of his No. 18 Dallara/Aurora in Turn 4 and spun very hard into the outside wall. Paul was admitted to Methodist Hospital in good condition with fractures to his right lower leg and left heel, out for several weeks as well.

Robby Gordon and Stephan Gregoire also spun before the day was over.

Amid the little decent weather experienced at the Speedway, Arie Luyendyk posted a quick lap of 220.297 miles per hour on Thursday, May 7.

On Saturday, May 10, the PPG Pole Award was up for grabs, with Luyendyk the favorite. The Dutchman delivered midway through the afternoon, with a run of 218.263 in the Wavephore-Sprint/PCS G-Force Aurora.

Earlier that morning, Tony Stewart had posted similar speeds in the Glidden/Menard's machine. There seemed to be a special rivalry shaping up between the veteran Luyendyk and the upstart Stewart, and both placed a premium on getting the pole.

Jim Guthrie (far right) and crew hoped the rain would end and racing would begin.

Tony Stewart led the most laps of the race (64), finishing in 5th place.

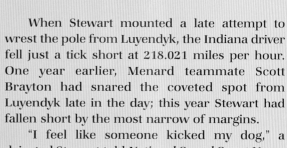

When Stewart mounted a late attempt to wrest the pole from Luyendyk, the Indiana driver fell just a tick short at 218.021 miles per hour. One year earlier, Menard teammate Scott Brayton had snared the coveted spot from Luyendyk late in the day; this year Stewart had fallen short by the most narrow of margins.

"I feel like someone kicked my dog," a dejected Stewart told *National Speed Sport News*.

A total of 21 drivers qualified the first day, with two more coming on Day 2 of time trials. The best second-day performance was recorded by sprint car superstar Steve Kinser, who ran 210.783 miles per hour for brother-in-law and crew chief Owen Snyder, realizing a long-term dream for both.

The week between qualifying weekends was hectic for A.J. Foyt. Indy's first four-time winner, now active as a team owner, scurried to replace the injured Sharp. He filled a third car with short

Mark Dismore's day ended after completing only 24 laps due to a four-car accident in Turn 4. Others involved in the melee were Roberto Guerrero, Eliseo Salazar, and Steve Kinser.

track veteran Billy Boat, who joined the already qualified Davey Hamilton.

After attempting to work a deal with NASCAR driver John Andretti that never came to fruition, Foyt chose Arizona driver Johnny O'Connell. But on Friday, May 16, O'Connell crashed the Conseco machine in Turn 1, suffering a foot injury that required surgery and sidelined him for the month.

Foyt then tabbed supermodified star Paul Durant, who eventually qualified 33rd in the Conseco entry.

In the days leading to the second weekend of qualifying, the hot topic of conversation in the garage centered around "exempt" positions. One year earlier, Indy officials had introduced a qualifying provision that helped protect IRL regulars from being bumped from the field. The so-called "25/8" rule resulted in two "non-exempt" cars being bumped by "exempt" entries that had posted slower speeds.

Following a tumultuous day of on-track activity, IRL Executive Director Leo Mehl announced that the two "bumped" cars of Lyn St. James and Johnny Unser would be added to the field, bringing the total number of starters to 35. It would be the first time since 1979 that more than 33 cars took the green flag on Race Day. Mehl also announced that the "25/8" rule would not be used at Indianapolis in 1998.

Rain was again a factor on the scheduled Race Day of Sunday, May 25. The cars were gridded and ready to go, but it began raining before the engines were fired. By 1:30 P.M., as they looked at a soaked race track and a forecast that called for more rain, officials postponed the event until Monday at 11:00 A.M. It marked the first time since 1986 that the event was postponed.

The following day, under threatening skies, the cars were underway on the pace lap when the entire fifth row of Stephan Gregoire, Affonso Giaffone, and Kenny Brack were eliminated in a bizarre low-speed crash.

Tony Stewart and Arie Luyendyk battle on the backstretch as Stewart forced Luyendyk into the grass.

1990 Indy 500 winner Arie Luyendyk led 61 laps on his way to his second victory.

The field regrouped and took the green flag, with Stewart boldly racing past Luyendyk to take command on the first lap. After just 15 circuits, the rains came again. They began as a light shower, giving hope that the event could be resumed. But it began to rain harder as the temperature began dropping, and officials set the restart for 11:00 A.M. the following day, Tuesday.

The rescheduling on a workday (Tuesday) brought some controversy to IMS President Tony George. But his decision proved to be prudent, as the following day dawned with clear skies and cool temperatures. (The following Saturday, which would have been the next choice, was rainy nearly all day in Indianapolis.)

The race resumed with Luyendyk nipping at Stewart's heels, and the two waged a ferocious duel throughout much of the race. Late in the day, as they diced through traffic, Luyendyk moved to the grass on the backstretch after running out of racing room while he and Stewart raced wheel-to-wheel.

Robby Gordon was out early with a fuel fire on Lap 20, and on the restart Kinser, Eliseo Salazar, and Mark Dismore were involved in a shunt, parking Dismore and slowing both Kinser and Salazar.

The engine reliability questions that had loomed earlier in the month were put to rest during the race. Cars raced aggressively throughout the event, resulting in 17 lead changes among nine drivers. Engine failures were no more a factor than in any other "500."

Stewart, Boat, Luyendyk, and Lazier (who had switched to Aurora power) took turns leading through the first half of the race. On Lap 114 the most serious crash of the day came when the cars of Billy Roe and Durant wrecked in Turn 3, with Durant taken to Methodist Hospital with a fractured pelvis and a concussion.

On lap 137, the caution waved for the cars of Jack Miller and Mike Groff, who were unhurt in a Turn 2 crash.

At this point rookie Jeff Ward took command in the FirstPlus Team Cheever entry. With three-fourths of the race finished, the serious strategy came into play.

As Ward held the lead, he was followed by five cars on the lead lap: Stewart, Luyendyk, Scott Goodyear (Luyendyk's Treadway Racing teammate), Lazier, and Menard driver Robbie Buhl.

The six staged a splendid battle throughout the final 125 miles. Ward, undaunted by the veterans snarling close behind, led until Lap 166, when Luyendyk took command. Then it was Ward regaining the lead two laps later, with at least one more stop needed for fuel.

Kinser, despite his earlier setback, had raced to ninth place late in the race when he clipped a lapped car on Lap 189 and spun, leaving Lyn St. James with nowhere to go.

With the caution out, Ward ducked into the pits on Lap 192 for a splash of fuel, giving the lead to Goodyear for just one lap. As the race resumed on Lap 193, Luyendyk swept past his teammate and took command.

On Lap 196, the caution waved for just one lap for debris. Luyendyk withstood Goodyear's challenge on the restart, then saw yellow again on lap 198 when Stewart brushed the wall in Turn 4 and continued underway.

As the cars came off Turn 4, USAC officials at the last minute decided to restart the race to avoid finishing under caution. As the starter waved the green flag, the yellow safety light remained illuminated around the track. Although confusion reigned for a moment, the clear-headed Luyendyk punched the throttle and raced away from the field.

At the checkered flag it was Luyendyk holding a .570-second lead over Goodyear, who recorded his second Indy 500 runner-up finish. Ward was third, Lazier fourth, and Stewart fifth.

Luyendyk's win was worth $1.568 million, and Ward was a shoe-in for the BankOne Rookie of the Year award.

"I had to work a lot harder today than in 1990," Luyendyk said later. "I drove hard all day." Luyendyk gave Firestone their second straight "500" victory.

Arie got the milk—and the Borg-Warner trophy!

Goodyear, who has lost two Indy 500s by a combined total of just over .6 seconds, was dejected.

"We didn't come here for second," he said.

Indianapolis is a daunting place, yet in 1997 the institution found itself humbled by rain, rain, and more rain. But give the old place credit; when the skies finally cleared, Indy fans were provided with enough close racing to last them a long time. Maybe until next May. May is when springtime comes to Indianapolis. Or so they say.

G FORCE/OLDSMOBILE AURORA
FIRESTONE

ARIE
LUYENDYK

#5 Wavephore/Sprint PCS/Miller Lite/Provimi
Entrant: Treadway Racing, LLC   Crew Chief: Skip Faul

Arie Luyendyk accomplished an impressive feat in winning his second Indianapolis 500.

He became the first driver in the 88-year history of the Speedway to surpass the $5 million mark in earnings.

His month of May wasn't a letter-perfect, "got-'em-covered" scenario. He and Treadway Racing had to work for it with the equality of the IRL's new cars and engines.

When the veterans got out on Day 4, Luyendyk turned a lap at 218.707 miles per hour, more than three miles per hour faster than Robby Gordon, who was second on the list. The next day, he reached 220.297, becoming the only driver during the month to reach the 220 bracket.

But on Day 6, he spun in the south short chute and grazed the Turn 2 wall. Still, he was the fastest at 217.318. On the day before Pole Day, he was fastest again at 218.325.

After heat played havoc with early qualifying runs, many chose to wait, Luyendyk among them. But when the time was right, the Treadway Racing crew pushed him in line. At 3:21 P.M., he rolled away and recorded a four-lap average of 218.263 that nobody else would touch.

"Testing would've helped us," he said. "The good thing for us was that we had no mechanical problems. We were able to run Tuesday, Wednesday, Thursday, and Friday. We had any track time we wanted. The data we had from past years helped us."

On Race Day, Tony Stewart got the drop on the start and led the first 50 laps. But Luyendyk stayed right in the hunt, leading four times before taking final command on Lap 194.

His margin of victory over runner-up Scott Goodyear was just .57 of a second, the third closest finish in Indy 500 history.

"I ran this thing hard all day," he said. "I've often said, in racing, there are not many highs and a lot of lows. You get hardened by it. I had to work a lot harder today than in '90. It was a lot more difficult today . . . therefore, more gratifying."

1997 INDY 500 PERFORMANCE PROFILE

Starting Position:	1
Qualifying Average:	218.263 MPH
Qualifying Speed Rank:	1
Best Practice Speed:	220.297 MPH 5/7
Total Practice Laps:	414
Number Practice Days:	7
Finishing Position:	1
Laps Completed:	200 145.827 MPH
Highest Position 1997 Race:	1
Fastest Race Lap:	108 215.115 MPH
1997 Prize Money:	$1,568,150
INDY 500 Career Earnings:	$5,027,329
Career INDY 500 Starts:	13
Career Best Finish:	1st 1990, '97

SCOTT
GOODYEAR

**G FORCE/OLDSMOBILE AURORA
FIRESTONE**

#6 Nortel/Sprint PCS/Quebecor Printing
Entrant: Treadway Racing, LLC   Crew Chief: Kevin Blanch

Scott Goodyear returned after a year's absence as a teammate to Arie Luyendyk with Treadway Racing, trying to win a race in which he had just missed Victory Lane twice.

After hovering in the top 10 in practice throughout the first week, he put together a four-lap average of 215.811 as the 10th qualifier of the month.

"The race car was pushing all over the place," Goodyear said. "The car got a big push in Turn 2 on the last lap. We're not really sure what was wrong. On the third lap coming out of Turn 4, it started pushing, and my helmet started slopping around. We're disappointed with the last lap and concerned about the engine. It's got 450 miles on it."

On Race Day, he started fifth while Luyendyk held down the pole. He took the lead from his teammate on Lap 141 and recaptured it later on Lap 193, just seven laps from the finish, with Luyendyk right behind.

But Luyendyk took command on Lap 194 and held the lead to the finish.

"I thought we were going to finish under the yellow," Goodyear said after finishing second by .57 of a second—the second time he has been the "500" runner-up by less than a second.

"I'm not sure if we would have had enough to pass him [Luyendyk] anyway," he added. "There was a little too much drag in the car. I'm just disappointed."

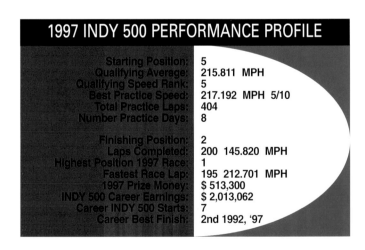

1997 INDY 500 PERFORMANCE PROFILE

Starting Position:	5
Qualifying Average:	215.811 MPH
Qualifying Speed Rank:	5
Best Practice Speed:	217.192 MPH 5/10
Total Practice Laps:	404
Number Practice Days:	8
Finishing Position:	2
Laps Completed:	200 145.820 MPH
Highest Position 1997 Race:	1
Fastest Race Lap:	195 212.701 MPH
1997 Prize Money:	$ 513,300
INDY 500 Career Earnings:	$ 2,013,062
Career INDY 500 Starts:	7
Career Best Finish:	2nd 1992, '97

3rd Place

G FORCE/OLDSMOBILE AURORA
GOODYEAR

JEFF
WARD

#52 FirstPlus Team Cheever
Entrant: FirstPlus Team Cheever   Crew Chief: Norm Johnson

Jeff Ward returned to Indy still a rookie as the second driver for driver/owner Eddie Cheever Jr. and acquitted himself well in his first "500" start. He had tried at Indy in 1995.

"It was a big jump for me, but I still have to start over," Ward said. "I just want to get on the track like everyone else."

His month of May didn't start all that well. On Day 4, he had an engine problem going into Turn 3 and hit the wall. He completed a 20-lap refresher test the day before Pole Day.

Ward then became the second qualifier of the month with a four-lap average of 214.517, good for seventh starting spot, second-best among rookies to front-row starter Sospiri.

"It feels great," Ward said. " [Danny] Sullivan came over and gave me a hug. It still hasn't sunk in. Eddie's great. Every day, he sits me down and talks with me. I want to go fast, and he tells me to take it one turn at a time."

On Race Day, Ward stayed with the leaders until he took the lead from Scott Goodyear on Lap 142. After turning it over to Arie Luyendyk, he reclaimed the point on Lap 169 for 24 laps. With victory in sight, he still needed a fuel stop, turning the lead back to Goodyear on Lap 193. Still, he finished third.

"It just went really well," Ward said. "We went really conservative but had a little bit of a push, so we went to a bigger stagger. The last 50 laps we hoped the yellows would go in our favor. If we hadn't taken that last splash-and-go pit stop, I'm sure we probably would've run out of fuel. I can't be disappointed. This is a dream come true. There is a great feeling out there."

1997 INDY 500 PERFORMANCE PROFILE

Starting Position:	7
Qualifying Average:	214.517 MPH
Qualifying Speed Rank:	9
Best Practice Speed:	215.631 MPH 5/10
Total Practice Laps:	223
Number Practice Days:	7
Finishing Position:	3
Laps Completed:	200 145.779 MPH
Highest Position 1997 Race:	1
Fastest Race Lap:	156 210.187 MPH
1997 Prize Money:	$414,250
INDY 500 Career Earnings:	$414,250
Career INDY 500 Starts:	1
Career Best Finish:	3rd 1997

4th Place

BUDDY LAZIER

DALLARA/OLDSMOBILE AURORA
FIRESTONE

#91 Delta Faucet-Montana-Hemelgarn Racing
Entrant: Hemelgarn Racing, Inc.   Crew Chief: Dennis LaCava

Buddy Lazier came back to Indianapolis as the defending champion, a new feeling, although he was again in the saddle for Hemelgarn Racing.

He was presented with a replica of the Borg-Warner Trophy in a public ceremony in the Speedway's Hall of Fame Museum, among other appearances befitting a "500" winner.

"To be the 57th different face on the trophy is absolutely awesome," he said. "The sculptor [artist William Behrends] did a great job. I paid him a lot of money to make me the best-looking guy on it."

On Pole Day, he was the next-to-last qualifier with a four-lap average of 214.286 miles per hour.

"My guys have been working really hard," Lazier said. "Thank God they're as good as they are. I think we'd have had a little bit better time, but I had too much push. We had to cram a month's worth into one day. The car is capable of 215s."

After starting 10th, he went to the front twice and was in the hunt. At the finish he was fourth, less than .2 of a mile an hour behind winner Arie Luyendyk over the 500-mile distance.

"The race car was wonderful," Lazier said. "We were in the position where we wanted to be and around 100 [laps] to go, the motor laid down. The tone changed. We went from 220 miles per hour to 201—203 in a slipstream. The engine builders did a good job because we made it to the finish, and we certainly wanted to make a run at the end. But it wasn't to be."

1997 INDY 500 PERFORMANCE PROFILE

Starting Position:	10
Qualifying Average:	214.286 MPH
Qualifying Speed Rank:	12
Best Practice Speed:	211.431 MPH 5/22
Total Practice Laps:	304
Number Practice Days:	9
Finishing Position:	4
Laps Completed:	200 145.705 MPH
Highest Position 1997 Race:	1
Fastest Race Lap:	42 211.273 MPH
1997 Prize Money:	$279,250
INDY 500 Career Earnings:	$2,119,980
Career INDY 500 Starts:	5
Career Best Finish:	1st 1996

TONY
STEWART

G FORCE/OLDSMOBILE AURORA
FIRESTONE

#2 Glidden/Menards/Special
Entrant: Team Menard, Inc.   Crew Chief: Bill Martin

Tony Stewart came to Indy for his second "500" after starting on the pole in 1996 and showing constant contention in all the Indy Racing League events to date.

He returned with Team Menard, which tested extensively at the Speedway in the weeks leading up to the month of May.

Stewart challenged Arie Luyendyk throughout the first week of practice and on Pole Day morning posted the fastest practice speed at 217.644 miles per hour.

When his qualifying time came, he took a shot at Luyendyk's pole figures but fell just short with a four-lap run of 218.021. In total time, it was less than .2 of a second behind Luyendyk over the four laps.

"I felt like someone kicked my dog," Stewart said. "Team Menard puts a lot of emphasis on the pole. To go out and run the lap like we did in practice, I was pretty excited. We had one more change we wanted to try before qualifications, but we ran out of time when everyone dashed for the qualifying line. It's just part of playing the game."

On Race Day, he got the drop on Luyendyk and led the first 50 laps of the race. In all, he led the most laps of any driver—64. He wound up fifth at the end.

"I don't mean to sound so happy because I finished fifth, but that was one of the most fun races I've ever had," Stewart said. "It was a great race. You had some slicing and dicing going on out there. If people say they didn't enjoy this Indy 500, then they aren't real race fans."

1997 INDY 500 PERFORMANCE PROFILE

Starting Position:	2
Qualifying Average:	218.021 MPH
Qualifying Speed Rank:	2
Best Practice Speed:	219.085 MPH 5/10
Total Practice Laps:	479
Number Practice Days:	11
Finishing Position:	5
Laps Completed:	200 145.490 MPH
Highest Position 1997 Race:	1
Fastest Race Lap:	105 215.626 MPH
1997 Prize Money:	$345,050
INDY 500 Career Earnings:	$567,103
Career INDY 500 Starts:	2
Career Best Finish:	5th 1997

6th Place

DAVEY
HAMILTON

G FORCE/OLDSMOBILE AURORA
GOODYEAR

#14 AJ Foyt PowerTeam Racing
Entrant: AJ Foyt Enterprises Crew Chief: John King

Davey Hamilton came to Indianapolis with his first "500" under his belt to make a second try under the tutelage of A.J. Foyt.

On the day before Pole Day, he was fourth fastest in practice with a lap at 215.853.

When his turn came in the qualifying line, he put the Foyt entry into the field at 214.484 as the ninth qualifier of the month.

"It's unfortunate we couldn't keep the 216s going but we'll be back for the race," Hamilton said. "On the third lap, we picked up a little push, came a little close to the wall. It caught me off guard."

The run put him eighth in the starting lineup, and by the 82nd lap, he was second behind Buddy Lazier. He finished sixth, one lap off the pace.

"We ran out of fuel twice early in the race," Hamilton said. "That caused us to lose a lap. We were in good shape. It was fun to finish, and we had no real problems. We got off on pit stops a little bit and tried to get our lap back but couldn't quite do it.

"We went in to win it, and I really thought we had the car to beat."

1997 INDY 500 PERFORMANCE PROFILE

Starting Position:	8
Qualifying Average:	214.484 MPH
Qualifying Speed Rank:	10
Best Practice Speed:	216.409 MPH 5/10
Total Practice Laps:	128
Number Practice Days:	8
Finishing Position:	6
Laps Completed:	199 145.058 MPH
Highest Position 1997 Race:	2
Fastest Race Lap:	194 209.849 MPH
1997 Prize Money:	$ 264,000
INDY 500 Career Earnings:	$ 448,003
Career INDY 500 Starts:	2
Career Best Finish:	6th 1997

DALLARA/OLDSMOBILE AURORA
GOODYEAR

BILLY
BOAT

#11 Conseco AJ Foyt Racing
Entrant: AJ Foyt Enterprises   Crew Chief: Craig Baranouski

Billy Boat went into the month of May with the possibility of a ride in a third A.J. Foyt entry and still got it after the Foyt team juggled its driver lineup in the wake of injuries to Scott Sharp and Johnny O'Connell.

He passed a 10-lap refresher test on the second qualifying day, and the Foyt team pushed the car into line at the end of the day. He took warmup laps but did not take the green with 3 minutes left in qualifying.

"We didn't plan on taking it," Boat said. "We made some changes to the car late in the day, and we just wanted to see how the car felt."

During the second week, he topped the speed charts three times among not-yet-qualified drivers. When the third time trial day arrived, he reeled off a four-lap average of 215.544, the first qualifier putting the car solidly in the show.

"I always had confidence in my race car and my race team," Boat said. "You just have to come here and do a job. I just told myself it's just going to be another race, just another qualifying run and tried not to remember that it's the biggest race in the world."

On Race Day, he started 22nd for his first "500" and took the lead for the 51st lap after Tony Stewart set the pace for the first quarter of the race. He wound up seventh at the end.

"[It was] everything I expected and more," Boat said. "We had a little problem early on. That got us a lap down. I was fast by myself, but when I was right behind cars, I was losing the front end. I came out without a ride and to leave with a top-10 finish is very satisfying. Next time, I'll be back for more."

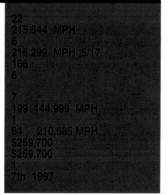

1997 INDY 500 PERFORMANCE PROFILE

Starting Position:	22
Qualifying Average:	215.544 MPH
Qualifying Speed Rank:	6
Best Practice Speed:	216.299 MPH 5/17
Total Practice Laps:	168
Number Practice Days:	6
Finishing Position:	7
Laps Completed:	199 144.999 MPH
Highest Position 1997 Race:	1
Fastest Race Lap:	64 210.585 MPH
1997 Prize Money:	$259,700
INDY 500 Career Earnings:	$259,700
Career INDY 500 Starts:	1
Career Best Finish:	7th 1997

ROBBIE
BUHL

G FORCE/OLDSMOBILE AURORA
FIRESTONE

#3 Quaker State/Special
Entrant: Team Menard, Inc.   Crew Chief: John O'Gara

Robbie Buhl came to Indy for his second

"500" as a member of the famed Menard team.

He quickly cracked the top three on the speed charts in practice twice and loomed as a contender for a high starting spot. In the morning practice on Pole Day, he turned the second fastest lap at 216.768 miles per hour.

On his first qualifying attempt, he waved off after three laps in the 214–215 bracket. On his second bid, he pulled in after a lap at 217.082. With 10 minutes left in Pole Day qualifying, he registered a four-lap average of 216.102, good for the inside of the second row.

"I hope we made it as exciting for the fans as we made it for the crew and myself," Buhl said. "We were probably going the fastest we've gone all week [on the second attempt] in Turn 1 of Lap 2 with the tailwind and time of day. In Turn 1, I tried to push the wall. In the third run, we just had to get it in."

On Race Day, he ran with the leaders throughout the first two-thirds of the race and went to the front for Laps 116–131. He finished eighth, one lap down.

"So close . . . shoulda been at the top," Buhl said. "Unfortunately, we got out of sequence in the pits with pitting under the green. Things must fall your way, and they did not. The guys did a great job. I'd love to race again tomorrow."

1997 INDY 500 PERFORMANCE PROFILE

Starting Position:	4
Qualifying Average:	216.102 MPH
Qualifying Speed Rank:	4
Best Practice Speed:	217.082 MPH 5/10
Total Practice Laps:	562
Number Practice Days:	11
Finishing Position:	8
Laps Completed:	199 144.989 MPH
Highest Position 1997 Race:	1
Fastest Race Lap:	129 211.521 MPH
1997 Prize Money:	$235,200
INDY 500 Career Earnings:	$430,603
Career INDY 500 Starts:	2
Career Best Finish:	8th 1997

G FORCE/OLDSMOBILE AURORA
GOODYEAR

ROBBIE
GROFF

#30 Alfa-Laval/Team Losi/McCormack Motorsports
Entrant: McCormack Motorsports, Inc.   Crew Chief: Phil McRobert

Robbie Groff followed in the footsteps of his brother Mike to Indianapolis and quickly set out to prove himself.

Driving for McCormack Motorsports, he was the second rookie of the month to pass his driver's test, with veterans Johnny Rutherford, Al Unser, and Johnny Parsons approving his final phase.

But on Pole Day, he brushed the wall on his second time-trial lap in the south short chute and waved off.

"The car is fine . . . just a lower wishbone," Groff said. "I'm lucky though. I've seen others a lot like it with much worse consequences."

On the second day of time trials, he waved off again before posting a four-lap run just 10 minutes from the close of qualifications at a four-lap average of 207.792 miles per hour.

"It's a terrible thing when you're down to your last attempt." Groff said. "Dennis [McCormack] did a great job of encouraging me and pumped me up and got me determined. I just put my head down and bit my teeth together."

After starting 21st, he ran a steady race, gaining ninth position on the 200th lap. That came after falling to 30th place, a lap down, on the first lap, after stopping on the backstretch with no power after the initial caution flag.

"I think the lap we were originally down hurt us," he said. "We were never really able to recover from that. It's a shame because the crew worked really hard."

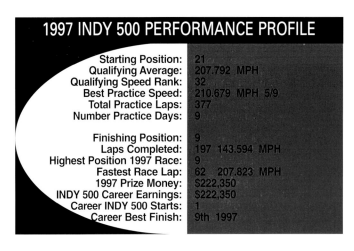

1997 INDY 500 PERFORMANCE PROFILE

Starting Position:	21
Qualifying Average:	207.792 MPH
Qualifying Speed Rank:	32
Best Practice Speed:	210.679 MPH 5/9
Total Practice Laps:	377
Number Practice Days:	9
Finishing Position:	9
Laps Completed:	197 143.594 MPH
Highest Position 1997 Race:	9
Fastest Race Lap:	62 207.823 MPH
1997 Prize Money:	$222,350
INDY 500 Career Earnings:	$222,350
Career INDY 500 Starts:	1
Career Best Finish:	9th 1997

10th Place

FERMIN VELEZ

DALLARA/OLDSMOBILE AURORA
GOODYEAR

#33 Old Navy Scandia Royal Purple Alta Xcel
Entrant: Team Scandia   Crew Chief: Brad McCanless

Fermin Velez, the first Spaniard to make a "500" field in 1996, returned with Team Scandia for a second crack at Indianapolis glory.

He went out with the other veterans on Day 4 and made the top 10 with a lap at 210.280 miles per hour.

He moved up to sixth-quickest on Day 5 with a lap at 214.174 and was fifth fastest the day before Pole Day at 215.760.

But, on a late afternoon run, he had engine trouble and waved off on the second circuit of his four-lap run.

Velez didn't show up again in practice until the day before the final qualifying weekend was to begin. But when time trials opened, he was third out and recorded a run of 206.512.

"We made the race," Fermin said. "That's what we wanted to do. Today was not as good as last week. The heat just slows down the car a little bit."

On Race Day, relegated to the 29th starting spot, he worked his way up steadily until he gained 10th place on the 200th lap.

"Not the way I wanted," he said. "I'm happy to finish. It's my first finish in this difficult Indy 500 race. I'm just happy for the crew. I'll take it, and next year, we'll go for it."

1997 INDY 500 PERFORMANCE PROFILE

Starting Position:	29
Qualifying Average:	206.512 MPH
Qualifying Speed Rank:	35
Best Practice Speed:	215.760 MPH 5/9
Total Practice Laps:	213
Number Practice Days:	7
Finishing Position:	10
Laps Completed:	195 142.039 MPH
Highest Position 1997 Race:	10
Fastest Race Lap:	100 205.479 MPH
1997 Prize Money:	$216,400
INDY 500 Career Earnings:	$396,053
Career INDY 500 Starts:	2
Career Best Finish:	10th 1997

11th Place

BUZZ CALKINS

**G FORCE/OLDSMOBILE AURORA
GOODYEAR**

#12 Bradley Food Marts
Entrant: Bradley Motorsports   Crew Chief: Steve Ritenour

Buzz Calkins returned to Indianapolis as the defending Indy Racing League co-champion.

He stayed in the top eight throughout most of the first week of practice but waved off his first attempt after three laps on Pole Day. He came back with 15 minutes remaining on the first time-trial day to register a four-lap run of 209.564 miles per hour.

"We had some engine problems," Calkins said. "A cracked head this morning and we ended up swapping engines. We had no horsepower and didn't get any practice. But we got in the field. We've got to put qualifying behind us and concentrate on the race."

The run was good enough for the 16th starting spot. Calkins ran as high as seventh on Lap 79 before a right rear half shaft broke less than 12 laps from the end, and he finished 11th.

"We ran out of gas on our second pit stop as we came in," Calkins said. "I can't believe this. We were in perfect position at that time. That put us out of sync for the rest of the race. The car wasn't perfect, but it wasn't bad."

1997 INDY 500 PERFORMANCE PROFILE

Starting Position:	16
Qualifying Average:	209.564 MPH
Qualifying Speed Rank:	27
Best Practice Speed:	213.792 MPH 5/7
Total Practice Laps:	505
Number Practice Days:	11
Finishing Position:	11
Laps Completed:	180 142.813 MPH
Highest Position 1997 Race:	7
Fastest Race Lap:	85 205.761 MPH
1997 Prize Money:	$201,000
INDY 500 Career Earnings:	$374,553
Career INDY 500 Starts:	2
Career Best Finish:	11th 1997

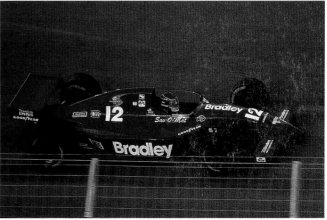

MIKE
GROFF

G FORCE/NISSAN INFINITI INDY FIRESTONE

#10 Jonathan Byrd's Cafeteria/Visionaire/Bryant
Entrant: Jonathan Byrd-Cunningham Racing LLC   Crew Chief: Mark Olson

Mike Groff went into the Indianapolis 500 with the Indy Racing League driver point lead and came out of it the same way with the Jonathan Byrd-Cunningham team.

Groff's consistency—he had been running at the finish of all four previous IRL events in the 1996–97 season—paid off again.

The veteran was the first of the month to qualify on Pole Day, putting together a four-lap run of 208.537 miles per hour. His lap times in the run were less than .2 of a second apart.

"We'll work next week on a better engine package and see what we can do," Groff said. "The engine is reliable, and that's a good sign for the race. We certainly didn't run the speed we wanted to. We ran comparable to what we ran in practice, and we were qualifying with an engine that had 400 miles on it."

On Race Day, after starting 18th, Groff moved to seventh by Lap 53. On Lap 137, he spun in the north short chute avoiding an accident involving Dr. Jack Miller. Still, he returned to finish 12th, the top finish for an Infiniti driver.

"The car had an understeer," Groff said. "If I got in traffic, it would misfire. We had a little bit of a problem with the engine yesterday. The crew changed everything overnight. It was running much better toward the end of the race."

1997 INDY 500 PERFORMANCE PROFILE

Starting Position:	18
Qualifying Average:	208.537 MPH
Qualifying Speed Rank:	31
Best Practice Speed:	209.585 MPH 5/8
Total Practice Laps:	392
Number Practice Days:	9
Finishing Position:	12
Laps Completed:	188 136.914 MPH
Highest Position 1997 Race:	7
Fastest Race Lap:	174 208.948 MPH
1997 Prize Money:	$197,300
INDY 500 Career Earnings:	$652,905
Career INDY 500 Starts:	4
Career Best Finish:	12th 1997

LYN
ST. JAMES

DALLARA/NISSAN INFINITI INDY
FIRESTONE

#90 Lifetime TV-Cinergy-Delta Faucet-Hemelgarn
Entrant: LSJ Racing/Hemelgarn Racing, Inc.   Crew Chief: Walter Gerber

---

Lyn St. James started out the month of May with a car and no engine but joined forces with Hemelgarn Racing to field an entry.

On Day 5, she took her first laps in a race car since the 1996 Indianapolis 500 after recovering from a broken right wrist she suffered during that event. The next day, two days before Pole Day, she was fourth fastest in practice with a lap at 212.565 miles an hour. She became the fifth qualifier of the month with a four-lap run of 210.145.

"It was not as quick as I thought it was going to be," St. James said. "It was solid. I picked up a big push in [Turn] 2. I was a little busier than I've been in past years. I had to adjust the bars. I just wish I had figured that out sooner."

The run held up until the final qualifying day when Alessandro Zampedri bumped his way back into the field and knocked St. James out. After qualifying, she was reinstated to the field and started in the 34th spot.

On Race Day, she reached ninth place by Lap 188. But she hit the fourth-turn wall trying to avoid Steve Kinser's accident and was placed 13th at the finish.

"It's really a disappointment," St. James said. "The car was running really good. Kinser touched with the red car, and I had nowhere to go. I drove harder today than I ever have. The fates are whatever. I guess that means I gotta come back next year."

1997 INDY 500 PERFORMANCE PROFILE

Starting Position:	34
Qualifying Average:	210.145 MPH
Qualifying Speed Rank:	26
Best Practice Speed:	212.776 MPH 5/13
Total Practice Laps:	216
Number Practice Days:	8
Finishing Position:	13
Laps Completed:	186 146.390 MPH
Highest Position 1997 Race:	9
Fastest Race Lap:	64 209.463 MPH
1997 Prize Money:	$188,000
INDY 500 Career Earnings:	$1,023,974
Career INDY 500 Starts:	6
Career Best Finish:	11th 1992

DALLARA/OLDSMOBILE AURORA
GOODYEAR

STEVE
KINSER

#44 SRS/One Call/Menards/Quaker State/St. Elmo's
Entrant: Sinden Racing   Crew Chief: Owen Snyder

Steve Kinser had tested an Indy-style car for A.J. Foyt once.

But the sprint-car legend didn't go for it in earnest until an opportunity came together with Sinden Racing Services for the 1997 Indianapolis 500.

On Day 7, he passed the last three regular phases and the final observation phase of his driver's test.

"Now we want to get this thing smoothed out and get some speed," Kinser said. "We'll try to get qualified and see what happens."

Juggling a bid at Indy with his World of Outlaws sprint-car schedule, Kinser became the first qualifier of the second day with a four-lap average of 210.793 miles per hour.

Al Unser (four-time "500" winner and IRL driver/coach) started working with me yesterday," Kinser said. "He really smoothed me out a lot. I got more relaxed in the car. The run felt really good."

On Race Day, after starting 20th, he survived a tangle with Eliseo Salazar, Mark Dismore, and Roberto Guerrero on Lap 23 and moved to fifth by Lap 52. But on Lap 189, he hit the wall in Turn 4.

"Other than hitting a car on a restart, then hitting another car with 15 laps to go, it wasn't too bad," Kinser said. "I'd sure love to run a few more IRL races. I'd hate to quit now. To run as good as we did on the spur of the moment, I'm very proud of everyone. I'm just disappointed in myself."

1997 INDY 500 PERFORMANCE PROFILE

Starting Position:	20
Qualifying Average:	210.793 MPH
Qualifying Speed Rank:	23
Best Practice Speed:	214.684 MPH 5/16
Total Practice Laps:	429
Number Practice Days:	8
Finishing Position:	14
Laps Completed:	185 146.265 MPH
Highest Position 1997 Race:	5
Fastest Race Lap:	184 206.110 MPH
1997 Prize Money:	$193,250
INDY 500 Career Earnings:	$193,250
Career INDY 500 Starts:	1
Career Best Finish:	14th 1997

DENNIS
VITOLO

DALLARA/NISSAN INFINITI INDY
FIRESTONE

#54 SmithKline Beecham/Kroger/Beck Motorsports
Entrant: Beck Motorsports   Crew Chief: Greg Beck

Dennis Vitolo returned to Indy after being absent from the field since 1994.

He was assigned to the Beck Motorsports ride on the second qualifying day and spent the second week of practice working up to speed.

Vitolo became the 28th qualifier of the month on the third day of time trials with a four-lap run of 207.626 miles per hour.

"The team did a great job in the short amount of time the team had to get dialed in," Vitolo said. "I told the team, 'Let's just get in and with, the little time left, work on race setup. The car's brand-new. They just built it up this week."

On Race Day, after starting 28th, he moved to 10th by the 48th lap before finishing 15th, despite being hampered by battery problems throughout the race.

"I'm happy to finish," Vitolo said. "We put a load of batteries in, but we finished. It's nice to take the checkered flag for once at Indy. I knew I was many laps down. I just wanted to stay out of the way of the leaders and let them run their race."

1997 INDY 500 PERFORMANCE PROFILE

Starting Position:	28
Qualifying Average:	207.626 MPH
Qualifying Speed Rank:	33
Best Practice Speed:	208.522 MPH 5/17
Total Practice Laps:	190
Number Practice Days:	6
Finishing Position:	15
Laps Completed:	173 125.970 MPH
Highest Position 1997 Race:	10
Fastest Race Lap:	41 202.543 MPH
1997 Prize Money:	$200,000
INDY 500 Career Earnings:	$343,862
Career INDY 500 Starts:	2
Career Best Finish:	15th 1997

16th Place

DALLARA/OLDSMOBILE AURORA
GOODYEAR

MARCO
GRECO

#22 Side Play Int'l Sport Scandia Alta Xcel
Entrant: Team Scandia   Crew Chief: Gilbert Lage

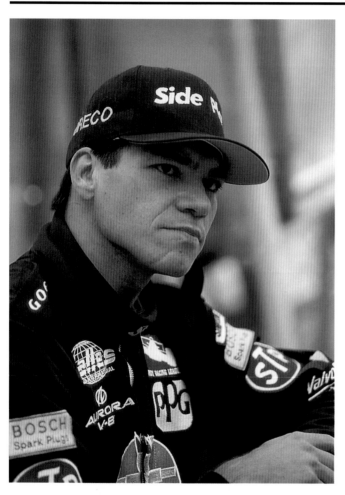

Marco Greco came to Indianapolis with Team Scandia in the heat of the Indy Racing League point battle with a string of steady finishes.

He didn't make a qualifying attempt the first weekend but put a machine in the field at an average speed of 210.322 miles per hour on the third qualifying day.

"We didn't expect high speeds," Greco said. "We didn't practice much. It's very tough, especially for myself, sitting in the garage and waiting.

I came to do my very best. I'm fourth in championship points. We never did six laps in a row without something happening."

The run was good for the 27th starting spot and Greco reached seventh place by Lap 139.

Gearbox problems ended his day after 166 laps, and he finished 16th.

"I think the gear on the driveshaft broke," Greco said. "The car was understeering a lot before the last pit stop, so we changed that and then the car broke when we went back out the last time."

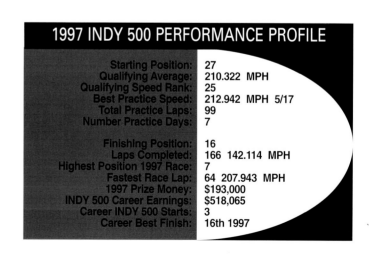

1997 INDY 500 PERFORMANCE PROFILE

Starting Position:	27
Qualifying Average:	210.322 MPH
Qualifying Speed Rank:	25
Best Practice Speed:	212.942 MPH 5/17
Total Practice Laps:	99
Number Practice Days:	7
Finishing Position:	16
Laps Completed:	166 142.114 MPH
Highest Position 1997 Race:	7
Fastest Race Lap:	64 207.943 MPH
1997 Prize Money:	$193,000
INDY 500 Career Earnings:	$518,065
Career INDY 500 Starts:	3
Career Best Finish:	16th 1997

DALLARA/OLDSMOBILE AURORA
GOODYEAR

VINCENZO
SOSPIRI

#8 Old Navy Scandia Royal Purple Alta Xcel
Entrant: Team Scandia   Crew Chief: Luke Wethington

Vincenzo Sospiri came to Indianapolis with Team Scandia a rookie to oval track racing.

On the first day of the USAC Rookie Orientation Program, he breezed through the first four phases, ran 78 laps, and reached 211.964.

"Little scary, really, but I like it," he said about the Speedway. "There's a lot more speed to catch out there, and I think we can go even faster than today. Since I was 14 1/2 and I started to watch Formula One, I've dreamed of being a world champion in Formula One and winning an Indy 500 as often as possible."

Two days later, he passed the observation phase under the watchful eyes of Johnny Rutherford, Al Unser, Sr. and Johnny Parsons. For the rest of the week, he searched for speed, reaching the top 10 the day before Pole Day with 213.498.

When qualifying came, he was the 11th of the month to complete a run, and his four-lap average was 216.822, putting him outside the front row for his first Indianapolis 500.

"[The] feeling is like a bullet in a gun," Sospiri said. "You go so close to the wall, and you go so fast; you are like a bullet."

In the race, he dropped back before finishing 17th as the last car running.

"We had a very good car to start with," he said. "I was comfortable in fifth, sixth, and seventh place. Unfortunately, we had some electronic problems. It took a long time to figure out because we didn't have it ever before. The problem was an electronic coil. We found the problem 20–30 laps from the end. We didn't get it fixed until four laps from the end."

1997 INDY 500 PERFORMANCE PROFILE

Starting Position:	3
Qualifying Average:	216.822 MPH
Qualifying Speed Rank:	3
Best Practice Speed:	217.056 MPH 5/10
Total Practice Laps:	231
Number Practice Days:	6
Finishing Position:	17
Laps Completed:	163 118.736 MPH
Highest Position 1997 Race:	3
Fastest Race Lap:	49 209.156 MPH
1997 Prize Money:	$196,250
INDY 500 Career Earnings:	$196,250
Career INDY 500 Starts:	1
Career Best Finish:	17th 1997

DALLARA/NISSAN INFINITI INDY
FIRESTONE

JOHNNY
UNSER

#9 Delta Faucet-Montana-Cinergy-Hemelgarn
Entrant: Hemelgarn Racing, Inc.   Crew Chief: Mike Colliver

Johnny Unser wanted his second year at Indy to be better than his first when he didn't complete a lap in 1996 because of transmission problems.

He got his chance when car owner Ron Hemelgarn announced on Pole Day that Unser would be in an Infiniti-powered car on his team.

Unser worked his way up to speed during the second week of practice and became the 32nd qualifier of the month with a four-lap average of 209.344 miles per hour as the first qualifier of the final time-trial day.

"We lost the engine yesterday morning, and I haven't had much time in the car since," Unser said. "We had a little bit of a problem in practice this morning—handling and electrical—so we didn't get a chance to test the setup. Qualifying was a bit of a gamble, but it was a gamble we had to take."

He had a topsy-turvy day. Claude Bourbonnais bumped him from the field a little more than two hours later. But he was reinstated at the end of the day as an added starter and took 35th position on the grid.

On Race Day, he moved to as high as third on Lap 52 before oil pressure problems sent him to the sidelines after 158 circuits.

"My engine blew," he said. "It just let go. Tyce [Carlson] was in front of me, and he spun. We didn't have any contact at all. It's great to see how many cars are still running out there right now."

1997 INDY 500 PERFORMANCE PROFILE

Starting Position:	35
Qualifying Average:	209.344 MPH
Qualifying Speed Rank:	28
Best Practice Speed:	210.773 MPH 5/22
Total Practice Laps:	112
Number Practice Days:	3
Finishing Position:	18
Laps Completed:	158 141.078 MPH
Highest Position 1997 Race:	3
Fastest Race Lap:	100 207.857 MPH
1997 Prize Money:	$158,000
INDY 500 Career Earnings:	$301,953
Career INDY 500 Starts:	2
Career Best Finish:	18th 1997

DALLARA/OLDSMOBILE AURORA
GOODYEAR

TYCE
CARLSON

#18 Klipsch Tnemec Overhead Door Pyle V-Line Earl's
Entrant: PDM Racing, Inc.   Crew Chief: John Pearson

Tyce Carlson started out the month of May with only a possible backup opportunity to improve from 1996 alternate to his first starting spot in the Indianapolis 500.

But when John Paul Jr. crashed the day before Pole Day and was ruled out for the month with leg injuries, PDM Racing decided on Day 11 that Carlson would replace him.

"I never wanted to get in the seat with the circumstances that happened, but I'm going to do my best job to win this race," Carlson said, "not for myself, but for the guys that have tried so hard to put this car in the field."

Leading up to the second weekend of time trials, he was a consistent runner in the top six of those not-yet-qualified. On the third time-trial day, he qualified for his first "500" at a four-lap average of 210.852 miles per hour.

"I've had 364 days [since being bumped in 1996] to wait for this moment," Carlson said. "When I got out of the car and saw my family and friends who have been behind me since I started racing, this is a dream come true."

After starting 26th, he ran as high as sixth before a Turn 2 accident left him sidelined in 19th.

"We were just trying to stay out there and bide our time," Carlson said. "I just got loose in the turn and lost it. I feel so sorry for those guys [the crew]. I have to go back and apologize."

1997 INDY 500 PERFORMANCE PROFILE

Starting Position:	26
Qualifying Average:	210.852 MPH
Qualifying Speed Rank:	22
Best Practice Speed:	213.802 MPH 5/17
Total Practice Laps:	155
Number Practice Days:	4
Finishing Position:	19
Laps Completed:	156 139.349 MPH
Highest Position 1997 Race:	6
Fastest Race Lap:	63 205.329 MPH
1997 Prize Money:	$173,250
INDY 500 Career Earnings:	$173,250
Career INDY 500 Starts:	1
Career Best Finish:	19th 1997

DR. JACK
MILLER

**DALLARA/NISSAN INFINITI INDY
FIRESTONE**

#40 AMS/Crest Racing/Trane/Spot-On
Entrant: Arizona Motorsports   Crew Chief: Joe Kennedy

Dr. Jack Miller came to Indy with the AMS/Crest Racing team to fulfill a lifelong dream.

The "Racing Dentist" from nearby Carmel, Indiana, was the first rookie to complete a phase of his driver's test and completed it the day before Pole Day.

"I'm very comfortable and as happy as I've ever been in a race car in my life," Miller said.

He was the third qualifier on Pole Day, checking in at a four-lap average of 209.250 miles per hour.

"Oh, man, it's the quickest I've gone," he said. "We did the quickest laps of the month during these qualification laps. I can probably go quicker than that. I was born and raised here in Indianapolis, and I have come to the Indy 500 since I was five. I took pictures for the Associated Press for five years in Turns 1 and 2, so I could learn the line there."

On Race Day, he started 17th and had a heart-stopper when he slid sideways in Turn 4 on the first parade lap. He ran as high as seventh on Lap 51 before bowing out in a Turn 3 accident after 131 circuits.

"I was running by myself in Turn 3, and the back end locked up and put me into the fence," Miller said.

1997 INDY 500 PERFORMANCE PROFILE

Starting Position:	17
Qualifying Average:	209.250 MPH
Qualifying Speed Rank:	29
Best Practice Speed:	209.497 MPH 5/10
Total Practice Laps:	219
Number Practice Days:	8
Finishing Position:	20
Laps Completed:	131 139.116 MPH
Highest Position 1997 Race:	7
Fastest Race Lap:	124 205.681 MPH
1997 Prize Money:	$171,250
INDY 500 Career Earnings:	$171,250
Career INDY 500 Starts:	1
Career Best Finish:	20th 1997

G FORCE/OLDSMOBILE AURORA
GOODYEAR

PAUL DURANT

#1 Conseco AJ Foyt Racing
Entrant: AJ Foyt Enterprises   Crew Chief: Craig Baranouski

Paul Durant spent most of the month trying to work out a ride. When the ride came, it was a fast, unusual journey.

When Johnny O'Connell, subbing for injured 1996 Indy Racing League co-champion Scott Sharp in the No. 1 Conseco AJ Foyt Racing entry, crashed the day before the final time-trial weekend, Foyt searched for a second replacement.

On the final qualifying day, he turned to Durant, a veteran supermodified competitor who had raced for years with Davey Hamilton, Foyt's other driver.

It didn't take long.

After Hamilton shook the car down, Durant climbed in it at 12:17 P.M.

By 12:39 P.M., he had 12 practice laps, and the team pushed the car into the technical inspection line. At 1:09 P.M., Durant had qualified at 209.149, just 52 minutes after saddling up.

"It really is exciting, considering that a little over an hour and a half ago, I thought I was going home," Durant told reporters. "The last couple of hours seem like a whirlwind. Racing has the highest highs and lowest lows, and in a matter of two hours, I've had both of them."

He started 33rd on Race Day and streaked to sixth by Lap 49. But on Lap 114, he tangled with Billy Roe in Turn 3, ending his day with a trip to Methodist Hospital with a broken pelvis.

1997 INDY 500 PERFORMANCE PROFILE

Starting Position:	33
Qualifying Average:	178,000 MPH
Qualifying Speed Rank:	30
Best Practice Speed:	211.015 MPH 5/18
Total Practice Laps:	66
Number Practice Days:	2
Finishing Position:	21
Laps Completed:	111 147.226 MPH
Highest Position 1997 Race:	6
Fastest Race Lap:	46 210.285 MPH
1997 Prize Money:	$178,000
INDY 500 Career Earnings:	$327,153
Career INDY 500 Starts:	2
Career Best Finish:	21st 1997

22nd Place

BILLY ROE

**DALLARA/OLDSMOBILE AURORA
FIRESTONE**

50 Sega/Progressive Electronics/KECO/U.J.T./Eurointernational
Entrant: Eurointernational Inc.   Crew Chief: Billy Bignotti

Billy Roe came to Indianapolis with a unique distinction: He may be the only driver who's driven a turbine car (sprinter at Phoenix International Raceway), an electric Indy-style car, and a piston-powered car.

He drove his first lap at Indy in an electric-powered machine in a demonstration on the same day that A.J. Foyt retired as a driver (May 15, 1993).

And this year he got the chance to take a crack at the "500" with the Eurointernational team.

Roe passed all five phases of his driver's test on Day 10 and became the second qualifier on the third time-trial day with a four-lap average of 212.752 miles per hour.

"I'm elated," Roe said. "I'd like to thank the good Lord for a great day and making this opportunity available. We've tried to simulate a qualifying run [in practice] and kept spewing water. I told the crew not to talk to me during qualifying unless I was under 212. I didn't hear from them, so I knew it was good enough."

After starting 24th on Race Day, he ran as high as 10th on Lap 112 before he and Paul Durant collided in Turn 3 to end his day in 22nd.

"They were racing real tight," Roe said. "I just hope Paul is okay."

1997 INDY 500 PERFORMANCE PROFILE

Starting Position:	24
Qualifying Average:	212.752 MPH
Qualifying Speed Rank:	18
Best Practice Speed:	213.381 MPH 5/17
Total Practice Laps:	291
Number Practice Days:	7
Finishing Position:	22
Laps Completed:	110 145.914 MPH
Highest Position 1997 Race:	10
Fastest Race Lap:	64 209.839 MPH
1997 Prize Money:	$ 150,250
INDY 500 Career Earnings:	$ 150,250
Career INDY 500 Starts:	1
Career Best Finish:	22nd 1997

23rd Place

EDDIE
CHEEVER JR.

G FORCE/OLDSMOBILE AURORA
GOODYEAR

#51 FirstPlus Team Cheever
Entrant: FirstPlus Team Cheever   Crew Chief: Mitch Davis

Eddie Cheever Jr. came to the Speedway as a driver/owner for the first time, fielding cars for himself and rookie Jeff Ward.

He did extensive pre-May testing at the track and when qualifying came, he recorded a four-lap average of 214.073, good for the 11th starting spot in the field.

"The track is almost a live organism," Cheever said. "It changes all the time. While the conditions were changing, I was sliding all the way around the track. Unfortunately, we didn't run in the beginning of the week, and that hurt us. I made a bad decision. I loosened up my car a lot. I also had a problem with my gearbox. I couldn't get it out."

On Race Day, he ran steadily until moving to sixth place on Lap 76 before a timing chain failed to end his day in 23rd. After that, he went to his team's pits and watched Ward go to the front in his team car.

"It was a real shame because I was going through traffic very easily," Cheever said. "This is the greatest race in the world, so it's a severe disappointment. The cookie crumbled."

And after watching Ward, he also talked about his rookie teammate's determined battle.

"Right to the end, I was convinced he was gonna win," said Eddie, the car owner. "He led the '500' with vigor."

1997 INDY 500 PERFORMANCE PROFILE

Starting Position:	11
Qualifying Average:	214.073 MPH
Qualifying Speed Rank:	13
Best Practice Speed:	216.909 MPH, 5/13
Total Practice Laps:	311
Number Practice Days:	5
Finishing Position:	23
Laps Completed:	84, 143.599 MPH
Highest Position 1997 Race:	6
Fastest Race Lap:	46, 208.948 MPH
1997 Prize Money:	$176,000
INDY 500 Career Earnings:	$1,528,652
Career INDY 500 Starts:	8
Career Best Finish:	4th 1992

83

24th Place

**DALLARA/OLDSMOBILE AURORA
GOODYEAR**

ELISEO
SALAZAR

#7 Copec/Cristal/Scandia
Entrant: Team Scandia   Crew Chief: Dane Harte

Eliseo Salazar returned to Indy with Team Scandia after a front-row start in 1996.

He reached the top 10 in practice on Day 5 of practice. But, as the sixth to attempt qualification on Pole Day, he hit a bird in Turn 3 on his third lap and pulled in. Later, he qualified with a four-lap average of 214.320 miles per hour.

"I live here, and I know what this place means," Salazar said. "This package is obviously new, and we will make improvements. In three or four years from now, they will be back up to 230 again, and they will need to slow up the cars again."

The run was good for ninth starting position on Race Day. However, he was involved in a tangle with Mark Dismore, Steve Kinser, and Roberto Guerrero in Turn 4 as the field came to the green after a caution.

A pit stop of 20 minutes, 4 seconds, got him back on the track. However, he brushed the wall and stopped in Turn 2 after 70 laps.

"Kinser hit me on the restart, and the right suspension broke," Salazar said. "The brake caliper seized, and that's the reason for the car to stop. We'll see if we can fix it and perhaps go out again."

However, his day was ended in 24th Place.

1997 INDY 500 PERFORMANCE PROFILE

Starting Position:	9
Qualifying Average:	214.320 MPH
Qualifying Speed Rank:	11
Best Practice Speed:	214.777 MPH 5/10
Total Practice Laps:	194
Number Practice Days:	5
Finishing Position:	24
Laps Completed:	70 112.721 MPH
Highest Position 1997 Race:	9
Fastest Race Lap:	59 206.531 MPH
1997 Prize Money:	$164,000
INDY 500 Career Earnings:	$611,253
Career INDY 500 Starts:	3
Career Best Finish:	4th 1995

25th Place

DALLARA/OLDSMOBILE AURORA
FIRESTONE

GREG
RAY

#97 Tobacco Free Kids
Entrant: Thomas Knapp Motorsport/Genoa   Crew Chief: Troy Stevens

---

Greg Ray came quickly onto the Indy Racing League scene and promptly passed the four regular phases and final observation phase of his driver's test on Day 4 at Indianapolis.

But Ray had the misfortune, on the second time-trial day, to run out of fuel on the final lap of a run that was in the 215-mile-an-hour bracket.

Things looked prosperous for him again as he led not-yet-qualified drivers on the day before the final qualifying weekend with a lap during practice at 215.069 miles per hour.

Misfortune, though, struck again. As first up on the third qualifying day, he had engine trouble on his warmup lap and couldn't take the green. But on the last qualifying day, he made his first "500" field with a four-lap average of 213.760.

"I didn't get worried until yesterday, when we blew the engine," Ray said of his tribulations. "Some of the guys were so down after we ran out of fuel [the first weekend], I went into the garage and gave them a pep talk. [Today] the car wasn't fast enough, but I kept my mouth shut and got the car safely in the show."

On Race Day, he started 30th and moved to 10th by the 43rd lap. But five laps later, water pump failure ended his day.

"I was looking forward to my rookie experience," Ray said. "We had a good car. Now it's all over."

1997 INDY 500 PERFORMANCE PROFILE

Starting Position:	30
Qualifying Average:	213.760 MPH
Qualifying Speed Rank:	14
Best Practice Speed:	215.595 MPH 5/11
Total Practice Laps:	255
Number Practice Days:	6
Finishing Position:	25
Laps Completed:	48 95.365 MPH
Highest Position 1997 Race:	10
Fastest Race Lap:	41 210.118 MPH
1997 Prize Money:	$171,250
INDY 500 Career Earnings:	$171,250
Career INDY 500 Starts:	1
Career Best Finish:	25th 1997

26th Place

JIM GUTHRIE

DALLARA/OLDSMOBILE AURORA
FIRESTONE

#27 Blueprint/Jacuzzi/Armour Golf/ERTL
Entrant: Blueprint Racing, Inc.   Crew Chief: Randy Ruyle

Jim Guthrie came to Indianapolis for his second "500" on a high after winning the 200-miler at Phoenix.

He was third fastest on Day 5, the second day of veteran practice, and looked to be a challenger. On Pole Day, he qualified with a four-lap average of 215.207 miles per hour. The run put him sixth in the starting lineup.

"In Turn 4 yesterday, the motor just quit," Guthrie said. "The timing chain had broken. The guys flew up to the shop in Chicago to work on the motor. This morning my crew showed up at 3:30 A.M. to put it together, and then, today, USAC noticed we had some fluid leaking. We fixed that and decided to go ahead and put it in the show."

After problems continued, Guthrie was one of five drivers who were allowed to make system check runs the day before the race.

On Race Day, Guthrie gained a position by the fifth lap. But on the seventh, he came to pit road with an engine problem.

"The car overheated, and the oil temperature went up," Guthrie said after rain delayed the race to the next day. "We were ready to go back out when the rain came."

The next day, engine troubles persisted, and he dropped out after completing 43 laps in 26th Place.

"Lady Luck wasn't with us," he said. "We tried some new things, and they didn't work. We don't know what went wrong. Things just weren't going our way."

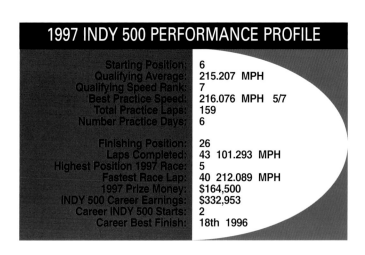

1997 INDY 500 PERFORMANCE PROFILE

Starting Position:	6
Qualifying Average:	215.207 MPH
Qualifying Speed Rank:	7
Best Practice Speed:	216.076 MPH 5/7
Total Practice Laps:	159
Number Practice Days:	6
Finishing Position:	26
Laps Completed:	43 101.293 MPH
Highest Position 1997 Race:	5
Fastest Race Lap:	40 212.089 MPH
1997 Prize Money:	$164,500
INDY 500 Career Earnings:	$332,953
Career INDY 500 Starts:	2
Career Best Finish:	18th 1996

27th Place

ROBERTO GUERRERO

DALLARA/NISSAN INFINITI INDY
GOODYEAR

#21 Pennzoil-Pagan Racing Dallara Infiniti
Entrant: Pagan Racing   Crew Chief: John Barnes

Roberto Guerrero came to Indy as one of the senior members of the driving cast, returning to Pagan Racing and working with the new Nissan Infiniti Indy engine.

After waving off an attempt just after taking the green in his primary car, he became the final qualifier of the first day in his backup with a four-lap run of 207.371 miles per hour.

"It's kind of tough, first of all, to say [about his speed holding up]," Guerrero said. "I don't know how many cars will have to qualify. It seems the second week around this place lots of race cars appear. We have another car ready if it's needed."

It was ruled the next day by USAC Chief Steward Keith Ward that Guerrero's backup could not be bumped from the field because it actually qualified as No. 21 and was a "locked in" starter. The run and the ruling put him 19th in the starting lineup.

Guerrero moved up to 11th spot by the 23rd lap, but he was involved in a four-car tangle in Turn 4 which ended his day in 27th Place.

"The car in front of me reacted to [Eliseo] Salazar spinning," Guerrero said. "He braked, and I didn't have enough time to stop. We changed the right front suspension, and we were going to check it out, but we couldn't even keep the car straight on the straightaway, so we decided to park it."

1997 INDY 500 PERFORMANCE PROFILE

Starting Position:	19
Qualifying Average:	207.371 MPH
Qualifying Speed Rank:	34
Best Practice Speed:	210.669 MPH 5/13
Total Practice Laps:	243
Number Practice Days:	8
Finishing Position:	27
Laps Completed:	25 134.725 MPH
Highest Position 1997 Race:	11
Fastest Race Lap:	4 202.206 MPH
1997 Prize Money:	$160,000
INDY 500 Career Earnings:	$2,338,763
Career INDY 500 Starts:	13
Career Best Finish:	2nd 1984, '87

87

MARK
DISMORE

DALLARA/OLDSMOBILE AURORA
GOODYEAR

#28 Kelley Automotive Mechanics Laundry Bombardier Grainger
Entrant: PDM Racing, Inc.   Crew Chief: Paul Murphy

Mark Dismore joined the new Kelley Racing team as PDM Racing pitched in to field a car. Their battle was against time.

Dismore took the track for the first time on Day 13 of the month after the PDM team prepared a car for Kelley in less than a week.

"I was real comfortable with those guys," Dismore said after being third fastest among potential second-weekend qualifiers with a lap at 210.389. "They took their time, and if something wasn't right, they made it right. We found out what we needed to find out, got out of the cars, and put 'em away."

The next day, Dismore turned a lap at 213.848 and posted the fastest lap of pre-qualifying practice on the third day of time trials at 217.360. His four-lap average was 212.423.

"This morning we did a 217," Dismore said. "I wish we could have qualified right then, but the track got hot. We lost the handle on the front end of the car. Tom [Kelley, the car owner] and me really didn't know each other until two weeks ago."

On Race Day, he started 25th and moved to 12th by the 22nd lap. His day ended, though, in a four-car melee off Turn 4, and he finished 28th.

"Everybody tries to win the race on the restart," Dismore said. "It doesn't matter what series it is. I'm really sick about it right now."

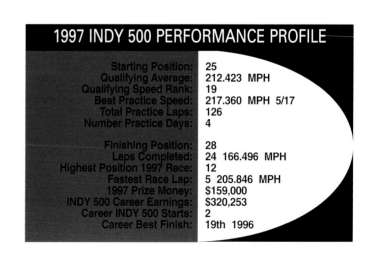

1997 INDY 500 PERFORMANCE PROFILE

Starting Position:	25
Qualifying Average:	212.423 MPH
Qualifying Speed Rank:	19
Best Practice Speed:	217.360 MPH 5/17
Total Practice Laps:	126
Number Practice Days:	4
Finishing Position:	28
Laps Completed:	24 166.496 MPH
Highest Position 1997 Race:	12
Fastest Race Lap:	5 205.846 MPH
1997 Prize Money:	$159,000
INDY 500 Career Earnings:	$320,253
Career INDY 500 Starts:	2
Career Best Finish:	19th 1996

29th Place

ROBBY
GORDON

G FORCE/OLDSMOBILE AURORA
GOODYEAR

#42 Coors Light
Entrant: Team Sabco   Crew Chief: Dave Forbes

Robby Gordon had a full plate for the month of May.

After switching to NASCAR's Winston Cup series, he still prepared for the Indianapolis 500 with SABCO Racing, his NASCAR team, fielding a car for him at Indy.

Gordon was fast in pre-May testing and was in the top six in practice every day leading to Pole Day. He was the month's 16th qualifier at 213.211, however, and started 12th.

"I'm surprised we ran for six laps," Gordon said. "That's the most we ran since we've been here. It's frustrating. I think I've run 95 laps or something before qualifying, and 60 of those were under 150, warming up."

On Race Day, he charged to the front. He gained six positions on the first lap and surged past Jim Guthrie for fifth on the second circuit.

He was challenging the leaders on Lap 20 when his car caught fire. He pulled to a stop in the third turn, jumped out, and rolled in the grass to extinguish the flames.

After the fire was out, Gordon got back in and was towed to the pits, but his crew couldn't repair the machine, and he finished 29th.

"I have no idea," Gordon said. "I was coming by [Arie] Luyendyk on the backstretch. I felt all this heat. I realized I was on fire. We were just cruisin'. We were going by Luyendyk pretty easy. Our car was so good."

1997 INDY 500 PERFORMANCE PROFILE

Starting Position:	12
Qualifying Average:	213.211 MPH
Qualifying Speed Rank:	15
Best Practice Speed:	215.993 MPH 5/7
Total Practice Laps:	375
Number Practice Days:	10
Finishing Position:	29
Laps Completed:	19 146.022 MPH
Highest Position 1997 Race:	4
Fastest Race Lap:	5 204.937 MPH
1997 Prize Money:	$ 139,500
INDY 500 Career Earnings:	$ 770,438
Career INDY 500 Starts:	4
Career Best Finish:	5th 1994, '95

30th
Place

CLAUDE
BOURBONNAIS

DALLARA/OLDSMOBILE AURORA
FIRESTONE

#72 Blueprint/Jacuzzi/Armour Golf/ERTL
Entrant: Blueprint Racing, Inc.   Crew Chief: Dale Wise

Claude Bourbonnais spent most of
the month of May "kicking tires" in Gasoline Alley, but
when his turn came, he made the most of it to gain a
spot in the "500" field.

Two days before the final weekend of time trials,
Bourbonnais was named to drive Blueprint Racing's
backup car to Jim Guthrie. He completed four phases of
the driver's test the same afternoon and the observation
phase the next day.

"I needed the rookie orientation to get back up to
speed, but I'm glad to have completed it," Claude said.
"I would've done exactly the same thing if I wouldn't
have had rookie orientation because I would've got up
to speed at the same rate."

But on the third qualifying day during practice,
Bourbonnais brushed the wall in Turn 2, and he drove
back to the pits on two wheels.

After the crew repaired the machine, he went out
and qualified less than 4 hours from the end of time
trials with a four-lap average of 210.523.

"The wind picked up, and we had a half-hour
window," Bourbonnais said. "I haven't been racing in a
year, so I'm a little rusty. I got some sleep last night but
the crew didn't."

After starting 32nd, he gained 14 spots in the first
nine laps, but the engine failed at that point, ending his
day in 30th.

"The engine just blew," he said. "We were at the
corner of [Turn] 4."

1997 INDY 500 PERFORMANCE PROFILE

Starting Position:	32
Qualifying Average:	210.523 MPH
Qualifying Speed Rank:	24
Best Practice Speed:	211.635 MPH 5/18
Total Practice Laps:	242
Number Practice Days:	6
Finishing Position:	30
Laps Completed:	9 184.710 MPH
Highest Position 1997 Race:	18
Fastest Race Lap:	8 194.016 MPH
1997 Prize Money:	$152,250
INDY 500 Career Earnings:	$152,250
Career INDY 500 Starts:	1
Career Best Finish:	30th 1997

31st Place

STEPHAN
GREGOIRE

G FORCE/OLDSMOBILE AURORA
GOODYEAR

#77 Chastain Motorsports-Estridge-Miller-Eads
Entrant: Chastain Motorsports   Crew Chief: Darrell Soppe

Stephan Gregoire came to Indianapolis with the new Chastain Motorsports team. It would be their third race together.

In addition to motorized racing, Gregoire finished 76th out of thousands in a mini-marathon in the week before qualifications.

"I'm from a town in France, and everybody runs," he said. "Being in shape is a big advantage to keep your concentration, so you won't make a big mistake."

Gregoire got in 259 laps of practice before qualifying and became the 14th to join the field on Pole Day after a run at 213.126 miles per hour.

"Today was not too bad," he said. "This morning we had a big problem with handling. At the end of the day yesterday, we made changes in spring settings. We went the wrong way. It had a big push, especially in Turns 1 and 2 because of the wind."

On the first of the three Race Days, after starting 13th, Gregoire's "500" ended early as he went out in a pace-lap tangle with Affonso Giaffone and Kenny Brack.

"I was on the bottom," he said. "I was running my line. Giaffone touched me, and I went right into the wall. All of us do not know what happened."

1997 INDY 500 PERFORMANCE PROFILE

Starting Position:	13
Qualifying Average:	213.126 MPH
Qualifying Speed Rank:	16
Best Practice Speed:	214.475 MPH 5/10
Total Practice Laps:	272
Number Practice Days:	6
Finishing Position:	31
Laps Completed:	0
Highest Position 1997 Race:	N/A
Fastest Race Lap:	N/A
1997 Prize Money:	$158,000
INDY 500 Career Earnings:	$494,706
Career INDY 500 Starts:	3
Career Best Finish:	19th, 1993

AFFONSO
GIAFFONE

DALLARA/OLDSMOBILE AURORA
GOODYEAR

#17 General Motors Brazil Chitwood Dallara
Entrant: Chitwood Motorsports, Inc.   Crew Chief: Mark Stainbrook

Affonso Giaffone came to his first Indianapolis 500 with the new Chitwood Motorsports team which bore the name and the legacy of "500" veteran Joie Chitwood.

On Day 4 of the month, he passed the first four phases of his driver's test in a scant few hours and completed the final observation phase by the end of the day.

By the day before Pole Day, he was seventh fastest. When qualifications opened, he became the fourth qualifier with a four-lap average of 212.974 miles per hour.

"I'm really happy being here for the first time," Giaffone said. "It's like a dream come true. I've been watching Indy on TV since I was a little boy, and I've got to say TV doesn't do it justice. I can't believe the size of this place. It's 10 times more awesome than you'd believe."

On Race Day, though, his run was short-lived as he went to the sidelines after tangling with Stephan Gregoire and Kenny Brack in Turn 4 before coming to take the green.

"I really don't know what happened," Giaffone said. "Just ran out of space. I think Kenny got off his line. It's a real disappointment to the team."

1997 INDY 500 PERFORMANCE PROFILE

Starting Position:	14
Qualifying Average:	212.974 MPH
Qualifying Speed Rank:	17
Best Practice Speed:	215.848 MPH 5/10
Total Practice Laps:	336
Number Practice Days:	8
Finishing Position:	32
Laps Completed:	0
Highest Position 1997 Race:	N/A
Fastest Race Lap:	N/A
1997 Prize Money:	$158,250
INDY 500 Career Earnings:	$158,250
Career INDY 500 Starts:	1
Career Best Finish:	32nd 1997

33rd Place

KENNY
BRACK

**G FORCE/OLDSMOBILE AURORA
GOODYEAR**

#4 Monsoon Galles Racing
Entrant: Galles Racing International   Crew Chief: Gary Armentrout

Kenny Brack came to the United States to join Galles Racing and start his Indy-style career at Phoenix, so the Indianapolis 500 would be only his second race in the new Indy Racing League machines.

The smiling Swede was the second to complete the first four phases of his driver's test and the first to pass the final observation phase.

On Day 2, he is believed to have set a unique record for the longest tow-in in Speedway history. His car stopped in the north short chute and needed a tow. When he was towed to pit road, he continued to hold the tow line, necessitating another trip around the 2 1/2-mile oval.

"Normally they tow you to the pit [in Europe]," Brack said with a laugh. "I didn't realize I was supposed to let go. No one told me."

On Pole Day, he became the seventh qualifier of the month with a four-lap run of 211.221.

"I think the run was good the first three laps, but then we got some oversteer and had to slow down," he said.

The run put him 15th, outside the fifth row for the race. He finished 33rd, tangling with Affonso Giaffone and Stephan Gregoire in Turn 4 as the field came to the green.

"I really don't know what happened," Brack said. "I got knocked out from behind."

1997 INDY 500 PERFORMANCE PROFILE

Starting Position:	15
Qualifying Average:	211.221 MPH
Qualifying Speed Rank:	21
Best Practice Speed:	215.074 MPH 5/16
Total Practice Laps:	402
Number Practice Days:	12
Finishing Position:	33
Laps Completed:	0
Highest Position 1997 Race:	N/A
Fastest Race Lap:	N/A
1997 Prize Money:	$202,250
INDY 500 Career Earnings:	$202,250
Career INDY 500 Starts:	1
Career Best Finish:	33rd 1997

34th Place

SAM
SCHMIDT

DALLARA/OLDSMOBILE AURORA
FIRESTONE

#16 Blueprint/HOPE Prepaid Fuel Card
Entrant: Blueprint Racing, Inc.   Crew Chief: Tommy O'Brien

Sam Schmidt came to Indy for his first "500" with the Blueprint Racing team and high hopes.

The Formula Ford 2000 veteran breezed through his driver's test and worked his way to the top of the speed chart for not-yet-qualified drivers on Day 13 with a lap at 211.989 miles per hour.

"I didn't think I would be the fastest," Schmidt said. "I guess the wind bothered everyone else more. Every day I've run, it's been windy."

When the third day of time trials arrived, he put the machine solidly in the show with a four-lap average of 215.141.

"It's a big relief to be qualified," he said. "We haven't run close to 215 since last Saturday. It's been a roller-coaster week."

On Race Day, problems returned. On the fifth caution lap after a fourth-turn accident before the start, Schmidt pulled to pit road with smoke coming from his mount.

"It was something in the motor," he said. "I don't know what, but it was blowing water out of the left bank. It was fine the first few laps. The pressures looked okay."

1997 INDY 500 PERFORMANCE PROFILE

Starting Position:	23
Qualifying Average:	215.141 MPH
Qualifying Speed Rank:	8
Best Practice Speed:	216.956 MPH 5/10
Total Practice Laps:	275
Number Practice Days:	9
Finishing Position:	34
Laps Completed:	0
Highest Position 1997 Race:	N/A
Fastest Race Lap:	N/A
1997 Prize Money:	$150,250
INDY 500 Career Earnings:	$150,250
Career INDY 500 Starts:	1
Career Best Finish:	34th 1997

35th Place

ALESSANDRO ZAMPEDRI

DALLARA/OLDSMOBILE AURORA
GOODYEAR

#34 Mi-Jack Scandia Royal Purple
Entrant: Team Scandia   Crew Chief: Jack Pegues

Alessandro Zampedri was on the comeback trail. He had been pointing to the Indianapolis 500 for his return for months, and he brought out applause when he first walked without crutches to pit road to join his teammates on a pre-May testing day.

After the first week of practice, the team waved off his first qualifying attempt on Pole Day; then he came back later to record a run of 209.094 miles per hour.

"It certainly feels great," Zampedri said. "A very tough year for me. I had to go through nine surgeries with lots of relapses. It really feels good to be back and running."

The feeling turned sour on the fourth qualifying day when Paul Durant bumped him from the field at 1 P.M. Just 2 hours and 14 minutes later, Zampedri went out in a backup car and posted a run of 211.757 to knock Lyn St. James from the field.

"This has been a really tough month," he said. "We did the best we could the first weekend, but it seems A.J. [Foyt, Durant's car owner] never runs out of cars. Yesterday and today, the team worked to put the backup car together. I was very confident with the car and knew if I had to take it out, we could make it."

On Race Day, Zampedri's scenario took another sour turn as he pulled to the pits without completing a lap.

"Timing chain broke," he said.

1997 INDY 500 PERFORMANCE PROFILE

Starting Position:	31
Qualifying Average:	211.757 MPH
Qualifying Speed Rank:	20
Best Practice Speed:	214.393 MPH 5/22
Total Practice Laps:	208
Number Practice Days:	6
Finishing Position:	35
Laps Completed:	0
Highest Position 1997 Race:	N/A
Fastest Race Lap:	N/A
1997 Prize Money:	$145,000
INDY 500 Career Earnings:	$583,253
Career INDY 500 Starts:	3
Career Best Finish:	4th 1996

For Those Who Tried . . . .

Scott SHARP

John PAUL JR.

Scott Sharp in the #1 Conseco AJ Foyt Racing entry hit the Turn 4 wall, slid 160 feet along the wall, and came to a stop near the main straightaway on Day 7. Sharp was taken to Methodist Hospital with a head injury. His best Indianapolis 500 finish was 10th in 1996.

John Paul Jr. lost his 500 chance on Day 7 when his #18 Klipsch Tnemec Overhead Door Pyle V-Line Earl's entry did a complete spin in Turn 4. Paul Jr. suffered a broken lower right leg and a broken left heel. He was expected to be wheelchair-bound in casts for six to eight weeks. Paul Jr. finished 9th in the Phoenix 200 in March. His best Indy 500 finish was 10th in 1992.

Scott HARRINGTON

Johnny O'CONNELL

On the fourth qualifying day, Scott Harrington in the #36 Johansson/Immke Motorsports entry lost control at the entrance to Turn 2, slid 600 feet with a half spin, hitting the outside wall with the left side, then sliding along the wall 270 feet backwards, stopping in the middle of the back straightaway. He was released and sent home with no injuries. Harrington finished 15th in the 1996 Indianapolis 500.

Johnny O'Connell was given a chance to drive for A.J. Foyt in place of Scott Sharp in the #1 Conseco AJ Foyt Racing entry. On Day 14, his engine blew and he hit the Turn 1 wall. O'Connell sustained minor facial cuts and a dislocated arch in his left foot.

Lone Star Event

By Mark Robinson

INAUGURAL INDY RACING LEAGUE EVENT

True Value ® 500

JUNE 7, 1997

TEXAS MOTOR SPEEDWAY

Well, they always say they do things up bigger in Texas. It is, after all, the land of J.R. Ewing, big spreads, oil wells, and slick million-dollar deals.

So when the Indy Racing League announced it was heading to Bruton Smith's sparkling new Texas Motor Speedway just outside Fort Worth for the first night-time Indy-car event in modern history, you just knew something special was in the mix. What no one could guess was that it would be a good ol' Saturday night at the fights, sparked by ol' Super Tex himself, A.J. Foyt.

The brief melee between Foyt, owner of the car driven by Billy Boat that took the checkered flag and cruised into Victory Lane for the supposed celebration of triumph, and Arie Luyendyk, whose car was declared the winner of the True Value 500K the following morning after a flaw in the electronic scoring system was uncovered, splashed the IRL across the headlines and put it atop sportscasts for days to come.

While the short-term reaction within the IRL camp was one of embarrassment over the incident—rightly so after Foyt, the winningest Indy-car driver in history, sucker-punched two-time Indy 500 champion Luyendyk from behind and then tossed him into a row of flowers—the long-lasting effects gave Tony George's growing open-wheel series a flavor of character previously lacking. Interest in the IRL picked up geometrically after the Texas tussle, which ended up a promoter's dream.

INDY RACING LEAGUE

The first night-time Indy car event in modern history was held at Texas Motor Speedway just outside Fort Worth before a crowd of more than 100,000.

Arie Luyendyk (left) and Eddie Cheever Jr. discussed the new Texas oval.

Billy Boat, still driving for the injured Scott Sharp, finished second.

"You hate to see something like that happen," mused Humpy Wheeler, general manager of Texas Motor Speedway's sister track at Charlotte, "unless you have the next race."

Perhaps the only real injustice done by the postrace pugilism was that it overshadowed some pretty fine racing on the gleaming high banks of TMS. Television cameras captured the dramatic midrace duel between Tony Stewart and Buddy Lazier, a pair of the IRL's top guns unwilling to give an inch as they battled side-by-

side for better than two laps. But it was just one of numerous true racing adventures that evening, many unseen by the TV audience because they didn't involve leaders but not unnoticed by the appreciative crowd of 100,000.

Early indications that there were problems with the United States Auto Club's timing and scoring system surfaced during the unique qualifying session on Wednesday night. The format, patterned after the Winston Cup night event at Charlotte, called for the IRL drivers to log two timed laps at full speed around the 1.5-mile superspeedway. At the completion of a third lap, drivers were to bring their cars to a designated pit box for a two-tire change before peeling across the finish line to stop the clock.

A pit speed limit of 120 miles per hour was set, a threshold for which drivers Robbie Buhl and Greg Ray originally had their qualifying attempts disallowed for exceeding. But, after comparing the electronic scoring with radar gun clockings in the pits, USAC chief steward Keith Ward reinstated the two attempts. That put Buhl outside of teammate and pole sitter Stewart on the first row and Ray on the outside of row three.

Much of that appeared academic because, as he had been at nearly every track to that point in 1997, Stewart was clearly the man to beat. In practice, the driver of the Team Menard G Force/Aurora/Firestone surpassed 217 miles per hour—almost 10 miles per hour more than IRL

officials had anticipated anyone going after they mandated specific aerodynamics for TMS that included a 6-degree minimum angle and 1-inch wickerbill on rear wings, as well as 8-inch minimums on the rear wing end plates.

In qualifying, Stewart's two hot laps exceeded 216 miles per hour and his total qualifying average, pit stop included, was 167.133. Buhl's runner-up effort was more than 1 mile per hour slower.

"I'm a night owl," said Stewart, the IRL's 26-year-old poster boy who came up through the USAC open-wheel ranks. "As soon as the sun goes down, I wake up."

Twenty-six cars were in the starting grid, but it was clearly a case of follow the leader. In this case, the leader was Stewart, who paced the first 68 laps before running out of fuel on his way to the pits.

It was five laps before that the scoring saga of Luyendyk began to unfold. The driver of the Treadway Racing G Force/Aurora/Firestone rolled into the pits on Lap 63, but the computerized scoring system didn't chart the lap for him when he crossed the start-finish line. His crew notified USAC almost immediately but received no remedy.

The same problem occurred with Luyendyk's teammate, Scott Goodyear, when he pitted three laps later. In all, there were five cars that developed electronic scoring glitches in the race. Besides Luyendyk and Goodyear, transponder gremlins also befell Eddie Cheever, Ray, and, ironically, Boat.

So, while the crowd was watching the lead change hands often among the likes of Jim Guthrie, Robbie Groff, Stewart, Lazier, and Boat, Luyendyk was a forgotten entity to everyone but

Pit crew members performed the final preparations on the cars.

Mike Groff's crew bid him a speedy recovery. Johnny Unser took over the Jonathan Byrd's Cafeteria Bryant Heating & Cooling entry for the True Value 500.

his own team. Though the scoreboard counted him laps down, his crew kept telling him to remain focused and drive on, that they would straighten out the confusion afterward.

Meanwhile, the list of contenders began to shrink on a regular basis. First it was Guthrie, victim of a cut tire on Lap 81. Then Lazier, whose engine expired two laps after his scintillating round-the-course duel with Stewart. Stewart, trying to unlap himself after a recent pit stop, eventually did so after a pair of pulsating, throttle-to-the-floor, drag-race circuits with Lazier.

"The thing broke when we were in [turns] one and two," Lazier said. "Stewart was trying to get his lap back, and I gave him plenty of room to race me. I was just being a gentleman, and all of a sudden, I didn't have any room."

Buhl's engine let go on the 167th of 208 laps. Groff's plant went 10 laps later.

At that point, 35 laps from the finish of the 500-kilometer event, the scoreboard showed the race was between Stewart, Boat, and Davey Hamilton, Boat's teammate with A.J. Foyt Racing. Luyendyk, though, was tailing Stewart for a number of laps. Finally, on Lap 190, Luyendyk roared past Stewart.

Stewart and his team paid no mind. They thought Luyendyk was two laps down. What they didn't know was that Luyendyk had actually made a pass for the lead. That, of course, wouldn't be sorted out until the next morning.

Bitten by bad luck so many times in the short history of the IRL, Stewart finally appeared to have victory in the bag in the waning laps. Boat and Hamilton were unable to cut into his lead, so Stewart was cruising at about 212 miles per hour per lap when, two laps shy of the checkered flag, his engine blew. Stewart's car spun in its own oil and hit the wall in Turn 1.

"To run that strong all day long and be that superior, we were disappointed," said Stewart, whose disappointment would end with a victory in the next IRL race at Pikes Peak. "We just have a little jinx right now."

That turned the spotlight on Boat, the unlikeliest of winners, the guy subbing for injured Scott Sharp, the guy who started the race dead last because of engine problems in qualifying. Boat led the final two laps under caution after Stewart's crash and maneuvered calmly to the victory stand for what would be a celebration more memorable than he could ever fathom.

Throughout the night, Luyendyk's crew had kept him calm by telling him the scoring would be righted immediately after the race. When he got out of his car and saw the victory party going on without him, the normally reserved Dutchman was beside himself.

Armed with a few Treadway team members, Luyendyk marched to the victory stand to find

chief steward Ward and halt what he was certain was an injustice. He found TMS general manager Eddie Gossage.

"Eddie, you can't give that trophy to Boat. I won the race!" Luyendyk demanded.

Gossage, in the midst of the victory presentation, barely recognized Luyendyk, who repeated his plea to whoever would listen.

"One of the Foyt guys heard what I said," Luyendyk would say later, "and he said something like, 'You were a lap down.' I said something like, 'You guys don't know how to count.'"

It was at that point that Luyendyk decided to head elsewhere to state his case. It wasn't quite soon enough.

Foyt, incensed that Luyendyk would try to taint his victory, caught Luyendyk from behind with a blow to the neck. He then grabbed the stunned Luyendyk around the neck and shoved him to the ground.

By then, a few Treadway team members and Tony George himself were holding Foyt back.

"You don't come in here and start mouthing somebody in Victory Circle," Foyt said. "He won Indy and probably thought he won this damned race. But he got down early and never made it up. I just wanted him to get out of Victory Circle and leave us alone."

What Foyt couldn't know at the time was that Luyendyk's assertions were correct. USAC officials, following a protest lodged by Treadway, reviewed their computer scoring, as well as telemetry and manual scoring from some teams. They found that Luyendyk actually completed 210 laps when it was supposed to be a 208-lap race.

The following morning, Ward announced Luyendyk as the true winner of the True Value 500K. The revised standings had Boat in second, Hamilton third, and Goodyear moved up to fourth (from ninth in the original standings).

"I think as a team we were very upset Saturday night, and it showed," said Luyendyk, who had some team members wonder privately if the results would have been changed had their driver not crashed the Foyt party. "The telemetry doesn't lie, and we were convinced that we won. I do have to respect USAC for stepping up to the plate and auditing the results."

Not only did USAC step up to the plate, it served itself up for dinner. Coming on the heels of another botched finish at Indianapolis—when the green flag was waved for a last-lap restart but yellow lights remained on around the course—the Texas debacle served as the final nail in USAC's coffin as the sanctioning body for IRL events. By the next race at Pikes Peak three weeks later, the IRL had brought its scoring and timing in house.

Just another Saturday night in Texas.

A First-Time Experience

By Bruce Martin

JUNE 27-29, 1997

INDY RACING LEAGUE

Winner Tony Stewart (center) shares Victory Circle with 2nd Place finisher Stephan Gregoire (right) and 3rd Place finisher Davey Hamilton (left).

Sometimes a person must lose before they can fully enjoy the fruits of victory.

Nobody knows that better than Tony Stewart.

It is conceivable Stewart could have won every race in the 10-race history of the Indy Racing League. But in the previous 9 IRL events, Stewart has been tantalized, then tormented, on his quest to make his first trip to victory lane in an Indy car.

Stewart has dominated practically every IRL event, but such problems as bad popoff valves in 1996, blown engines in 1997, and just bad racing luck have kept victory lane out of the driver's reach.

That all changed in the June 29 Samsonite 200, as Stewart finally broke through to reach victory lane at Pike's Peak International Raceway.

Stewart had waited his entire life for this moment. So had Team Menard team manager Larry Curry. And so had team owner John Menard, the 57-year-old home improvement king who has invested tens of millions of dollars for this moment.

When Stewart crossed the finish line under the checkered flag, the "Poster Boy of Indy Racing League" finally scored his first victory in an Indy car.

In a race where nine cars were running on the lead lap, and 12 of the 22 cars were running at the finish, it was marred with a crash that left pole winner Scott Sharp in serious condition with a sub-dural brain hemorrhage at Penrose Hospital in Colorado Springs. Sharp crashed in the second turn on the opening lap of the race.

Affonso Giaffone
(#17), Billy Boat
(#18), Robbie
Groff (#30), and
Vincenzo Sospiri
(#22) battle for
position.

For Stewart, the victory was something the 26-year-old driver from Rushville, Indiana, has dreamed of, worked for, and obsessed over.

"I've been racing for 18 years, and every win is a special win," Stewart said. "What makes this win special is I did it with these two guys (Curry and Menard) and all the guys on the team. These guys have never griped one time about working 16-hour days, seven days a week. They always go home with smiles on their faces. With all the disappointments, those guys have been cheering me up and keeping me pumped up about winning a race when I probably should have been doing the opposite. I should have been doing it for them. Those guys have poured their hearts and souls in it. It made me feel better I finally got one for those guys as much as for myself."

Before the race it was said Stewart had a monkey on his back that had grown into a gorilla. After winning the race, Stewart said, "That monkey is off our back now. He's in the zoo!"

For Menard, who owns a large midwestern chain of home improvement stores called Menard's, it took 18 years of owning Indy cars and spending large sums of money to finally visit victory lane at an Indy car race. "I entered my first race in 1979 with Herm Johnson as the driver," Menard recalled. "I think that was before Tony was even born. I hope this is not a once every 18 years occurrence. It feels really, really great. It shows that perseverance pays off.

"Right now, we have as good a team as any and today, we proved we are better than everybody. We have a great bunch of guys. We kept coming back, getting so close, getting all discouraged, coming back time after time, and it is just a great feeling."

When Menard was asked how much money he has spent in his career as an Indy car team owner, Stewart chimed in and said, "They don't have that many zeroes." But to Menard, it was worth every penny.

"We've had support from our sponsors all along, but I've spent some of my own money, too," Menard said. "It's in the millions of dollars. I really don't want to think about money right now."

And for Curry, it's a reward for the countless hours of testing, preparation, and a little blood, sweat and tears. "Finally," Curry said. "I can't explain it right now. Some things you get easy. We never got anything easy. This kid has been the class of the IRL, and he got his just due today. Tony was up to the task."

Stewart dominated the race and led three times for 193 of the 200 laps. But it was not an easy win for the former USAC midget, sprint, and Silver Crown champion as he finished just 0.222 seconds ahead of Stephan Gregoire of France. Davey Hamilton was third followed by Eddie Cheever and Buzz Calkins. Stewart's victory, worth $161,000,

was witnessed by a crowd of and an announced crowd of 38,100 fans who were on hand for the first-ever IRL race at the new 1.0-mile facility.

The race was slowed nine times for 82 laps of caution, which dropped the average speed to 100.128 miles an hour.

It also increased the tension level for Team Menard as Stewart had to fight off Cheever, and later Gregoire, on the final three restarts in the last 28 laps of the race. On Lap 172, when the green flag came out, Stewart said Cheever was using a rolling start to get a run of momentum on Stewart at the start/finish line. The yellow came out on Lap 181 when Kenny Brack crashed in the fourth turn wall.

An anxious Menard stood on the back of an equipment box in the pit area and said, "It's just nerve-racking."

The green flag waved on the 187th lap, and Cheever, again, tried the rolling start, but Stewart was able to retain the lead. With 10 laps to go, Cheever began to block the third-place car of Gregoire, but the Frenchman finally returned the favor with a pass for second in the second lap one lap later.

Robbie Groff brought out the final caution flag on the 194th lap when he spun on the back straight. With three laps remaining, the green flag was about to come out, and Menard said, "Tony will need a midget start on this one because Gregoire is looking pretty impressive."

As the green flag came out on the 198th lap, Stewart stayed in front, and Hamilton went low in the first turn in a three-wide battle to pass Cheever for third place.

After being tantalized so many times for his first Indy car win only to suffer heartache, Stewart raced to the checkered flag, sending his team into pandemonium.

Roberto Guerrero qualified 5th fastest after switching to Aurora power.

Treadway Racing's fuel man Brian Hornick is ready for the next pit stop.

Rookie Jimmy Kite (#33) made his IRL debut at Pikes Peak. Kite had the fastest lap of the race at 167.715 miles per hour.

"I just feel elated," Menard said. "This has been years in the making. To finally have it happen, I can't even think about it before now. It's the top of the mountain right now; it's really great."

The race also gave added credibility to the IRL, which conducted its first-ever event without the United States Auto Club (USAC) serving as the sanctioning body and officiating the race. This came after two-straight races mired in controversy from USAC decisions.

For Menard, Curry, and public relations director Becky Brayton, the win had added significance. On May 17, 1996, Team Menard driver Scott Brayton lost his life when he crashed in practice at the Indianapolis Motor Speedway preparing for the 80th Indianapolis 500. His death was the first time the pole winner for the Indy 500 lost his life before the race.

"This one is for Scott," Menard said. "I know he is up there watching and grinning. That day at the Indianapolis Motor Speedway was probably the lowest point in my life and the closest I ever came to quitting in all my years of racing."

Becky Brayton, Scott's widow, had a smile on her face and tears in her eyes. "This is real special, considering everything," Brayton said. "I'm glad I

stuck with this. I have been, even before now."

Before Scott Sharp suffered a head injury that left him in a Colorado Springs Hospital after a first-lap crash in the Samsonite 200, the defending co-Indy Racing League champion had a chance to enjoy a spectacular comeback.

Sharp suffered a brain hemorrhage when he crashed his Conseco-sponsored, A.J. Foyt Enterprises car in practice at Indianapolis Motor Speedway on May 9. The brain injury forced him to miss the 81st Indianapolis 500 and the June 7 True Value 500 at Texas Motor Speedway.

As Sharp began to heal, he returned to the cockpit of his G-Force/Oldsmobile Aurora during an open test session at Charlotte Motor Speedway in mid-June.

Sharp's time away from the race car only fueled his hunger to return to the IRL. And Sharp displayed that hunger on June 23 when he won the pole for the Samsonite 200 IRL event at Pike's Peak International Raceway. He captured the pole with a lap of 176.117 miles an hour at the 1.0-mile oval located at the base of Pike's Peak.

"It feels good," Sharp said. "My fire has been burning, and it has certainly made me hungry to come back a little sooner than they wanted me too,

"I went to Charlotte to test, and there was a little apprehension when I first got going, 'How long is this going to take?' 'How comfortable is this going to feel?'" Sharp said. "About the fourth lap by, I ran 210 so it was pretty comfortable right away. It seems like maybe our luck is going to change a little bit."

During his time out of the car, he has had to watch Billy Boat drive his racing machine. Sharp said that was one of the toughest things he has ever had to do in racing. "It is tough every day to sit there and watch anyone driving your car," Sharp said. "It is tough to miss the Indy 500; it is tough to miss Texas. Any day your car is on the race track, even if it is a test day, it is not fun to be out of it."

Sharp had a hunch before he took his first qualification lap that he had a car capable of winning the pole. "My last warm-up lap was pretty quick; it was the fastest lap I had turned all week," Sharp said. "I knew right then and there, as long as it didn't start to push too much, we could run it pretty hard.

"It's great to be back, and this is a great way to repay the team a little bit. Hopefully, we can turn this pole into something more on Sunday."

Sharp's performance pleased his team owner, the tough to please A.J. Foyt. "One thing about Scottie, he will push the button when the car is working," Foyt said. "I'm just glad to have Scott back with the team and not at the hospital."

Unfortunately, those words would prove to be prophetic on Race Day.

Pikes Peak International Raceway

Front row drivers Scott Sharp (#1) and Tony Stewart (#2) paced the field, followed by Davey Hamilton (#14).

When Tony Stewart crossed the finish line under the checkered flag, he finally scored his first victory in an Indy car.

but nevertheless, it is great to be back. The crew has worked hard. We had a tough month of May. We changed a lot of things last night, and I'm just happy for the whole team."

Sharp admitted when a race driver is out of action for several races, there is a question in the back of their mind how long it will take for him to get back up to speed. Sharp had the answer to that question as he knocked Tony Stewart off the pole after the Team Menard driver had previously qualified at 175.021 miles per hour.

Invading the South

By Dave Argabright

INDY RACING LEAGUE

It didn't have quite the historical impact of Sherman's march through the south some 140 years before, but it was certainly more constructive.

The invading "northerners" of the Indy Racing League made a ground-breaking trip to Charlotte Motor Speedway in late July, bringing Saturday night Indy car racing to the south for the first time in many years.

The result was a spectacular race in which the nearly 80,000 on hand were on their feet for much of the night. It proved that the IRL machines can race effectively on the banked 1.5-mile Charlotte quad-oval, and it virtually guaranteed that the IRL's appeal is broad enough to reach knowledgeable stock car fans throughout the south.

Buddy Lazier made a thrilling run to take the win, his first since winning the Indianapolis 500 in 1996. He fought off a growing crowd of young, surging open wheel racers who seem to explode onto the IRL scene, lending more promotional appeal to the IRL with every event.

Prior to the event, there was no guarantee that the race would sell well at Charlotte. The center of the NASCAR Winston Cup universe, the famed track has always enjoyed terrific fan support thanks to the promotional efforts of the respected general manager H. A. "Humpy" Wheeler and his staff.

Stock car fans are accustomed to tight, tough racing with close finishes and tend to be extremely knowledgeable. So a strong product would need to be presented, one that entertained in a fresh new way.

Nearly 80,000 were on hand to watch the first IRL race at Charlotte Motor Speedway, traditionally a favorite stock car venue.

Buddy Lazier (center) celebrated his victory as team owner Ron Hemelgarn (far right) looked on. Billy Boat (right) and Scott Goodyear (left) finished 2nd and 3rd, respectively.

Wheeler and his staff went to work, aggressively promoting the event. They hoped that they could appeal to "transplanted" northerners who had settled in the booming city, as well as Winston Cup fans. Their advertising and promotional budget for the event was reportedly 25 percent more than for one of their Winston Cup events.

One of the promotional opportunities came in May, when Tony Stewart toured the CMS oval during Coca-Cola 600 activities, in front of a packed house. As Stewart roared around the course, fans gave him a light show as thousands of flashbulbs recorded the event.

"I haven't seen that many flash cubes except at a rock concert," Stewart said later. "I did a burnout out of the pits to get their attention."

Then on June 19, the speedway held an IRL test under the lights and promoted it as "Fast and Free Night" at the track. Nearly 3,000 fans turned out for an autograph session and a free preview of the July event.

The publicity caught the eye of at least one Winston Cup team. Richard Childress, owner of the legendary Goodwrench No. 3 wheeled by Dale Earnhardt, was involved as a sponsor on Greg Ray's No. 31.

Danny "Chocolate" Meyers, the well-known fuel man for Childress and Earnhardt, suited up to fuel Affonso Giaffone's GM Brasil machine.

The result of this carefully planned blitz was a very large crowd, more than even the most optimistic person projected.

There was no lack of contenders for the event. Stewart, still beaming after his win at the prior IRL event at Pikes Peak International Raceway, was very fast in pre-race testing. He took the pole in the Glidden/Menard entry and was once again the pre-race favorite.

But A.J. Foyt driver Davey Hamilton held a five-point lead in the IRL point standings, and he was eager to score his first win for Foyt.

Roberto Guerrero had switched from Infinity to Aurora power, immediately boosting his test speeds and becoming a contender.

But a relatively new name had shocked the IRL scene. Jimmy Kite, an enthusiastic young driver originally from Georgia, had landed a ride with Team Scandia. Just one year earlier, Kite had moved to the Midwest to pursue sprint car and midget rides and in the season opener won the USAC Silver Crown event at Phoenix.

That was a stunning win for Kite, who drove

past seasoned veterans on his way to the win. He backed up the performance with strong runs in the next several Silver Crown events, and he caught the eye of Team Scandia boss Andy Evans. Their discussions resulted in a five-year accord, bringing the smiling, ebullient Kite to Charlotte for just his second IRL start. Just one week before the event, in fact, he won a 50-lap NAMARS midget event at the historic high-banked Salem Speedway.

His pre-race testing speeds were strong, over 213 miles per hour. But he struggled during qualifying, relegating him to a 13th-place starting position.

At the onset, Stewart made it look like he would dominate. He led all but one of the first 75 laps before losing radio communications with his crew and the handling of the car began to go away.

As Stewart pulled away from the field, Wheeler worried that the race would be a snoozer.

"The first 30 laps or so," he later told *National Speed Sport News*, "I was thinking we were in for a long night."

But as Stewart faded, the competition on the track went from a slow simmer to a boil. Cars raced three- and four- wide on the 24-degree CMS banking, bringing the crowd to their feet for nearly the entire second half of the race.

Lazier gave notice early that he was in the hunt for the win. As Stewart began to fade, Lazier powered the Delta Faucet/Cinergy entry into the lead.

Charlotte Motor Speedway's Lug Nut was on hand to entertain the crowd.

Fans were able to view the new chassis built by Riley & Scott Inc. of Indianapolis. Mark Dismore (#28), in the Bombardier Business Aircraft Grainger entry, was one of the first drivers to use the new chassis.

The success of the VisionAire 500 proved that IRL machines can race effectively on the banked 1.5-mile Charlotte quad-oval.

113

John Paul Jr. (#18) makes a comeback at Charlotte, finishing 11th. He is followed by 5th Place finisher Kenny Brack (#4).

Vincenzo Sospiri (#22) and his crew are featured on the "big screen" at Charlotte Motor Speedway.

Behind him, serious dicing and racing continued to shuffle the order of the top 10.

But Lazier suffered a setback when he lost a lap near the halfway point of the race. At that point it was Boat and Guerrero trading the lead.

The road Boat traveled to get to Charlotte was full of twists and turns and uncertainty. He had earlier subbed in the Conseco/Foyt entry at

Indianapolis after Scott Sharp was injured and nearly won the Texas event, but he was replaced by Sharp at Pikes Peak.

Boat caught a ride at PPIR with PDM racing, and in that event Sharp was reinjured. Foyt was quick to retain Boat for Charlotte, and it was later revealed that he will finish the year for Foyt.

He drove as if his job depended on it, however, and was sensational on the CMS banks. A veteran of midgets and sprint cars, Boat is accustomed to high-banked race tracks, and his comfort level was obvious.

The racing was interrupted only four times for cautions, the first coming for debris on Lap 74. Mark Dismore, who had posted a splendid run to the top five after starting 10th in the Bombardier Aircraft entry, lost an engine and oiled the track on lap 99.

Guerrero and Hamilton were racing wheel to wheel on Lap 144 when they got together, both spinning into the Turn 2 concrete. Guerrero was third at the time after leading for 27 laps at the midway point of the race.

Kite was sensational, and he rocketed into the lead on two different occasions. But his night came to an end on Lap 163 when he crashed the Old Navy/Royal Purple entry in Turn 4.

The 21-year-old driver was very fast at that point, and his crash with just over 40 laps to go made it a two-car battle between Lazier and Boat.

"He was racing me very hard," Lazier later said of Boat.

Lazier took the lead after Kite's accident, with Boat chasing him and narrowing the lead. The two defined intensity when they locked up in a duel with just 12 laps to go and then encountered lapped traffic.

Boat used the traffic to slip past Lazier, but Lazier returned the favor in much the same fashion just one lap later. They were wheel-to-wheel, mere inches from one another, at over 200 miles per hour. The crowd stood as if in awe, cheering lustily.

That would be the end of Boat's challenge. His car had developed a push, and he could only watch helplessly as Lazier began to pull away slightly. At the flag Lazier held a 3.3-second lead.

The scene in Victory Lane was emotional and enthusiastic. The win was Lazier's first in over a year, and he admitted, "I was getting kind of worried."

While everyone was pleased with the strong showing in front of a new generation of southern fans, Lazier insisted that the win was especially satisfying.

"To me, it's an incredible win because my lady and I and my whole family are huge Winston Cup fans," he said. "To be watching races here for as long as I can remember and then being able to come here and run in an open wheel format is awesome and then to be able to win; it's just unbelievable."

Boat was happy with second, followed by Scott Goodyear who was one lap down. Two laps back were Affonso Giaffone and Kenny Brack, their best IRL finishes to date.

Stewart soldiered home to seventh and, in the process, wrested the points lead from Hamilton.

Among the enthusiastic crowd, there was perhaps no one more excited than Wheeler, who saw his group's PR efforts rewarded with a memorable show.

"I don't think anybody here tonight will ever forget Buddy Lazier," Wheeler told *National Speed Sport News*. "I think he made a hero out of himself tonight.

"Jimmy Kite, what a show he put on. If you looked at the grandstands, the fans really got into this thing.

"People go to see people race, and that is what these guys are doing in this series. It is going to get better and better."

The IRL brought Saturday night Indy car racing to the South for the first time in many years.

Buddy Lazier (#91) cornering in on the finish. Jimmy Kite (#33) and Eliseo Salazar (#7) follow.

The Magic Mile

By Jonathan Ingram

AUGUST 17, 1997

INDY RACING LEAGUE

New Hampshire International Speedway is a difficult 1.0-mile oval where drivers and crews alike are put to the test.

When Robbie Buhl races at the New Hampshire International Speedway, it's like old home week. Before owner Bob Bahre created the "Magic Mile" oval, the facility was a road circuit where aspiring driver Buhl used to pay a $35 fee once a week to test his Sports Renault in between classes at the nearby New England College.

After graduation, Buhl turned out to be an able pupil when it came to racing, scoring victories in almost every series he entered, including championship seasons in the Barber Dodge and Indy Lights series. So naturally, whenever Buhl returns to the New Hampshire track, some of his old college buddies always turn out to cheer him on.

In the Pennzoil 200, his buddies got to see Buhl come home to Victory Lane. The win aboard Team Menard's G Force-Aurora was special because it was Buhl's first victory as an Indy car driver. "Any time you win it's good, but it feels great to win up here," said Buhl, who turned 34 two weeks after his inaugural Indy Racing League triumph.

After hectoring the rear wing of Eddie Cheever's leading G Force-Aurora as the final laps wound down in the 200-mile race, Buhl was looking for a way past. When Cheever's gearbox gave up three laps from the finish, Buhl took the lead and held on to beat the oncoming Vincenzo Sospiri, who had suddenly closed up when Buhl hit the brakes to avoid Cheever's fatally wounded machine. Buhl's first victory in an Indy car came

Winner Robbie Buhl joined Tony Stewart on John Menard's team for the 1997 season.

Robbie Buhl came back home to win the Pennzoil 200 at New Hampshire International Speedway. Buhl used to pay $35 once a week to test his Sports Renault in between classes at the nearby New England College. It was his first victory as an Indy car driver.

by the closest margin in the Indy Racing League's two-year history, 0.064 seconds, and returned his gratitude to the team which had kept his vacant car awaiting until he recovered from a testing accident two months earlier at the Pikes Peak International Raceway. A crash there left Buhl with a brain contusion, or bruise.

As an experienced oval driver, Buhl knows accidents and injuries are part of the high-speed game surrounded by walls. His biggest problem while missing two races during his recovery was patience. "Just like when I'm healthy, I want to get out and run," he said.

It wasn't the first time Buhl had paid some dues. In 1993, he went to the Indy 500 for the first time with an ill-prepared team and crashed twice, suffering a concussion. He then went back to the minor leagues of Indy Lights—where he won the championship in 1992—while trying to land a ride with a front-line Championship Auto Racing Team entrant.

Buhl's break came with the formation of the Indy Racing League in 1996. A driver looking to prove himself, Buhl exemplified IRL founder Tony George's view that American driving talent needed more opportunities on ovals.

True Value 200, August 18, 1996

Buhl spent 1996 with the team of Greg Beck where his first appearance in an IRL race at New Hampshire did not go smoothly, or far. He spun on the first lap at the "Magic Mile's" 1996 inaugural event, where eventually Scott Sharp won aboard one of A.J. Foyt's Lola-Fords by executing a fuel strategy to beat Buzz Calkins and Michele Alboreto. That race was best remembered for Tony Stewart's incredible drive—and bad luck. With a two-lap lead, his Menard V-6 engine expired 18 laps from the finish.

This year Buhl joined Stewart on John Menard's team. Despite his injury and layoff, when he returned to New Hampshire, there was no apprehension about returning to Menard's Quaker State-backed entry. But his goals were relatively modest. "Today I was just trying to stay on the lead lap and show that I could stay on the pace," said Buhl, who qualified seventh. "To get a win for these guys was really great."

The dramatic finish was another milestone for the IRL whose formula of cars powered by atmospheric V-8s again provided an outstanding race of close competition on the difficult confines of the New Hampshire mile.

The IRL's main attraction of unpredictable results due to evenly matched cars was also evident in qualifying, where Brazilian Marco Greco won his first pole in the series. Driving the Galles Racing International's Monsoon G Force-Aurora on Goodyear tires, Greco averaged 160.594 miles per hour.

At Galles, alongside fellow F-3000 series graduate and teammate Kenny Brack, who qualified third, Greco found a more comfortable home after switching from Team Scandia. "I'm progressing as a driver because there is an emphasis on both [Galles] cars," said Greco, who joined the Galles team for the first time at the Pikes Peak round in June.

Greco also found a team familiar with tackling the wiley ways of the New Hampshire track. It's a difficult mile oval due to the tight entry and exits necessary to negotiating each end of the track. It's the only mile oval where drivers actually use the brakes entering the corners. For that reason and the fact drivers must accelerate so hard off the corners, getting the proper chassis set-up is a challenge.

Come Race Day, Team Cheever had the best grip on how to get around New Hampshire, even though driver/owner Eddie Cheever qualified 18th due to a poor choice on gear ratios. With that gearing choice corrected and some other suspension adjustments, Cheever was scything through the field once the green flag fell. "It's the engineers and crew members and what experience that they have that makes the difference here," said Cheever.

Brazilian Marco Greco won his first pole in the series. Driving the Galles Racing International's Monsoon G Force-Aurora, Greco averaged 160.594 miles per hour.

119

As Greco dashed away to a 3.3-second lead over Scott Goodyear in the first 34 laps, Cheever carefully picked his way up to 14th place on a track tricky to pass on due to the tight corners. But after Greco (destined for an oil line failure) led eight other cars on the lead lap into the pits during the day's third caution on Lap 34, Cheever began to strut his stuff.

Unlike those leaders who were pitting early for fresh tires and chassis adjustments, Goodyear, Buhl, Arie Luyendyk, Cheever, and John Paul Jr. stayed on the track in pursuit of a more traditional two-stop strategy. By the time those five made their first trip into the pits on Lap 61 during the fourth caution brought out by Greco's spin when his oil line broke, Cheever had jumped to second behind Goodyear.

Since the cars on a three-stop strategy had stayed out of the pits during that fourth caution, at the re-start Cheever was 13th in line and holding ninth place with Buhl just behind him in 10th. From there, it took chargin' Cheever just 30 laps to vault into first place, including one three-wide pass of Sospiri where he used the slower G Force of Johnny Unser as a pick.

Cheever then held the lead for 38 laps with Goodyear and Buhl staying within three seconds until all three made their second and final pit stops. When leader Eliseo Salazar and the others on the ill-conceived three-stop strategy pitted, Cheever again took the lead 45 laps from the finish, this time with Buhl on his rear wing after the departure of Goodyear with a blown engine.

As the laps wound down, the suspense went up as Buhl whittled a 1.5-second deficit down to a single car length with 22 laps to go. The margin between Cheever, on Goodyear tires, and Buhl, on Firestones, see-sawed because they each worked better on opposite ends of the track. "I was going better through Turns 3 and 4, and he was faster in Turns 1 and 2," said Cheever. "I had to slide the car up the track in One and Two to stay ahead of him. But that was a problem in traffic, and I didn't want to do that if I didn't have to."

For 15 laps, Buhl was within one to three car lengths of Cheever, depending on lapped cars, but unable to make his way past. "The only way I was going to get by him was to stay close and hope for a break in traffic," said Buhl. Then Cheever's gearbox broke—and his heart temporarily along with it—at the exit of Turn 4 with three laps to go. Incredibly, the race suddenly got even tighter with Sospiri closing in.

The Italian, who began the season in F-1 with Lola before switching to Team Scandia at the Indy 500, was making a valiant effort to make the three-stop effort work on fresher Goodyear tires. On Lap 195 he set the fastest race lap and had already passed the other remaining front runner on a the two-stop strategy, Luyendyk. "When Eddie's car broke, they came on the radio and told me Sospiri was trying to pass for position," said Buhl, "and I was on the brakes [to avoid Cheever]."

So now it was a two-lap sprint between a faster car on fresh tires and leader Buhl, still paying his dues, with only a car length separating them. After getting his bogged engine back up to speed, Buhl held Sospiri in check for one lap. But on the final circuit lapped traffic loomed in Turn 3 in the form of Robbie Groff's G Force.

Buhl aggressively dove inside Groff at the entrance of the turn, and Sospiri chose the outside route. "I wanted to go on the outside line," said Sospiri, "because that was the fastest line for me. But I was just a little too wide." Indeed. As Sospiri's car came alongside Buhl in the final corner, he slid up the track, and Buhl beat him to the exit. Sospiri pulled his Team Scandia entry alongside once again on the inside at the finish line but fell half a car length short—and 0.064 seconds.

At long last, it was time for Buhl, sporting a new goatee beard to change his luck, to stop paying dues and start celebrating.

Neither of the two drivers leading the points championship, on the other hand, was much in a celebratory mood at race's end. Leader

Buddy Lazier (#91) and Roberto Guerrero (#21) fight for position.

Pit crews prepare the cars for the race ahead at New Hampshire's "Magic Mile."

Stewart, Buhl's usually more heralded teammate, couldn't find the handle on his G Force-Aurora after the first day of practice and spent much of the Race Day out of the top five until his engine expired. Fortunately for Stewart, points contender Davey Hamilton had virtually the same experience, but the engine in his G Force-Aurora blew up first. Stewart gained three points and led Hamilton, driver of an A.J. Foyt entry, by 10 points headed into the final round of the championship in Las Vegas.

One Last Gamble

By Jonathan Ingram

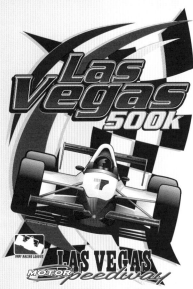

OCTOBER 11, 1997

INDY RACING LEAGUE

Las Vegas, brightly welcomed IRL race fans to the second Las Vegas 500k.

The final race of the 1996–97 schedule was a crowning moment for the Indy Racing League. In a race where Eliseo Salazar became the ninth different winner in ten races, Team Menard driver Tony Stewart won the championship by six points over Davey Hamilton, taking an arduous route to the title by manhandling a recalcitrant chassis through a cold, windy night. By winning his first major league open-wheel championship, Stewart confirmed his status as one of the brightest of America's young racers.

Las Vegas 500k, September 15, 1996

Stewart's drive to the title also reconfirmed the status of the IRL as a home to fresh American driving talent. It was just about a year earlier at the first IRL race on the 1.5-mile banked Las Vegas oval that another young driver also established his credentials. At the age of 25, Richie Hearn won his first Indy car race in the inaugural event on the magnificent new facility just north of Las Vegas' famed strip. Driving a Reynard 95I chassis powered by a Ford Cosworth turbo, Hearn edged Michel Jourdain by 1.693 seconds. That race in September of 1996, the second in the 1996–97 season, was the last event run by the IRL before the introduction of its new generation of chassis especially designed for ovals and 4.0-liter, normally-aspirated V-8 engines.

When the drivers gathered in October of 1997 for the season finale at the Las Vegas Motor track, Stewart had more on the line than any other. Since his debut in the IRL, the 26-year-old was regarded

Eliseo Salazar (center) celebrated his first IRL victory with team manager Dick Simon (left) and team owner Andy Evans (right).

as the epitome of the young American driver the series was designed to attract. A graduate from the sprint car and midget ranks, Stewart had brilliantly demonstrated that the transition can be made from driving open-wheel cars on dirt and asphalt short tracks to piloting rear-engined racers on superspeedways.

Entering the finale at Las Vegas as the championship points leader by a margin of 10, Stewart intended to make another big step in his quest to become the next A.J. Foyt. With plans to run in both the IRL and NASCAR in the future, Stewart needed the championship if he was to continue along the path as a potential rival to Foyt's record of success in a diversity of American disciplines. The fact he had won his first Indy car race during the season, had claimed four poles, and led 812 laps would not be remembered or recognized nearly as well as a championship trophy.

Ironically, it was Foyt driver Davey Hamilton that Stewart had to beat for the title. Their initial skirmish came in qualifying, where the stakes were the two points available to the pole winner. Stewart's teammate Robbie Buhl threw down the gauntlet with a provisional pole lap of 205.074 miles per hour in a G Force-Aurora on Firestone tires. Fourteen spots further down the qualifing order, Hamilton responded with an impressive effort of 205.300 miles per hour in a G Force-Aurora on Goodyears. That was good enough to put him on the provisional pole and put his team owner Foyt into a qualifying dilemma.

Foyt's other car, a Dallara-Aurora driven by Billy Boat, was still in the qualifying line and further back was Stewart's G Force-Aurora. In a classic Vegas-style showdown, the Texan had to decide whether to gamble that Hamilton's time would stand up versus Stewart—or send Boat out to increase the pole speed and put it out of Stewart's reach.

Foyt elected to turn Boat loose and the veteran midget driver earned his first IRL pole in six attempts with a lap of 207.413 miles per hour, blowing away Hamilton's speed. Alas, Stewart turned a lap of 205.113 miles per hour, which was .036 seconds slower than Hamilton's mark. That put him on the second row, inside teammate Buhl.

Had Foyt not given Boat the green light, the championship gap would have been eight points instead of 10. "If we do win the gamble, Davey gets two points," said Foyt. "But I could not afford to do that with Tony Stewart sitting behind us [in the qualifying line]. We didn't have no choice but [for Boat] to go for it. Davey will tell you I'm not going to play sides, not like they do in F-1."

Race night on Saturday arrived with rapidly dropping temperatures on the heels of a stiff desert wind. Even though the wind mercifully died down just prior to the start, an IRL record starting field of 31 cars took several additional warm-up laps to get heat in the tires by running three laps under yellow.

Since teams had not tested or practiced in such conditions, there was bound to be a shuffling of the field. Boat immediately was passed by Hamilton, who then developed a loose chassis condition that would eventually cost him a lap that he never regained. Boat himself would eventually retire due to an electrical problem without ever leading a lap under green.

Stewart's opening stints were comfortable and consistent, and he trailed the leader Buhl by 4.1 seconds after the first round of pit stops. But then the car's handling went haywire, and he too would not lead a lap under green. "It didn't respond to any of the changes we made to it, so I think it must have broken a shock," Stewart would say afterward. He lost his first lap when he nearly found the wall on the 96th circuit and slowed down dramatically on the backstraight. He pitted on schedule 20 laps later but then returned to the pits after only six more green flag laps, again searching for a cure to the problem.

A series of four yellows over the final 90 laps was a godsend for Stewart, enabling him to close up on each re-start as well as make another long unscheduled pit stop. That one came after just 23 more laps of green during the sixth caution for the blown engine of Eddie Cheever. The re-start that followed found Stewart in 11th place, one lap and four positions behind Hamilton. Was the points leader concerned that he might not make it to the finish, since the 20 cars still running meant a DNF would cost him the points title? "Every one of the five times I almost hit the wall," replied Stewart.

Teams prepared for the Las Vegas 500k during a colorful Nevada sunset.

Buzz Calkins' day ended when he tangled with Sam Schmidt and Dr. Jack Miller on lap 60, finishing 28th.

Tony Stewart's crew made final preparations for the Las Vegas 500k. Stewart finished 11th in the race and became the 1996–97 IRL Champion with 278 total points.

Winner Eliseo Salazar spins the money wheel hoping to double his prize money.

IRL drivers Robbie Buhl and Robbie Groff, among others, signed autographs for fans before the race.

Stewart's car was pushing like a sidewinder rattlesnake on desert sand, which a rejuvenated wind kept blowing up by the wall. "I kept trying to use a lot of brakes but not too much to keep it from sliding," said Stewart of his battle to keep the car out of the dust and wall. "I was having trouble from the middle of the corner on out. It was like running a Silver Crown car on the [dirt] mile at Springfield."

While the points battle never quite warmed up—unless one counts Stewart's harrowing adventures with the wall—the joust for the victory began to pick up along with the wind. Rookie of the year winner Jim Guthrie (9 laps), Kenny Brack (6 laps), Salazar (21 laps), and then Buhl (1 lap) all ran in the lead before the Chilean took over for the final 49 circuits.

Buhl became testimony to the tricky conditions when his Quaker State-backed Menard entry got cocked sideways in the dust at the start-finish on the re-start after the seventh caution flag, which snapped in the wind due to the stalled car of Johnny Unser, one of three drivers powered by an Infiniti V-8. Running third behind Salazar, Buhl dropped to fifth before returning to third by race's end.

Roberto Guerrero's accident 12 laps from the finish, which brought out the final caution, could be attributed to the difficulty of running high speed on a 1.5-mile oval. Coming out of Turn 2, the Columbian was preparing to pass the G Force-Aurora of Marco Greco. Greco's car suddenly lost fuel pressure, then balked in the groove. Guerrero's car was launched over Greco's left rear tire as he tried to evade him. The Dallara-Aurora hit the grass upside down, digging through the dirt before it came to a stop, and the driver quickly scrambled out unhurt.

The safety crews hurried to clean up the mess, leaving four more laps of green and one last chance for Mark Dismore, running second behind Salazar in Kelly Racing's Dallara-Aurora. Dismore had led twice for 45 laps earlier in the event and had pulled within half a second of Salazar with 30 laps to go. "I started to hustle [the car] by trying different lines," said Dismore. "I turned in later at the corners and got down by the white lines." But the valiant Dismore could not ever coax enough speed from his Dallara-Aurora to catch Salazar. "I blistered the right rear tire," he said. "By the end I was just trying to hang on." Finally, the tire gave way entering the last lap, enabling Scott Goodyear, who finished second, Buhl, and Guthrie to get past.

For winner Salazar, the victory aboard his Dallara-Aurora on Goodyear tires by a margin of 1.2 seconds was salve for his wounds. The Chilean national hero, who began running Indy cars in 1995, broke his leg at the outset of the inaugural IRL season in a test crash in Orlando then suffered a broken back in a test accident at Orlando in 1997. "I need milk for all my broken bones," joked Salazar about the post-race tradition at the Indy 500.

Despite those problems, Salazar came back to the IRL as soon as he was physically fit. The victory was also salvation for his engineer Dick Simon. As a driver and team owner, Simon had struggled to win an Indy car race without success, eventually selling his operation to Team Scandia and owner Andy Evans to take on the role of engineer.

For his part, Hamilton was stoic to the end after coming home seventh, three positions ahead of Stewart. Only a victory would have beaten Stewart's 10th-place finish. "We were off at the start and just fell a little short," said Hamilton, who finished more races—eight—than any other driver.

The race itself was a typically competitive IRL event where 10 different drivers exchanged the lead 13 times before Salazar headed to victory lane and Stewart headed off into the cold night toting his fourth open-wheel championship and one of the most promising careers in American racing.

"I thought it would be pretty hard to top winning three USAC championships in the '95 season," said Stewart, "but I think the pressure that's involved in a series like the IRL means this is definitely the biggest thing I've won yet. It will get me a lot of recognition. They're a lot of variables to running a series like this, and that's what makes it so gratifying."

The colorful desert was the setting for the second Las Vegas 500k.

Roberto Guerrero's accident 12 laps from the finish brought out the final caution. His Dallara-Aurora landed upside down, digging through the dirt before it came to a stop. Guerrero was unhurt.

1997 INDY RACING LEAGUE SPONSORS

OFFICIAL PACE CAR

OFFICIAL MOTOR OIL

OFFICIAL CLOTHIER

OFFICIAL WEBSITE PROVIDER

OFFICIAL TRAILER

OFFICIAL HARDWARE

Other Participating Companies

American Dairy Association	Holmatro	PPG Industries
Bart Wheels	J.C. Carter	Pennzoil
Robert Bosch Corp.	KECO Coatings	Perkin Elmer
Champion Spark Plug	Kruse International	Raybestos
Coors Brewing Company	Lincoln Electric	STP
Crower Motorsports	MBNA Motorsports	Sun Industries
Earl's Performance Products	Miller Electric	True Value
Emco Gears	Nissan	Valvoline
Fastlane Footwear	Oldsmobile	Weld Wheels

500 Contingency Awards

PPG INDUSTRIES
$495,000

PENNZOIL PRODUCTS CO.
$125,000

VALVOLINE, INC.
$75,000

ROBERT BOSCH CORP.
$45,000

AURORA BY OLDSMOBILE
$40,000

FIRESTONE
$35,000

RAYBESTOS BRAKE PARTS
$30,000

QUAKER STATE
$25,000

EARL'S PERFORMANCE PRODUCTS
$22,500

STP RACING/FIRST BRANDS CORP.
$20,000

CHAMPION SPARK PLUG
$20,000

CANON U.S.A.
$12,000

PREMIER FARNELL CORP.
$10,000

SIMPSON RACE PRODUCTS
$10,000

LOCTITE CORPORATION
$9,500

J.C. CARTER CO.
$7,500

KECO COATINGS
$6,500

BG OIL
$5,000

BELL HELMETS
$6,000

BART WHEELS
$5,000

EMCO GEARS, INC.
$5,000

HYPERCO, INC.
$5,000

IDEAL DIVISION/STANT CORP.
$5,000

KLOTZ SPECIAL
FORMULA PRODUCTS, INC.
$5,000

MECHANIX WEAR
$5,000

NISSAN
$5,000

PROLONG SUPER LUBRICANTS
$5,000

OIL CHEM RESEARCH CORP.
$5,000

MOBIL OIL CORPORATION
$5,000

SNAP-ON TOOLS
$5,000

STANT MANUFACTURING, INC.
$5,000

500 Race Day Awards

BORG-WARNER TROPHY AWARD
$130,000 plus trophy replica - Borg-Warner
Automotive, Inc.
Arie Luyendyk

OLDSMOBILE OFFICIAL PACE CAR
AWARD
1997 Aurora V-8 Official Pace Car -
Oldsmobile
Arie Luyendyk

COORS INDY PIT STOP CHALLENGE
$70,000 - Coors Brewing Company
(contest held May 22, 1997)
Kenny Brack

SCOTT BRAYTON DRIVER'S TROPHY
$25,000 - Royal Purple Motor Oil
(awarded to driver who most
exemplifies the attitude,spirit and
competitive drive of Scott Brayton)
John Paul Jr.

AMERICAN DAIRY AWARDS
$13,750 - American Dairy Association
(winner, fastest rookie,
winning chief mechanic)
Arie Luyendyk, Vincenzo Sospiri, Skip Faul

LOCTITE AWARDS
$10,500 - Loctite Corporation and
Permatex Fast Orange
(winner, winning chief mechanic,
pole position)
Arie Luyendyk, Skip Faul, Arie Luyendyk

BANK ONE "ROOKIE OF THE YEAR"
AWARD
$10,000 - Bank One, Indianapolis
Jeff Ward

FASTLANE FOOTWEAR "FASTEST RACE
LAP" AWARD
$10,000 - Fastlane Footwear
Tony Stewart

KODAK "PHOTO FINISH" AWARD
$10,000 - Eastman Kodak Company
(race winner)
Arie Luyendyk

MBNA "LAP LEADER" AWARD
$10,000 - MBNA Motorsports
(awarded to the driver who leads
the most laps in the race)
Tony Stewart

NBD "LEADERS' CIRCLE" AWARD
$10,000 - NBD Bank
(awarded to the driver who leads
the most laps in the race)
Tony Stewart

NATIONAL CITY BANK "CHECKERED
FLAG" AWARD
$10,000 - National City Bank, Indiana
(race winner)
Arie Luyendyk

PENNZOIL PERFORMAX™ 100
"Performance" Award
$10,000 - Pennzoil Products Company
(winning chief mechanic)
Skip Faul

PREMIER/D-A "MECHANICAL
ACHIEVEMENT" AWARD
$10,000 - Premier Industrial Corp.
Paul Durant

CLINT BRAWNER "MECHANICAL
EXCELLENCE" AWARD
$5,000
Clint Brawner Mechanical Excellence
Award Foundation
Vincenzo Sospiri

CRAFTSMAN TRACTOR AWARD
$5,000 - Frigidaire Home Products
Arie Luyendyk

THE GEAR SHED "TOP FINISHING CREW"
AWARD
$5,000 - The Gear Shed
Fermin Velez

INDIANA OXYGEN "PERSEVERANCE"
AWARD
$5,000 - Indiana Oxygen
(team who exemplifies the most
exceptional sportsmanship in
a non-winning effort)
(Buddy Lazier) Hemelgarn Racing

JACUZZI WINNERS AWARD
$5,000 - U.S. Industries, Inc.
Arie Luyendyk

KRUSE "HIGHEST FINISHING ROOKIE"
AWARD
$10,000 - Kruse International
Jeff Ward

LINCOLN ELECTRIC "HARD CHARGER"
AWARD
$5,000 - Lincoln Electric
(lowest qualifier to lead the race)
Billy Boat

MONROE AUTO "EFFICIENCY" AWARD
$5,000 - Monroe Auto Equipment
Company
(awarded to the driver that runs the most
miles between pit stops)
Billy Boat

MOTORSPORTS SPARES/GOODRIDGE
"PERSISTENCE PAYS" AWARD
$5,000 - Motorsports Spares Int'l,
Inc./Goodridge
(highest finishing last day qualifier)
Johnny Unser

"STIHL THE LEADER" AWARD
$5,000 - Stihl, Inc.
(awarded to the team on the
leading edge of technology)
Monsoon Galles Racing (Kenny Brack)

SUN INDUSTRIES "COMPETITIVE SPIRIT"
AWARD
$5,000 - Sun Industries
(awarded to the lowest position
car still running at the finish)
Vincenzo Sospiri

SYSCO "MAKING THE GRADE" AWARD
$5,000 - SYSCO
(race winner)
Arie Luyendyk

THUNDERBIRD "WINNER'S" AWARD
$5,000 plus a Formula 271-SR-1 boat -
Thunderbird Products
(race winner)
Arie Luyendyk

TRUCKERS TOY STORE "RACE
TRANSPORTER" AWARD
$5,000 - Truckers Toy Store, Inc.
(best tractor, trailer and
tractor/trailer combination)
Jonathan Byrd/Cunningham Racing,
AJ Foyt Enterprises,
AJ Foyt PowerTeam Racing

500 Qualifying Awards

PPG Pole Award - $100,000
PPG Industries
Plus a 1997 customized Chevrolet van ($40,000 value)
Arie Luyendyk

GTE "Front Runner" Award - $30,000
($10,000 awarded to each front row driver)
GTE
Arie Luyendyk, Tony Stewart, Vincenzo Sospiri

True Value "Pole Winning Chief Mechanic" Award - $10,000
COTTER AND COMPANY
Skip Faul

Sure Start/Automotive Armature
"On The Bubble" Award - $10,000
(awarded to the driver "on the bubble"
at close of qualifying)
SURE START, INC.
Claude Bourbonnais

Ameritech "Youngest Starting Driver" Award - $7,500
AMERITECH
Tony Stewart

American Dairy "Fastest Qualifying Rookie" Award - $5,000
AMERICAN DAIRY ASSOCIATION
Vincenzo Sospiri

Buckeye Machine/Race Spec "Final Measure"
Award - $5,000
(awarded to last team to pass inspection
and qualify for the race)
BUCKEYE MACHINE/RACE SPEC
Paul Durant

Citadel Group "Overachiever" Award - $5,000
(awarded to the team who achieves the greatest qualifying
success with limited resources)
CITADEL GROUP
Robbie Groff

Ferguson Steel "Most Consistent Veteran Qualifier"
Award - $5,000
FERGUSON STEEL COMPANY
Tony Stewart

T.P. Donovan "Top Starting Rookie" Award - $5,000
OLINGER DISTRIBUTING COMPANY, INC.
Vincenzo Sospiri

S R E Industries "My Bubble Burst" Award - $5,000
(awarded to the last driver to be bumped on last day of
qualifying)
SRE INDUSTRIES
Lyn St. James

Snap-On Tools/CAM "500 Top Wrench" Award - $5,000
(awarded to the chief mechanic demonstrating
outstanding skill and expertise during qualifying)
SNAP-ON TOOLS/CHAMPIONSHIP ASSOCIATION OF
MECHANICS, INC.
Mark Weida

Mi-Jack "Top Performer" Award - $5,000
(awarded to the driver recording the
fastest single qualifying lap)
MI-JACK PRODUCTS
Arie Luyendyk

Loctite "Permatex Fast Orange" Award - $5,000
(awarded to the pole position winner)
LOCTITE CORPORATION
Arie Luyendyk

Official Box Score
Indy Racing League
True Value 200
August 18, 1996

New England August 18, 1996

FP	*SP	Car	Driver	Car Name	YR/C/E/T	Qual. Speed	Laps Comp.	Running/ Reason Out	IRL Pts.	*IRL Awards	Designated Awards	Total Awards
1	12	1	Scott Sharp	Conseco/AJ Foyt Racing Lola	95/L/F/G	168.867	200	(130.934)	35	$100,000	$18,000	$118,000
2	10	12	Buzz Calkins	Bradley Motorsports/Bradley Food Marts	95/R/F/F	169.831	200	Running	33	82,000	5,250	87,250
3	2	33	Michele Alboreto	Scandia Rio Hotel & Casino Perry Ellis Royal Purple	95/R/F/G	175.125	200	Running	32	69,000	12,750	81,750
4	9	10	Mike Groff	Jonathan Byrd's Cafeteria	95/R/F/F	170.638	199	Running	31	57,000	7,500	64,500
5	17	14	Davey Hamilton	AJ Foyt Power Team Racing Lola	95/L/F/G	165.903	196	Running	30	52,000	3,000	55,000
6	18	21	Roberto Guerrero	Pennzoll Pagan Racing Ford	95/R/F/G	164.477	196	Running	29	47,000	10,000	57,000
7	15	40	Marco Greco	Scandia International Sports Limited Perry Ellis	95/L/F/G	166.287	196	Running	28	46,000	3,250	49,250
8	14	22	Stephan Gregoire	Scandia Perry Ellis	95/L/F/G	168.322	192	Running	27	45,000	250	45,250
9	6	7	Eliseo Salazar	Cristal/Copec Mobil Scandia Xcel Alta Perry Ellis	95/L/F/G	171.197	190	Running	26	44,000	250	44,250
10	11	18	John Paul Jr.	V-Line Earl's Performance Products/Crowne Plaza	93/L/M/G	169.416	190	Running	25	43,000	3,250	46,250
11	16	28	R Tyce Carlson	Earl's Performance Products/Harrah's Resorts	93/L/M/G	165.975	187	Running	24	42,000	14,500	56,500
12	7	2	Tony Stewart	Glidden Menards Special	95/L/M/F	171.190	182	Electrical	24	41,000	0	41,000
13	3	5	Arie Luyendyk	The Mi-Jack Products/Bryant Heating & Cooling Special	95/R/F/F	174.643	170	Running	22	40,000	0	40,000
14	1	4	Richie Hearn	Ralphs/Food4Less/Fuji Film/Della Penna Motorsports	95/R/F/G	175.367	166	Engine	23	39,000	22,000	61,000
15	51	51	Eddie Cheever	First Plus Team Cheever	95/L/M/G	170.852	166	Running	20	38,000	0	38,000
16	20	30	Stan Wattles	Spirit of San Antonio/McCormack Motorsports	94/L/F/G	161.842	163	Low Fuel Pressure	19	37,000	0	37,000
17	22	15	David Kudrave	Tempero-Giuffre Racing	93/L/B/G	150.867	118	Clutch	18	14,000	0	14,000
18	23	9	Brad Murphey	Hemelgarn Racing	94/R/F/F	No Time	79	Handling	17	13,000	2,000	15,000
19	4	91	Buddy Lazier	Hemelgarn Racing/Delta Faucet/Super Fitness	95/R/F/F	172.664	66	Accident	16	34,000	0	34,000
20	5	3	Mark Dismore	Quaker State Menards Special	95/L/M/F	172.056	43	Clutch	15	33,000	0	33,000
21	21	96	Joe Gosek	ABF Motorsports/Manaras/United Airlines	92/L/B/G	154.196	30	Accident	14	10,000	0	10,000
22	13	54	Robbie Buhl	Original Coors/Beck Motorsports	94/L/F/F	168.710	0	Accident	13	32,000	0	32,000
23	19	27	Jim Guthrie	Team Blueprint Racing, Inc.	93/L/M/F	164.031	0	Accident	12	32,000	0	32,000
		64	Johnny Unser	Ruger Titanium Hawaiian Tropic Project Indy	95/R/F/G				0	10,000	0	10,000
									Total-	$1,000,000	$102,000	$1,102,000

Margin of Victory: 20.4 seconds **Fastest Lap/Leading Lap:** #2 Tony Stewart: 166.439 mph on Lap 179

Time of Race: 1:36:57.912 **Average Speed:** 130.934 mph **Margin of Victory:** 20.4 mph **Engine Legend:** F-Ford Cosworth; M-Menard V6; B-Buick **Tire Legend:** F-Firestone; G-Goodyear

Legend: FP-Finish Position; SP-Start Position; R-Rookie

Chassis Legend: L-Lola; R-Reynard

*Top 20 entrant qualifiers earn bonus of $22,000 each.

Lap Leaders:

Lap	1-6	#4 Richie Hearn
Lap	7-13	#5 Arie Luyendyk
Lap	14-37	#2 Tony Stewart
Lap	38-41	#5 Arie Luyendyk
Lap	42-182	#2 Tony Stewart
Lap	183-200	#1 Scott Sharp

Lap Leader Summary:

Driver	Times	Total
Tony Stewart	2	165
Scott Sharp	1	18
Arie Luyendyk	2	11
Richie Hearn	1	6

Caution Flags:

Lap	1-5	Accident 1 #54 & 4 #27
Lap	35-40	Accident 4 #96
Lap	68-78	Accident 4 #91
Lap	123-125	Debris/Rain/Red Flag

Official Box Score
Indy Racing League
Las Vegas Motor Speedway
September 15, 1996

FP	SP	Car	Driver	R	Car Name	YR/C/E/T	Qual. Speed	Laps Comp.	Running/Reason Out	IRL Pts.	Total IRL Pts.	*IRL Awards	Designated Awards	Total Awards
1	8	4	Richie Hearn		Ralph's/Food4Less/Fuji Film	95/R/F/G	221.511	200	Running	36y	59	$100,000	$20,000	$120,000
2	22	22	Michel Jourdain Jr.		Herdez Viva Mexico!	94/L/F/G	212.615	200	Running	33	33	82,000	13,250	95,250
3	6	10	Mike Groff		Jonathan Byrd's Cafeteria/Visionaire	95/R/F/F	222.359	199	Running	32	63	69,000	11,250	80,250
4	9	21	Roberto Guerrero		Pennzoil Pagan Racing Ford	95/R/F/G	220.687	198	Running	31	60	57,000	18,000	75,000
5	18	33	Michele Alboreto		Scandia Rio Hotel & Casino Perry Ellis Royal Purple	95/R/F/G	215.139	197	Running	30	62	52,000	3,500	55,500
6	16	12	Buzz Calkins		Bradley Motorsports/Bradley Food Marts	95/R/F/F	215.991	197	Running	29	62	47,000	500	47,500
7	13	7	Eliseo Salazar		Cristal/Copec Mobil Scandia Xcel Alta Perry Ellis	95/L/F/G	217.672	196	Running	28	54	46,000	500	46,500
8	15	54	Robbie Buhl		Original Coors/Beck Motorsports	94/L/F/F	216.285	195	Running	27	40	23,000	2,750	25,750
9	24	40	Marco Greco		Scandia International Sports Limited Perry Ellis	95/L/F/G	210.190	191	Running	26	54	44,000	250	44,250
10	23	34	Affonso Giaffone	R	Hype/Quaker State/Scandia	94/L/F/G	211.243	190	Running	25	25	21,000	250	21,250
11	5	14	Davey Hamilton		AJ Foyt Power Team Racing Lola	95/L/F/G	222.818	187	Running	24	54	42,000	2,250	44,250
12	11	6	Johnny O'Connell		The Mi-Jack/Bryant Heating & Cooling Special	94/R/F/F	219.646	183	Accident	23	23	19,000	3,000	22,000
13	19	27	Jim Guthrie	R	Team Blueprint Racing, Inc.	93/L/B/F	214.968	182	Wheel Bearing	22	34	18,000	2,000	20,000
14	3	50	Robby Gordon		Valvoline Cummins Craftsman Special	95/R/F/G	223.371	179	Wheel Bearing	21	21	17,000		17,000
15	12	18	John Paul Jr.		V-Line Earl's Performance Products/Crowne Plaza	93/L/M/G	219.477	170	Running	20	45	38,000	10,000	48,000
16	7	1	Scott Sharp		Conseco/AJ Foyt Racing Lola	95/L/F/G	222.332	168	Wheel Bearing	19	54	37,000		37,000
17	10	3	Mark Dismore		Menards/Quaker State/Special	95/L/M/F	219.718	149	Accident	18	33	36,000		36,000
18	21	30	Stan Wattles	R	Spirit of San Antonio/McCormack Motorsports	94/L/F/G	213.161	119	Accident	17	36	35,000		35,000
19	28	15	J.C. Carbonell	R	YPF/Sharp/Newsweek/Camare	93/L/B/G	181.208	112	Overheating	16	16	34,000		34,000
20	1	5	Arie Luyendyk		The Mi-Jack/Bryant Heating & Cooling Special	95/R/F/F	226.491	106	Accident	17x	39	33,000	20,000	53,000
21	2	2	Tony Stewart		Menards/Glidden/Special	95/L/M/F	224.225	77	Accident	14	38	32,000		32,000
22	20	64	Johnny Unser		Ruger Titanium Hawaiian Tropic Project Indy	95/R/F/G	213.624	67	Wheel Bearing	13	13	10,000		10,000
23	14	28	Tyce Carlson	R	Earl's Performance Products/Harrah's Resorts	93/L/M/G	217.496	53	Accident	12	36	32,000	2,500	34,500
24	4	91	Buddy Lazier		Hemelgarn Racing/Delta Faucet	95/R/F/F	222.938	35	Handling	11	27	32,000		32,000
25	27	51	Eddie Cheever		First Plus Team Cheever	95/L/M/G	192.836	27	Accident	10	30	32,000		32,000
26	25	8	Stephan Gregoire		Scandia Team Perry Ellis	95/L/F/G	209.978	27	Accident	9	36	10,000		10,000
27	26	9	Brad Murphey	R	Hemelgarn Racing	94/R/F/F	205.958	26	Accident	8	25	32,000		32,000
28	17	16	Johnny Parsons		Team Blueprint Racing, Inc.	93/L/B/F	215.853	7	Accident	7	7	10,000		10,000
										Total-		$1,040,000	$110,000	$1,150,000

Time of Race: 2:36:17.345 **Average Speed:** 115.171 mph **Margin of Victory:** 1.693 seconds

Fastest Lap: #4 Hearn, 219.191 mph on Lap 53 **Fastest Leading Lap:** #50 Gordon, 217.453 mph on Lap 51

Legend: FP- Finish Position; SP- Start Position; R- Rookie **IRL Points Bonus:** x- 2 points PPG Pole; y- 1 point most laps lead.

***IRL Awards:** Top 20 entrant point leaders earn bonus of $22,000

Chassis Legend: L- Lola; R- Reynard. **Engine Legend:** F- Ford Cosworth; M- Menard V6; B- Buick. **Tire Legend:** F- Firestone; G- Goodyear.

Caution Flags:

Lap-Lap	Laps	Incident
9-18	10	#16 Parsons accident T4
30-46	17	#9, #51, #8 accident T2
55-62	8	#28 Carlson accident T2
78-87	10	#2 Stewart accident T2
107-115	9	#5 Luyendyk accident T2
125-138	14	#30 Wattles accident T4
152-160	9	#3 Dismore accident T4
161-165	4	Debris
185-186	2	Red Flag: #6 O'Connell accident FS (20 min.)

Total: 83

Lap Leaders:

Laps	Car	Driver
1-25	#5	Arie Luyendyk
26-57	#50	Robby Gordon
58-79	#18	John Paul Jr.
80-99	#50	Robby Gordon
100-110	#4	Richie Hearn
111-111	#6	Johnny O'Connell
112-153	#4	Richie Hearn
154-155	#6	Johnny O'Connell
156-160	#4	Richie Hearn
161-168	#50	Robby Gordon
169-200	#4	Richie Hearn

Lap Leader Summary:

Driver	Times	Total
Richie Hearn	4	90
Robby Gordon	4	60
Arie Luyendyk	1	25
John Paul Jr.	1	22
Johnny O'Connell	2	3

Official Box Score
Indy Racing League
Indy 200 at Walt Disney World
Presented by Aurora
January 25, 1997

FP	SP	CAR	DRIVER	CAR NAME	C/E/T	QUAL. SPEED	LAPS COMP	RUNNING/ REASON OUT	IRL PTS.	TOTAL IRL PTS.	IRL AWARDS	DESIGNATED AWARDS	TOTAL AWARDS
1	5	51	Eddie Cheever Jr.	FirstPlus Team Cheever	G/A/G	163.547	149	Running	35	65	$128,000	$42,000	$170,000
2	14	10	Mike Groff	Jonathan Byrd's Cafeteria Bryant Heating & Cooling	G/I/F	159.355	149	Running	33	96	103,600	15,250	118,850
3	6	6	Scott Goodyear	Treadway Racing/NORTEL	G/A/F	163.332	149	Running	32	32	63,900	5,000	68,900
4	4	1	Scott Sharp	Conseco/AJ Foyt Racing	D/A/F	163.785	149	Running	31	85	69,600	4,250	73,850
5	11	91	Buddy Lazier	Delta Faucet-Hemelgarn-Montana	D/I/F	161.341	149	Running	30	57	40,800	4,750	45,550
6	9	27	R Jim Guthrie	Blueprint Racing, Inc.	D/A/F	162.272	148	Running	29	63	56,000	7,250	63,250
7	7	14	Davey Hamilton	AJ Foyt/Power Team Racing	D/A/G	163.280	148	Running	28	82	54,600	250	54,850
8	12	22	Marco Greco	Intl Sports Ltd/Scandia/Alta/Xcel/Royal Purple	D/A/G	160.214	147	Running	27	81	53,300	10,250	63,550
9	10	33	R Fermin Velez	Mi-Jack Scandia Alta Xcel Royal Purple	D/A/G	161.638	147	Running	26	26	51,900	250	52,150
10	1	2	Tony Stewart	Glidden/Menard/Special	G/A/F	166.013	146	Accident T3	28xy	66	50,550	32,750	83,300
11	3	12	W Buzz Calkins	Bradley Motorsports	G/A/G	164.046	144	Engine	24	86	49,200	5,000	54,200
12	2	5	Arie Luyendyk	Treadway Racing/WavePhore	G/A/F	164.964	97	Accident T1	23	62	47,800		47,800
13	16	17	Danny Ongais	Trane Heating/Cooling/Allied Specialty Ins.	D/A/G	151.483	94	Suspension	22	22	24,500		24,500
14	15	30	R Jeret Schroeder	Purity Farms McCormack Motorsports	G/A/G	154.859	93	Accident T1	21	21	45,100		45,100
15	18	40	R Jack Miller	AMS Crest Racing	D/A/F	—	85	Suspension	20	20	43,750		43,750
16	8	4	R Jeff Ward	Monsoon-Galles Racing	G/A/G	162.660	63	Gearbox	19	19	20,400	2,500	22,900
17	17	21	Roberto Guerrero	Pennzoil Dallara Infiniti	D/I/G	—	56	Fuel pump	18	78	41,000	5,000	46,000
18	13	18	John Paul Jr.	Earl's Performance/V-Line/Tnemec/KECO	D/A/G	159.553	46	Oil pump	17	62	39,700	3,000	42,700
19	19	77	Stephan Gregoire	Miller-Eads Co/Chastain Motorsports	G/A/G	—	2	Fuel pump	16	52	16,300		16,300
											$1,000,0000	$137,500	$1,137,5000

Time of Race: 1:06:43.145 Average Speed: 133.995 Margin of Victory: Under caution Fastest Lap/Leading Lap: #2 Tony Stewart, Lap 5 of 22.579 sec., 159.440 mph

PPG Pole Winner: Tony Stewart Coors Pit Performance Winner: Tony Stewart True Value Pole Winning Chief Mechanic: John O'Gara/Team Menard, Inc.

MBNA Motorsports Lap Leader: Tony Stewart IRL Points Bonus: x - 2 points PPG Pole; y - 1 point most laps led
#22 Marco Greco 2-65 sec./Team Scandia

Chassis Legend: D - Dallara; G - G Force Engine Legend: A - Oldsmobile Aurora; I - Nissan Infiniti Tire Legend: F - Firestone; G - Goodyear

IRL Point Leaderss

Groff 96, Calkins 86, Sharp 85,
Hamilton 82, Greco 81, Guerrero 78,
Stewart 66, Cheever 65, Guthrie 63
Luyendyk 62

Caution Flags:

Laps	Incident
99-106	#30 Schroeder & #5 Luyendyk T1
146-149	#2 Stewart Accident T3
150	Rain, Red Flag

Lap Leaders:

Lap-Lap		
1-130	#2	Tony Stewart
131-144	#12	Buzz Calkins
145	#2	Tony Stewart
146-149	#51	Eddie Cheever Jr.

Lap Leader Summary:

Driver	Times	Total
Tony Stewart	2	131
Buzz Calkins	1	14
Eddie Cheever Jr.	1	4

1997 Official Box Score
Indy Racing League
Phoenix 200
March 23, 1997

FP	SP	CAR	DRIVER	CAR NAME	C/E/T	QUAL. SPEED	LAPS COMP	RUNNING/ REASON OUT	IRL PTS.	TOTAL IRL PTS.	IRL STANDINGS	IRL AWARDS	DESIGNATED AWARDS	TOTAL AWARDS
1	2	27 R	Jim Guthrie	Blueprint Racing	D/A/F	169.484	200	Running	35	98	8	$115,600	$54,500	$170,100
2	1	2	Tony Stewart	Glidden/Menard/Special	G/A/F	170.012	200	Running	36xy	102	7	94,000	51,500	145,500
3	14	14	Davey Hamilton	AJ Foyt/Power Team Racing	G/A/G	162.448	200	Running	32	114	2	78,400	5,500	83,900
4	8	22	Marco Greco	Int'l Sports Ltd/Scandia/Alta/Xcel/Royal Purple	D/A/G	163.495	199	Running	31	112	4	64,000	500	64,500
5	19	77	Stephan Gregoire	Miller-Eads Co/Chastain Motorsports	G/A/G	154.939	199	Running	30	82	11	36,000	4,000	40,000
6	16	10	Mike Groff	Jonathan Byrd's Cafeteria Bryant Heating & Cooling	G/I/F	159.858	195	Running	29	125	1	52,000	7,250	59,250
7	10	21 W	Roberto Guerrero	Pennzoil Racing	D/I/G	163.080	194	Running	28	106	5	50,800	3,250	54,050
8	22	12	Buzz Calkins	Bradley Foodmarts	G/A/G	164.032	187	Running	27	113	3	49,600	2,500	52,100
9	11	18	John Paul, Jr.	Klipsch Tnemec V-Line Earl's	D/A/G	162.896	179	Running	26	88	9	48,400	2,250	50,650
10	6	16 R	Sam Schmidt	Blueprint Racing	D/A/F	163.837	176	Accident T4	25	25	27	25,200	250	25,450
11	9	4 R	Kenny Brack	Monsoon Galles Racing	G/A/G	163.436	145	Accident T4	24	24	29	24,000	3,250	27,250
12	7	51	Eddie Cheever Jr.	FirstPlus Team Cheever	G/A/G	163.510	120	Over Heating	23	88	10	44,800	250	45,050
13	21	17 R	Affonso Giaffone	General Motors of Brazil/Chitwood/Dallara	D/A/G	NS	114	Half Shaft	22	47	19	21,600		21,600
14	15	33 R	Fermin Velez	Mi-Jack Scandia Alta Xcel Royal Purple	D/A/G	161.907	94	Electrical	21	47	20	42,400		42,400
15	17	50 R	Billy Roe	Eurointernational Dallara Aurora	D/A/F	158.940	82	Accident T3	20	20	33	19,200		19,200
16	20	1	Scott Sharp	Conseco/AJ Foyt Racing	G/A/G	NS	65	Engine	19	104	6	40,000		40,000
17	3	6	Scott Goodyear	Treadway Racing/NORTEL	G/A/F	166.044	52	Engine	18	50	18	38,800		38,800
18	5	3	Robbie Buhl	Menard/Quaker State/Special	G/A/F	163.964	51	Accident T1	17	57	16	15,600		15,600
19	12	30 R	Jeret Schroeder	McCormack Motorsports	G/A/G	162.631	51	Accident T1	16	37	21	36,400		36,400
20	18	40 R	Jack Miller	AMS Crest Racing	D/A/F	158.040	33	Fuel Pickup	15	35	24	35,200		35,200
21	13	91	Buddy Lazier	Delta Faucet-Montana-Hemelgarn Racing	D/I/F	162.543	31	Engine	14	71	13	34,000		34,000
22	4	5 W	Arie Luyendyk	Treadway Racing/WavePhore	G/A/F	165.784	11	Mechanical	13	75	12	34,000		34,000
											TOTAL-	$1,000,000	$135,000	$1,135,000

Time of Race: 2:14:32 **Average Speed:** 89.190 mph **Margin of Victory:** .854 sec. **Fastest Lap/Leading Lap:** #2 Tony Stewart, Lap 11 of 22.135 sec., 162.638 mph

PPG Pole Winner: Tony Stewart **True Value Pole Winning Chief Mechanic:** Bill Martin/Team Menard, Inc.

MBNA Motorsports Lap Leader: Tony Stewart **Coors Pit Performance Winner:** #27 Guthrie 2 - 78 sec./Blueprint Racing, Inc. **IRL Points Bonus:** x - 2 points PPG Pole; y - 1 point most laps led

Legend: W - Former Winner; R - Indy Racing League Series Rookie **Chassis Legend:** D - Dallara; G - G Force **Engine Legend:** A - Oldsmobile Aurora; I - Nissan Infiniti **Tire Legend:** F - Firestone; G - Goodyear

Caution Flags:

Laps	Incident
2-6	#21 Guerrero Tow In
13-18	#5 Luyendyk Back Straight Away
36-44	#91 Lazier Oiling
52-60	#3 Buhl & #30 Schroeder T1
69-75	Oil on Track
85-98	#50 Roe T3
117-132	Oil on Track
146-154	#4 Brack T4
180-190	#16 Schmidt T4

Lap Leaders:

Lap-Lap	Driver
1-41	#2 Stewart
42	#27 Guthrie
43-55	#17 Giaffone
56-61	#2 Stewart
62-65	#1 Sharp
66-94	#2 Stewart
95-120	#27 Guthrie
121	#2 Stewart
122-145	#4 Brack
146-153	#2 Stewart
154-200	#27 Guthrie

Lap Leader Summary:

Driver	Times	Total
Stewart	5	85
Guthrie	3	74
Brack	1	24
Giaffone	1	13
Sharp	1	4

1997 Daily Practice Laps
81st Indianapolis 500
May 27, 1997

#	Driver		5/04	5/05	5/06	5/07	5/08	5/09	5/10	5/11	5/12	5/13	5/14	5/15	5/16	5/17	5/18	5/22	TOTAL
1	Paul Durant	G/A/G															56	10	66
1	Davey Hamilton	G/A/G															11		11
1	Johnny O'Connell	G/A/G												18	14				32
1T	Scott Sharp	G/A/G			21	17													38
1T	Billy Boat	D/A/G								19									19
1T	Scott Sharp	D/A/G															11	12	23
2	Tony Stewart	G/A/F			33	38	9	23	28										193
2T	Tony Stewart	G/A/F			13	26	41	54	21		40	61	56	27	27		9	20	286
3	Robbie Buhl	G/A/F			44		44	75	46		89	97	11	29	58			21	265
3T	Robbie Buhl	G/A/F					9	11	9										313
4	Kenny Brack	G/A/G	67	23	41	47			67									24	271
4T	Kenny Brack	G/A/G													100	2			402
5	Arie Luyendyk	G/A/F			64	47	26	52	73		73		63					16	413
6	Scott Goodyear	G/A/F			35	24	23	62	84		64	101		62			61	16	404
7	Eliseo Salazar	D/A/G			31	21		49	28		55					5	17	21	194
8	Vincenzo Sospiri	D/A/G	78		22	12		48	22								40	30	231
10	Mike Groff	G/I/F			36	27		55	25		24	60			103			27	183
10T	Mike Groff	G/I/F					38	30									12		209
11	Billy Boat	D/A/G						22		4	36	21	17	69	37	15	7	12	149
12	Buzz Calkins	G/A/G		43	27	53	31	23	43		22	53	41	69	37	73	10	16	505
14	Davey Hamilton	G/A/G			14	7		12	24		16		21	11	44			12	106
14T	Davey Hamilton	D/A/G								11									11
16	Sam Schmidt	D/A/F	7		26	7	23	66	21		61			17	32	15	7	29	275
17	Affonso Giaffone	D/A/G			89	37	7	35	36			42		39	9	68		25	336
18	Tyce Carlson	D/A/G			53	57											14		155
18	John Paul Jr.	D/A/G					44	9										25	163
21	Roberto Guerrero	D/I/G			39	20	34	19	33			46		27		12			64
21T	Roberto Guerrero	D/I/G					10	24				14							179
22	Marco Greco	D/A/G			3		5	49	54						18			18	99
27	Jim Guthrie	D/A/G			6	45								24		69		20	159
28	Mark Dismore	D/A/F											28		13				126
30	Robbie Groff	G/A/G	56		78	40	4	38	31	71								9	377
33	Fermin Velez	D/A/G			47	28		30	25					22	15	22		34	213
34	Alessandro Zampedri	D/A/G			15		4	31	35	43						31	31	18	159
34T	Alessandro Zampedri	D/A/F															28		49
36	Scott Harrington	D/A/F													17	48			93
36T	Scott Harrington	D/A/F															30		30
40	Dr. Jack Miller	D/A/G	32				10	76	32		12		14	4	31			8	219
42	Robby Gordon	G/A/G			37	25	18	13	25		66	58	29	76			22	6	375
44	Steve Kinser	D/A/G					44	98	24	44	89	48	81	39	30			21	429
50	Billy Roe	D/A/F						18		2	34	67	43		28	15		30	262
51	Eddie Cheever Jr.	G/A/G						67				22				57	12		266
51T	Eddie Cheever Jr.	G/A/G															44		44
51T	Jeff Ward	G/A/G	16						27				37		26		29		108
52	Jeff Ward	D/I/F		2				43			1							27	115
54	Dennis Vitolo	D/I/F										19		64	43	45		18	190
72	Claude Bourbonnais	G/A/G												92	36	68	46		242
77	Stephan Gregoire	D/I/F					30	35	49	38	46	53	29		36		32	13	272
90	Lyn St. James	G/A/G			34	33	27		23				37	5			44	9	216
91	Buddy Lazier	D/I/F			21		8	10	42		9					10	27		44
91	Johnny Unser	D/I/F																32	112
91T	Buddy Lazier	D/A/F										35	26	43	71	36	28	24	259
97	Greg Ray	D/A/F		12	84			16	34	43					10	20		24	255

1997 Daily Best Speeds
81st Indianapolis 500
May 27, 1997

Car	Code	Driver	5/04	5/05	5/06	5/07	5/08	5/09	5/10	5/11	5/12	5/13	5/14	5/15	5/16	5/17	5/18	5/22
1	G/A/G	Paul Durant															211.015	207.469
1	G/A/G	Davey Hamilton															212.927	
1	G/A/G	Johnny O'Connell																
1T	G/A/G	Scott Sharp			214.041	217.402								207.054	212.922			
1T	D/A/G	Scott Sharp																215.502
2	D/A/G	Billy Boat						214.148	219.085	204.026								211.213
2T	G/A/F	Tony Stewart			214.337	215.750	212.399	217.355	213.225		212.039	214.439	216.466	201.916	216.388		213.407	
2T	G/A/F	Tony Stewart																
3	G/A/F	Robbie Buhl			213.412	211.705	215.822	216.899	217.082		214.659	214.884		197.598	214.388		213.225	
3T	G/A/F	Robbie Buhl			213.843		214.900	214.352	125.574				170.474			119.201		
4	G/A/G	Kenny Brack	204.997		209.434	212.821	215.708	211.466	212.846		212.670	211.566	212.525	200.579	215.074			212.741
4T	G/A/G	Kenny Brack																
5	G/A/F	Arie Luyendyk		205.597	218.707	220.297	217.318	218.325	219.587		217.103						216.195	212.054
6	G/A/F	Scott Goodyear			211.282	214.123	209.966	212.424	217.192		216.092	216.513					141.347	212.972
7	D/A/G	Eliseo Salazar			209.366	212.465		214.690	214.777							207.097	210.709	209.893
8	D/A/G	Vincenzo Sospiri	211.964		209.268	211.332	209.585	213.498	217.056								194.452	202.94
10	G/I/F	Mike Groff			206.115	208.923		208.338	208.943		207.035	209.908	215.151		211.134	216.299		204.578
10T	G/I/F	Mike Groff						204.685										
11	D/A/G	Billy Boat			212.339	213.792	211.248	207.833	209.839	199.978	212.334	214.133	212.309	210.320	213.013	211.268	204.904	205.044
12	D/A/G	Buzz Calkins			208.512	210.941		215.853	216.409		210.482	213.346			210.852		206.835	207.963
14	G/A/G	Davey Hamilton									213.199		215.972					204.843
14T	D/A/F	Davey Hamilton												211.456				
16	D/A/F	Sam Schmidt	180.386	198.325	204.685	202.789	209.864	211.129	216.956	206.706				211.989	213.564	216.159	136.258	209.922
17	D/A/G	Affonso Giaffone			209.098	211.600	200.205	215.162	215.848			213.660				213.802	209.839	201.663
18	D/A/G	Tyce Carlson			212.555	212.079	211.640	209.536						210.59	212.846			
18	D/I/G	John Paul Jr.			204.341						214.367		214.367					208.035
21	D/I/G	Roberto Guerrero			110.043	207.680	210.664	209.254				210.669		207.216				
21T	D/I/G	Roberto Guerrero			189.143		183.035	209.293				210.079						
22	D/A/G	Marco Greco				216.076	183.173	211.496	215.848						211.775	212.942		202.211
27	D/A/F	Jim Guthrie	191.759		207.035	208.633	191.595							210.389	213.848	217.360		
28	D/A/G	Mark Dismore			210.280													206.806
30	G/A/G	Robbie Groff			201.068	214.174	179.322	210.679	208.208	209.045			206.531	188.166	209.844	209.108	204.332	207.819
33	D/A/G	Fermin Velez							210.752									205.044
34	D/A/G	Alessandro Zampedri						215.675								214.393	213.716	
34T	D/A/G	Alessandro Zampedri						211.367	211.456	210.822							214.061	211.854
36	D/A/F	Scott Harrington													169.351	200.316		
36T	D/A/F	Scott Harrington																
40	D/A/G	Jack Miller	194.246	99.635			178.671	208.169	209.497		201.315		196.601	110.179	208.011		205.526	189.561
42	G/A/G	Robby Gordon			215.569	215.993	212.229	215.326	213.574		212.565	215.574	213.838	211.164			211.839	135.170
44	D/A/G	Steve Kinser					190.251	206.536	206.954	211.854	206.096	214.444	214.276	210.936	214.684			210.389
50	D/A/F	Billy Roe								101.458		209.888	210.669		212.409	208.522		209.966
51	G/A/G	Eddie Cheever Jr.						178.243	215.631		215.600	216.909				210.379	209.190	
51T	G/A/G	Eddie Cheever Jr.														213.381		
51T	G/A/G	Jeff Ward						212.665	215.631							213.073	209.210	
52	G/A/G	Jeff Ward	205.780										212.294		213.043			
54	D/I/F	Dennis Vitolo			205.315			209.404			33.300	196.002		200.615				208.996
72	D/A/F	Claude Bourbonnais					208.386	213.326	214.475				213.528	203.841			211.635	197.360
77	G/A/G	Stephan Gregoire				211.307	212.565		211.198			212.776	209.702				211.426	205.030
90	D/I/F	Lyn St. James			207.168			205.573		211.441				206.536		204.834		209.795
91	D/I/F	Buddy Lazier			214.128		209.327								207.569			210.773
91	D/I/F	Johnny Unser																
91T	D/A/F	Buddy Lazier						209.570	215.352		214.398	217.040	216.570	208.497	215.028	215.430	210.202	211.431
97	D/A/F	Greg Ray	185.494		205.255				209.766	215.595					215.069	215.260	213.939	214.807

1997 Qualification Attempts Chronological Summary

OA	TIME		CAR	DRIVER	LAP 1	LAP 2	LAP 3	FOUR-LAP LAP 4	AVERAGE	SR	SP
Saturday, May 10, 1997 - Pole Day											
1	11:00	A.M.	10	Mike Groff	208.068	208.720	208.420	208.943	208.537	31	18
2	11:06		52	Jeff Ward	215.631	214.813	213.980	213.655	214.517	9	7
3	11:13		40	Dr. Jack Miller	208.773	209.302	209.429	209.497	209.250	29	17
4	11:19		17	Affonso Giaffone	215.848	212.766	211.695	211.640	212.974	17	14
5	11:29		3	Robbie Buhl	215.476	214.982	214.551	waved off			
6	11:51		7	Eliseo Salazar	214.429	209.190	Hit bird, T3, waved off				
7	12:00	P.M.	90	Lyn St. James	209.996	209.903	210.261	210.423	210.145	26	34
8	12:06		21	Roberto Guerrero	waved off						
9	12:13		30	Robbie Groff	208.208	Brushed wall, south chute, waved off					
10	3:21		5	Arie Luyendyk	218.659	218.108	218.182	218.103	218.263	1	1
11	3:41		4	Kenny Brack	211.506	212.389	211.984	209.035	211.221	21	15
12	3:53		27	Jim Guthrie	214.367	215.455	215.162	215.848	215.207	7	6
13	3:58		14	Davey Hamilton	216.242	215.218	212.982	213.523	214.484	10	8
4	4:06		33	Fermin Velez	210.723	waved off					
15	4:15		6	Scott Goodyear	215.203	217.103	216.149	214.802	215.811	5	5
16	4:23		8	Vincenzo Sospiri	216.737	217.056	216.659	216.836	216.822	3	3
17	4:28		2	Tony Stewart	217.986	217.823	218.113	218.161	218.021	2	2
18	4:41		34	Alessandro Zampedri	206.759	203.957	waved off				
19	4:45		7	Eliseo Salazar	214.777	214.736	214.219	213.554	214.320	11	9
20	4:49		3	Robbie Buhl	217.082	pulled in					
21	5:00		12	Buzz Calkins	209.648	209.614	208.391	waved off			
22	5:06		77	Stephan Gregoire	214.475	213.543	212.615	211.889	213.126	16	13
23	5:12		51	Eddie Cheever Jr.	214.459	214.818	213.767	213.255	214.073	13	11
	5:18		91	Buddy Lazier	Made presentation, did not take green						
24	5:30		42	Robby Gordon	213.574	213.220	213.215	212.836	213.211	15	12

QA	Time	Car	Driver	Lap 1	Lap 2	Lap 3	Lap 4	4-Lap Avg	SP	SR
25	5:35	34	Alessandro Zampedri	211.307	209.405	208.788	206.925	209.094	27	25
26	5:45	12	Buzz Calkins	209.839	209.702	209.244	209.473	209.564	4	16
27	5:50	3	Robbie Buhl	215.595	216.175	216.263	216.377	216.102	12	4
28	5:55	91T	Buddy Lazier	215.352	214.828	214.516	212.470	214.286	34	10
29	6:00	21	Roberto Guerrero	208.454	208.280	207.455	205.325	207.371		19

Sunday, May 11, 1997 - Second Qualifying Day

QA	Time	Car	Driver	Lap 1	Lap 2	Lap 3	Lap 4	4-Lap Avg	SP	SR
30	12:11 P.M.	44	Steve Kinser	210.872	211.074	211.347	209.883	210.793	23	20
31	1:05	30	Robbie Groff	202.156	201.505	waved off				
32	5:47	97	Greg Ray	214.813	215.332	215.595	waved off, out of fuel			
33	5:50	30	Robbie Groff	208.938	207.431	207.459	207.349	207.792	32	21
	5:57	11	Billy Boat	Made presentation, did not take green						

Saturday, May 17, 1997 - Third Qualifying Day

QA	Time	Car	Driver	Lap 1	Lap 2	Lap 3	Lap 4	4-Lap Avg	SP	SR
34	11:35 A.M.	11	Billy Boat	214.485	216.299	215.714	215.688	215.544	6	22
35	11:42	50	Billy Roe	212.204	213.270	212.159	213.381	212.752	18	24
36	11:47	33	Fermin Velez	209.108	207.612	204.932	204.466	206.512	35	29
37	11:54	18	Tyce Carlson	212.264	211.680	210.827	208.671	210.852	22	26
38	11:59	54	Dennis Vitolo	207.488	207.531	207.660	207.823	207.626	33	28
39	12:05 P.M.	28	Mark Dismore	214.895	213.756	211.879	209.249	212.423	19	25
40	12:12	16	Sam Schmidt	216.159	214.782	214.449	215.182	215.141	8	23
41	12:19	22	Marco Greco	212.942	210.684	209.127	208.589	210.322	25	27

Sunday, May 18, 1997 - Bubble Day

QA	Time	Car	Driver	Lap 1	Lap 2	Lap 3	Lap 4	4-Lap Avg	SP	SR
42	12:00 P.M.	9	Johnny Unser	210.202	209.746	207.871	209.570	209.344	28	35
43	2:07	97	Greg Ray	213.939	213.822	213.614	213.665	213.760	14	30
44	1:00 P.M.	1	Paul Durant	208.493	209.453	209.815	208.841	209.149	30	33

(Bumps #34 Alessandro Zampedri)

QA	Time	Car	Driver	Lap 1	Lap 2	Lap 3	Lap 4	4-Lap Avg	SP	SR
45	2:08	72	Claude Bourbonnais	208.996	211.273	210.207	211.635	210.523	24	32

(Bumps #9 Johnny Unser)

QA	Time	Car	Driver	Lap 1	Lap 2	Lap 3	Lap 4	4-Lap Avg	SP	SR
46	2:14	34T	Alessandro Zampedri	213.088	212.344	211.690	209.932	211.757	20	31

(Bumps #90 Lyn St. James)

QA	Time	Car	Driver	Lap 1	Lap 2	Lap 3	Lap 4	4-Lap Avg	SP	SR
47	5:51	36	Scott Harrington	214.061	Accident, T2					

#9 Johnny Unser, #90 Lyn St. James added to field.

QA = Qualification Attempt   SR = Overall Speed Rank   SP = Starting Position

1997 Scoring Positions at 10-Lap Intervals 81st Indianapolis 500 May 27, 1997

CAR NO.	DRIVER	SP	1	10	20	30	40	50	60	70	80	90
5	Arie Luyendyk	1	2	2	2	3	3	6	2	1	6	1
2	Tony Stewart	2	1	1	1	1	1	1	1	2	2	2
8	Vincenzo Sospiri	3	3	5	6	7	7	13	5	9	4	7
3	Robbie Buhl	4	4	3	3	2	2	8	3	3	9	5
6	Scott Goodyear	5	7	6	7	6	6	4	7	6	3	4
27	Jim Guthrie	6	5	30	29	28	25	25	25	26	26	26
52	Jeff Ward	7	8	7	4	5	5	12	6	5	10	6
14	Davey Hamilton	8	10	8	8	9	9	3	10	8	5	8
7	Eliseo Salazar	9	9	9	9	25	26	26	26	24	24	24
91	Buddy Lazier	10	11	10	5	4	4	2	4	4	1	3
51	Eddie Cheever Jr.	11	12	16	24	19	17	17	9	7	11	22
42	Robby Gordon	12	6	4	28	29	29	29	29	29	29	29
77	Stephan Gregoire	13	30	31	31	31	31	31	31	31	31	31
17	Affonso Giaffone	14	31	32	32	32	32	32	32	32	32	32
4	Kenny Brack	15	32	33	33	33	33	33	33	33	33	33
12	Buzz Calkins	16	13	11	11	8	8	14	8	10	7	12
40	Dr. Jack Miller	17	16	19	19	21	22	10	21	22	21	21
10	Mike Groff	18	18	24	22	23	23	11	19	20	15	18
21	Roberto Guerrero	19	14	15	14	26	27	28	28	28	28	28
44	Steve Kinser	20	15	12	10	20	20	9	20	17	13	15
30	Robbie Groff	21	33	29	27	24	24	18	22	21	17	20
11	Billy Boat	22	19	17	15	14	10	5	11	11	8	10
16	Sam Schmidt	23	34	34	34	34	34	34	34	34	34	34
50	Billy Roe	24	17	13	12	11	11	23	15	13	14	16
28	Mark Dismore	25	20	14	13	27	28	27	27	27	27	27
18	Tyce Carlson	26	23	20	20	13	14	16	12	16	22	19
22	Marco Greco	27	21	23	18	12	16	19	16	12	18	11
54	Dennis Vitolo	28	25	25	23	18	19	21	23	23	23	23
33	Fermin Velez	29	22	21	17	10	13	20	14	19	20	17
97	Greg Ray	30	24	18	16	15	12	24	24	25	25	25
34	Alessandro Zampedri	31	35	35	35	35	35	35	35	35	35	35
72	Claude Bourbonnais	32	26	28	30	30	30	30	30	30	30	30
1	Paul Durant	33	27	22	21	17	15	15	17	15	16	9
90	Lyn St. James	34	28	27	25	16	18	22	13	14	19	13
9	Johnny Unser	35	29	26	26	22	21	7	18	18	12	14

Race Average Speed: 184.820 116.054 120.587 135.363 144.077

199.904 105.565 131.140 138.351 148.197

100	110	120	130	140	150	160	170	180	190	FINISH 200	LAPS COMP	RUNNING OR REASON OUT
1	2	4	2	1	3	2	4	4	4	1	200	Running
2	1	2	3	3	2	3	5	3	3	5	200	Running
7	19	18	19	19	20	20	19	19	19	17	163	Running
5	5	1	1	6	6	6	6	6	6	8	199	Running
4	4	5	4	2	4	4	3	2	2	2	200	Running
26	26	26	26	26	26	26	26	26	26	26	43	Engine
6	6	3	5	4	1	1	1	1	1	3	200	Running
10	10	8	7	8	7	7	7	8	7	6	199	Running
24	24	24	24	24	24	24	24	24	24	24	70	Accident T2
3	3	6	6	5	5	5	2	5	5	4	200	Running
23	23	23	23	23	23	23	23	23	23	23	84	Timing Chain
29	29	29	29	29	29	29	29	29	29	29	19	Fire
31	31	31	31	31	31	31	31	31	31	31	0	Accident T4
32	32	32	32	32	32	32	32	32	32	32	0	Accident T4
33	33	33	33	33	33	33	33	33	33	33	0	Accident T4
16	16	10	13	11	11	13	11	11	11	11	188	Rt. Half Shaft
20	20	17	17	17	18	19	20	20	20	20	131	Accident T3
21	21	19	18	18	17	17	16	14	14	12	188	Running
28	27	27	27	27	27	27	27	27	27	27	25	Steering Gear
12	11	11	10	12	10	10	10	10	12	14	185	Accident T4
19	18	15	15	13	13	12	12	12	9	9	197	Running
9	7	9	9	7	8	8	8	7	8	7	199	Running
34	34	34	34	34	34	34	34	34	34	34	0	Engine
17	13	21	22	22	22	22	22	22	22	22	110	Accident T3
27	28	28	28	28	28	28	28	28	28	28	24	Accident T4
18	17	12	12	15	16	16	17	17	18	19	156	Accident T2
8	9	7	8	9	9	9	13	15	15	16	166	Gearbox
22	22	22	21	20	19	18	18	18	16	15	173	Running
14	14	14	14	14	14	14	14	13	13	10	195	Running
25	25	25	25	25	25	25	25	25	25	25	48	Water Pump
35	35	35	35	35	35	35	35	35	35	35	0	Oil Leak
30	30	30	30	30	30	30	30	30	30	30	9	Engine
11	8	20	20	21	21	21	21	21	21	21	111	Accident T3
15	15	13	11	10	12	11	9	9	10	13	186	Accident T4
13	12	16	16	16	15	15	15	16	17	18	158	Oil Pressure
144.133		142.342		141.811		145.471		146.578		145.827		
	148.513		142.260		142.654		144.077		147.518			

Official Prize List Times & Averages
81st Indianapolis 500
May 25, 1997

FP	SP	CAR	YR	DRIVER	CAR NAME	C/E/T	QUAL. SPEED	LAPS COMP	RUNNING/ REASONS	IRL PTS.	IMS PRIZE	PARADE	LAP PRIZES	DESIGNATED AWARDS	TOTAL AWARDS
1	1	5	WF	Arie Luyendyk	Wavephore/Sprint PCS/Miller Lite/Provimi	G/A/F	218.263	200	145.827	37	$869,900	$300	$27,450	$670,500	$1,568,150
2	5	6	F	Scott Goodyear	Nortel/Sprint PCS/Quebecor Printing	G/A/F	215.811	200	145.820	33	447,700	300	900	64,400	513,300
3	7	52	R	Jeff Ward	FirstPlus Team Cheever	G/A/G	214.517	200	145.779	32	294,700	300	22,050	97,200	414,250
4	10	91	WF	Buddy Lazier	Delta Faucet-Montana-Hemelgarn Racing	D/A/F	214.286	200	145.705	31	228,700	300	3,150	47,100	279,250
5	2	2	F	Tony Stewart	Glidden/Menards/Special	G/A/F	218.021	200	145.490	31	216,700	300	28,800	99,250	345,050
6	8	14	R	Davey Hamilton	AJ Foyt PowerTeam Racing	G/A/G	214.484	199	Running	29	208,700	300		55,000	264,000
7	22	11	F	Billy Boat	Conseco AJ Foyt Racing	D/A/G	215.544	199	Running	28	203,700	300	450	55,250	259,700
8	4	3	F	Robbie Buhl	Quaker State/Special	G/A/F	216.102	199	Running	27	192,700	300	7,200	35,000	235,200
9	21	30	RF	Robbie Groff	Alfa-Laval/Team Losi/McCormack Motorsports	G/A/G	207.792	197	Running	26	196,700	300		25,350	222,350
10	29	33	F	Fermin Velez	Old Navy Scandia Royal Purple Alta Xcel	D/A/G	206.512	195	Running	25	182,700	300		33,400	216,400
11	16	12	F	Buzz Calkins	Bradley Food Marts	G/A/G	209.564	188	Rt Half Shaft	24	179,700	300		21,000	201,000
12	18	10	F	Mike Groff	Jonathan Byrd's Cafeteria/Visionaire/Bryant	G/I/F	208.537	188	Running	23	175,700	300		21,300	197,300
13	34	90	F	Lyn St. James	Lifetime/TV-Cinergy-Delta Faucet-Hemelgarn	D/I/F	210.145	186	Accident, T4	22	150,700	300		37,000	188,000
14	20	44	R	Steve Kinser	SRS/One Call/Menards/Quaker State/St. Elmo's	D/A/G	210.793	185	Accident, T4	21	173,000	0		20,250	193,250
15	28	54	F	Dennis Vitolo	SmithKline Beecham/Kroger/Beck Motorsports	D/I/F	207.626	173	Running	20	166,700	300		33,000	200,000
16	27	22	F	Marco Greco	Side Play Int'l Sport Scandia Alta Xcel	D/A/G	210.322	166	Gearbox	19	164,700	300		28,000	193,000
17	3	8	RF	Vincenzo Sospiri	Old Navy Scandia Royal Purple Alta Xcel	D/A/G	216.822	163	Running	18	139,700	300		56,250	196,250
18	35	9	F	Johnny Unser	Delta Faucet-Montana-Cinergy-Hemelgarn	D/I/F	209.344	158	Oil Pressure	17	137,700	300		20,000	158,000
19	26	18	RF	Tyce Carlson	Klipsch Themec Overhead Door Pyle V-Line Earl's	D/A/G	210.852	156	Accident, T2	16	157,700	300		15,250	173,250

Fin	St	No		Driver	Car Name / Entrant	C/E/T	Q Speed	Status	Laps			Prize	Award	Total
20	17	40	RF	Dr. Jack Miller	AMS/Crest Racing/Trane/Spot-On	D/I/F	209.250	Accident, T3	131	15	300	155,700	15,250	171,250
21	33	1	F	Paul Durant	Conseco AJ Foyt Racing	G/A/G	209.149	Accident, T3	111	14	300	153,700	24,000	178,000
22	24	50	R	Billy Roe	Sega/Progressive Elect./KECO/U.J.T/Eurointernat'l	D/A/F	212.752	Accident, T3	110	13	300	134,700	15,250	150,250
23	11	51	F	Eddie Cheever Jr.	FirstPlus Team Cheever	G/A/G	214.073	Timing Chain	84	12	300	149,700	26,000	176,000
24	9	7	F	Eliseo Salazar	Copec/Cristal/Scandia	D/A/G	214.320	Accident, T2	70	11	300	148,700	15,000	164,000
25	30	97	R	Greg Ray	Tobacco Free Kids	D/A/F	213.760	Water Pump	48	10	300	150,700	20,250	171,250
26	6	27	F	Jim Guthrie	Blueprint/Jacuzzi/Armour Golf/ERTL	D/A/F	215.207	Engine	43	9	300	146,700	17,500	164,500
27	19	21	F	Roberto Guerrero	Pennzoil-Pagan Racing Dallara Infiniti	D/I/G	207.371	Steering Gear	25	8	300	144,700	15,000	160,000
28	25	28	F	Mark Dismore	Kelley Automotive Mechanics Laundry Bombardier Grainger	D/A/G	212.423	Accident, T4	24	7	300	143,700	15,000	159,000
29	12	42	G	Robby Gordon	Coors Light	G/A/G	213.211	Fire	19	6	300	121,700	17,500	139,500
30	32	72	R	Claude Bourbonnais	Blueprint/Jacuzzi/Armour Golf/ERTL	D/A/F	210.523	Engine	9	5	300	125,700	26,250	152,250
31	13	77	F	Stephan Gregoire	Chastain Motorsports-Estridge-Miller-Eads	G/A/G	213.126	Accident, T4	0	4	300	142,700	15,000	158,000
32	14	17	RF	Affonso Giaffone	General Motors Brazil Chitwood Dallara	D/A/G	212.974	Accident, T4	0	3	300	142,700	15,250	158,250
33	15	4	RF	Kenny Brack	Monsoon Galles Racing	G/A/G	211.221	Accident, T4	0	2	300	141,700	60,250	202,250
34	23	16	R	Sam Schmidt	Blueprint/HOPE Prepaid Fuel Card	D/A/F	215.141	Engine	0	1	300	129,700	20,250	150,250
35	31	34	F	Alessandro Zampedri	Mi-Jack Scandia Royal Purple	D/A/G	211.757	Oil Leak	0	1	300	129,700	15,000	145,000
				John Paul Jr.									25,000	25,000
												$6,750,000	$10,200	$90,000	$1,792,250	$8,642,450

Time of Race: 3:25:43.388   Average Speed: 145.827 mph   Margin of Victory: .570 sec.

Fastest Lap: #2 Tony Stewart, Lap 105 - 215.626   Fastest Leading Lap: #5 Arie Luyendyk, Lap 108 - 215.115

Legend: FP - Finishing Position; SP - Starting Position; R - Indy 500 Rookie; W - Former Winner; F - Officially In The Field.   Tires: F - Firestone; G - Goodyear.

Chassis: D - Dallara; G - G Force.   Engine: A - Oldsmobile Aurora V-8; I - Nissan Infiniti Indy V-8.

Lap Leaders:

Laps	No	Driver
1-50	#2	Tony Stewart
51-51	#11	Billy Boat
52-62	#2	Tony Stewart
63-78	#5	Arie Luyendyk
79-79	#2	Tony Stewart
80-82	#91	Buddy Lazier
83-109	#5	Arie Luyendyk
110-111	#2	Tony Stewart
112-115	#91	Buddy Lazier
116-131	#3	Robbie Buhl
132-140	#5	Arie Luyendyk
141-141	#6	Scott Goodyear
142-166	#52	Jeff Ward
167-168	#5	Arie Luyendyk
169-192	#2	Tony Stewart
193-193	#6	Scott Goodyear
194-200	#5	Arie Luyendyk

Lap Leader Summary:

No	Driver	Laps	$
#2	Tony Stewart	64	$28,800
#5	Arie Luyendyk	61	$27,450
#52	Jeff Ward	49	$22,050
#3	Robbie Buhl	16	$7,200
#91	Buddy Lazier	7	$3,150
#6	Scott Goodyear	2	$900
#11	Billy Boat	1	$450

Caution Flags:

Pace Lap, Accident, #17 Giaffone, #4 Brack, #77 Gregoire T4 (4 Caution Laps)
Laps 10-10 Smoking Car; #72 Bourbonnais
Laps 11-14 Moisture Reported
Lap 15 Red Flag, Moisture, Postponed
Laps 16-18 Race Continues Under Caution - 5/27/97
Laps 20-28 #42 Gordon Stops in T1
Laps 59-62 #27 Guthrie Stalls on Front Straight
Laps 94-99 #7 Salazar Stops in T2
Laps 114-123 Accident, #50 Roe & #1 Durant T3
Laps 138-142 Accident, #40 Miller North Short Chute
Laps 165-169 #18 Carlson, Spin T2
Laps 189-193 Accident, #44 Kinser T4
Laps 196-197 Debris
Lap 199 Debris

1997 Official Box Score
Indy Racing League
True Value 500 at
Texas Motor Speedway
June 7, 1997

FP	SP	CAR	DRIVER	CAR NAME	C/E/T	QUAL. SPEED	LAPS COMP	RUNNING/ REASON OUT	IRL PTS.	TOTAL IRL PTS.	IRL STANDINGS	IRL AWARDS	IRL DESIGNATED AWARDS	TOTAL AWARDS
1	11	5	Arie Luyendyk	Treadway Racing/Wavephore	G/A/F	158.791	208	Running	35	147	5	$109,000	$44,500	$153,500
2	21	1 R	Billy Boat	Conseco AJ Foyt Racing	G/A/G	NS	207	Running	33	61	22	89,400	10,750	100,150
3	9	14	Davey Hamilton	AJ Foyt PowerTeam Racing	G/A/G	159.103	207	Running	32	175	1	75,500	7,000	82,500
4	5	6	Scott Goodyear	Treadway Racing/Nortel	G/A/F	165.293	207	Running	31	114	11	62,600	3,250	65,850
5	1	2	Tony Stewart	Glidden/Menards/Special	G/A/F	167.133	206	Engine/Contact	33 xy	166	2	79,200	40,750	119,950
6	7	51	Eddie Cheever Jr.	FirstPlus Team Cheever	G/A/G	161.606	206	Running	29	129	8	51,900	2,250	54,150
7	22	7	Eliseo Salazar	Copec/Cristal/Scandia	D/A/F	NS	205	Running	28	93	14	50,800	250	51,050
8	6	97 R	Greg Ray	Thomas Knapp Motorsports	D/A/F	162.125	204	Running	27	37	31	27,700	2,250	29,950
9	17	8 R	Vincenzo Sospiri	Old Navy Scandia Royal Purple Alta Xcel	D/A/G	151.010	204	Running	26	44	28	26,600	1,250	27,850
10	23	10	Johnny Unser	Jonathan Byrd's Cafeteria Bryant Heating & Cooling	G/I/F	NS	203	Running	25	55	25	46,100	5,250	51,350
11	14	28	Mark Dismore	Kelley Racing Bombardier Grainger Mech. Laundry	D/A/G	153.856	203	Running	24	64	20	24,500	750	25,250
12	26	34	Alessandro Zampedri	Mi-Jack Scandia Royal Purple	D/A/G	NS	201	Running	23	24	38	21,900	250	22,150
13	15	21	Roberto Guerrero	Pennzoil-Pagan Racing Dallara Infiniti	D/I/G	152.873	201	Running	22	136	7	44,300	0	44,300
14	25	18 R	Tyce Carlson	Klipsch Overhead Door Jacuzzi Earl's V-Line	D/A/G	NS	184	Running	21	73	18	41,800	0	41,800
15	13	30 R	Robbie Groff	McCormack Motorsports	G/A/G	154.652	173	Engine	20	46	27	42,200	2,000	44,200
16	2	3	Robbie Buhl	Menards/Quaker State/Special	G/A/F	165.946	167	Engine	19	103	13	48,100	0	48,100
17	4	91	Buddy Lazier	Delta Faucet-Montana-Hemelgarn Racing	D/A/F	165.318	157	Engine	18	120	10	40,000	0	40,000
18	3	4	Kenny Brack	Monsoon Galles Racing	G/A/G	165.480	118	Water Leak	17	43	29	17,000	2,500	19,500
19	10	12	Buzz Calkins	Bradley Food Marts	G/A/G	158.792	98	Head Gasket	16	153	3	37,900	0	37,900
20	16	17 R	Affonso Giaffone	General Motors of Brazil	D/A/G	152.745	82	Engine Fire	15	65	19	14,800	0	14,800
21	8	27 R	Jim Guthrie	Blueprint Racing/Jacuzzi/Armour Golf/ERTL/Dallara	D/A/F	160.997	81	Tire/Contact	14	121	9	35,700	0	35,700
22	18	44 R	Allen May	SRS/Young Chevrolet	D/A/G	149.586	36	Accident	13	13	48	13,700	0	13,700
23	20	16 R	Sam Schmidt	HOPE Prepaid Fuel Card	D/A/F	134.136	36	Accident	12	38	30	13,700	0	13,700
24	19	40 R	Dr. Jack Miller	AMS/Crest Racing	D/I/F	149.197	24	Electrical	11	61	23	35,700	0	35,700
25	24	33 R	Fermin Velez	Old Navy Scandia Royal Purple Alta Xcel	D/A/G	NS	1	Driver Illness	10	82	17	34,200	0	34,200
26	12	22	Marco Greco	Side Play Int'l Scandia Alta Xcel	D/A/G	158.496	0	Engine/Spin	9	140	6	35,700	0	35,700
												$1,120,000	$123,000	$1,243,000

Time of Race: 2:19:48 **Average Speed:** 133.903 **Margin of Victory:** Under caution
Fastest Lap: #2 Tony Stewart (Lap 97, 218.094 mph) **Fastest Leading Lap:** #2 Tony Stewart (Lap 57, 217.488 mph)
PPG Pole Winner: Tony Stewart **Coors Pit Performance Winner:** Arie Luyendyk 3-94 sec./Treadway Racing, LLC **IRL Points Bonus:** x - 2 points PPG Pole; y - 1 point most laps led
MBNA America Lap Leader: Tony Stewart **True Value Pole Winning Chief Mechanic:** Bill Martin/Team Menard, Inc.
Legend: R - Indy Racing League Rookie **Chassis Legend:** D - Dallara; G - G Force **Engine Legend:** A - Oldsmobile Aurora; I - Nissan Infiniti **Tire Legend:** F - Firestone; G - Goodyear

Lap Leaders:

Lap-Lap	Driver	Car		Lap-Lap	Driver	Car
1-68	Tony Stewart	#2		126-132	Billy Boat	#1
69-71	Eliseo Salazar	#7		133	Tony Stewart	#2
72-75	Davey Hamilton	#14		134-157	Buddy Lazier	#91
76-81	Jim Guthrie	#27		158-169	Tony Stewart	#2
82-84	Billy Boat	#1		170	Arie Luyendyk	#5
85-87	Robbie Groff	#30		171-189	Tony Stewart	#2
88-120	Buddy Lazier	#91		190-208	Arie Luyendyk	#5
121-125	Eddie Cheever Jr.	#51				

Caution Flags:

Laps	Reason/Incident
1-18	#22 Greco, Engine T1
24-26	#40 Miller, Stopped Back Straight
37-46	#44 May, Accident T2 / #16 Schmidt, Accident T2
81-91	#27 Guthrie, Accident Front Straight / #17 Giaffone, Engine Fire T4
137-141	#4 Brack, Blown Engine
143-148	#18 Carlson & #6 Goodyear, Contact Front Straight
168-171	#3 Buhl, Engine T4
207-208	#2 Stewart, Accident T1
	Total Caution Laps 59

Lap Leader Summary:

Driver	Times	Total
Tony Stewart	4	100
Buddy Lazier	2	57
Arie Luyendyk	2	20
Billy Boat	2	10
Jim Guthrie	1	6
Eddie Cheever Jr.	1	5
Davey Hamilton	1	4
Eliseo Salazar	1	3
Robbie Groff	1	3

1997 Official Box Score
Indy Racing League
Samsonite 200 at Pikes Peak International Raceway
June 29, 1997

JUNE 27-29, 1997

FP	SP	CAR		DRIVER	CAR NAME	C/E/T	QUAL. SPEED	LAPS COMP.	RUNNING/ REASON OUT	IRL PTS.	TOTAL IRL PTS.	IRL STANDINGS	IRL AWARDS	DESIGNATED AWARDS	TOTAL AWARDS
1	2	2		Tony Stewart	Glidden/Menards/Special	G/A/F	175.021	200	100.128	36 y	202	2	$106,000	$55,500	$161,500
2	11	77		Stephan Gregoire	Estridge-Moen-Nutone-Porter Paint-Jack K Elrod	G/A/G	171.608	200	Running	33	119	13	64,700	10,500	75,200
3	4	14		Davey Hamilton	AJ Foyt Power Team Racing	G/A/G	173.879	200	Running	32	207	1	72,700	6,500	79,200
4	13	51		Eddie Cheever Jr.	FirstPlus Team Cheever	G/A/G	171.282	200	Running	31	160	6	59,700	3,500	63,200
5	7	12		Buzz Calkins	Bradley Foodmarts	G/A/G	172.496	200	Running	30	183	3	54,300	2,500	56,800
6	18	22	R	Vincenzo Sospiri	Old Navy Scandia Royal Purple Alta Xcel	D/A/G	169.356	200	Running	29	73	23	48,900	1,250	50,150
7	3	6		Scott Goodyear	Treadway Racing-NORTEL	G/A/F	174.224	200	Running	28	142	10	47,900	2,250	50,150
8	12	91		Buddy Lazier	Delta Faucet Montana Hemelgarn Racing	D/A/F	171.551	198	Running	27	147	9	46,800	250	47,050
9	10	17	R	Affonso Giaffone	General Motors of Brazil Chitwood Dallara	D/A/G	171.608	196	Running	26	91	16	45,700	250	45,950
10	16	30	R	Robbie Groff	Team Losi Serv-All Laval McCormack Motorsports	G/A/G	170.438	193	Spin Back Straight	25	71	24	44,600	2,250	46,850
11	21	28		Mark Dismore	Bombardier Business Aircraft Grainger	D/A/G	162.602	192	Running	24	88	17	43,600	1,000	44,600
12	14	7		Eliseo Salazar	Copec-Cristal Scandia	D/A/G	171.282	190	Running	23	116	14	42,500	0	42,500
13	22	70		Marco Greco	Side Play Int'l-Galles	G/A/G	No Time	190	Running	22	162	5	19,400	2,000	21,400
14	6	4	R	Kenny Brack	Monsoon Galles Racing	G/A/G	173.553	179	Accident T4	21	64	26	40,300	2,500	42,800
15	8	5		Arie Luyendyk	Treadway Racing-WavePhore Sprint PCS	G/A/F	172.364	163	Accident T2	20	167	4	39,200	0	39,200
16	20	40	R	Dr. Jack Miller	AMS/Crest Racing	D/I/F	165.320	141	Accident T2	19	80	20	38,200	5,000	43,200
17	17	97		Greg Ray	Thomas Knapp Motorsports	D/A/F	169.988	108	Accident T4	18	55	29	15,100	0	15,100
18	5	21		Roberto Guerrero	Pennzoil Racing	D/A/G	173.770	85	Accident T4	17	153	7	36,000	250	36,250
19	15	18	R	Billy Boat	Klipsch Overhead Door V-Line Earl's Performance	D/A/G	171.103	83	Accident T4	16	77	21	34,900	0	34,900
20	9	33	R	Jimmy Kite	Old Navy Scandia Royal Purple Alta Xcel	D/A/G	171.731	39	Accident T4	15	15	46	33,900	2,000	35,900
21	19	10		Johnny Unser	Jonathan Byrd's Cafeteria Bryant Heating & Cooling	G/I/F	165.487	23	Accident T2	14	69	25	32,800	0	32,800
22	1	1		Scott Sharp	Conseco AJ Foyt Racing	D/A/G	176.117	0	Accident T2	15 x	119	12	32,800	22,500	55,300
													$1,000,000	$120,000	$1,120,000

Time of Race: 1:59:50 **Average Speed:** 100.128 mph **Margin of Victory:** 0.222 sec.
Fastest Lap: #33 Jimmy Kite (Lap 15, 167.715 mph) **Fastest Leading Lap:** #2 Tony Stewart (Lap 60, 165.753 mph)
PPG Pole Winner: Scott Sharp **True Value Pole Winning Chief Mechanic:** Craig Baranouski/AJ Foyt Enterprises
MBNA America Lap Leader: Tony Stewart **Coors Pit Performance Winner:** #2 Stewart 2-59 sec./Team Menard **IRL Points Bonus:** x - 2 points PPG Pole; y - 1 point most laps led
Legend: R - Indy Racing League Rookie **Chassis Legend:** D - Dallara; G - G Force **Engine Legend:** A - Oldsmobile Aurora; I - Nissan Infiniti **Tire Legend:** F - Firestone; G - Goodyear

Lap Leaders:

Lap-Lap	Driver
1-89	#2 Tony Stewart
90	#5 Arie Luyendyk
91-95	#77 Stephan Gregoire
96-148	#2 Tony Stewart
149	#6 Scott Goodyear
150-200	#2 Tony Stewart

Caution Flags:

Laps	Reason/Incident	Laps	Reason/Incident
1-10	#33 Sharp, Accident T2	164-170	#5 Luyendyk, Accident T2
25-36	#10 Unser, Accident T2	181-186	#4 Brack, Accident T4
41-56	#33 Kite, Accident T4	194-197	#30 Groff, Spin Back Straight
87-97	#21 Guerrero & #18 Boat, Accident T4		
113-118	#97 Ray, Accident T4		Total Caution Laps 82
146-155	#40 Miller, Accident T4		

Lap Leader Summary:

Driver	Times	Total
Tony Stewart	3	193
Stephan Gregoire	1	5
Arie Luyendyk	1	1
Scott Goodyear	1	1

1997 Official Box Score
Indy Racing League
Inaugural VisionAire 500 at Charlotte Motor Speedway
July 26, 1997

FP	SP	CAR		DRIVER	CAR NAME	C/E/T	QUAL. SPEED	LAPS COMP	RUNNING/ REASON OUT	IRL PTS.	TOTAL IRL PTS.	IRL STANDINGS	IRL AWARDS	DESIGNATED AWARDS	TOTAL AWARDS
1	5	91		Buddy Lazier	Delta Faucet Cinergy Hemelgarn Racing	D/A/F	211.948	208	Running	35	182	6	$109,200	$43,500	$152,700
2	3	1	R	Billy Boat	Conseco AJ Foyt Racing	G/A/G	212.440	208	Running	33	110	17	89,900	13,750	103,650
3	8	6		Scott Goodyear	Treadway Racing NORTEL Quebecor Printing	G/A/G	209.408	207	Running	32	174	8	75,600	6,000	81,600
4	16	17	R	Affonso Giaffone	General Motors of Brazil Chitwood Dallara	D/A/G	207.333	206	Running	31	122	14	62,400	2,250	64,650
5	18	4	R	Kenny Brack	Monsoon Galles Racing International	G/A/G	207.198	206	Running	30	94	20	34,900	2,750	37,650
6	15	51		Eddie Cheever Jr.	FirstPlus Team Cheever	G/A/G	208.406	206	Running	29	189	3	51,500	10,250	61,750
7	1	2		Tony Stewart	Glidden/Menards/Special	G/A/F	217.164	205	Running	31 xy	233	1	50,400	32,750	83,150
8	9	77		Stephan Gregoire	Chastain Motorsports	G/A/G	209.310	202	Running	27	146	11	27,300	250	27,550
9	11	70		Marco Greco	Monsoon Galles Racing International	G/A/G	209.116	202	Running	26	188	4	26,200	2,250	28,450
10	14	7		Eliseo Salazar	Copec-Cristal-Scandia	D/A/G	208.567	200	Running	25	141	13	47,100	250	47,350
11	21	18		John Paul Jr.	Klipsch Overhead Door Earl's Performance V-Line	D/A/G	203.183	198	Running	24	112	16	46,000	0	46,000
12	6	27		Jim Guthrie	Jacuzzi Armour Golf Odyssey Golf ERTL Collectibles	D/A/F	210.436	197	Running	23	144	12	44,900	0	44,900
13	20	30	R	Robbie Groff	Serv-All/Team Losi/McCormack Motorsports	G/A/G	205.105	189	Half Shaft	22	93	21	43,800	0	43,800
14	22	10		Mike Groff	Jonathan Byrd's VisionAire Bryant Heating & Cooling	G/A/F	198.624	176	Running	21	169	10	42,700	0	42,700
15	13	33	R	Jimmy Kite	Old Navy-Scandia-Royal Purple-Alta-Xcel	D/A/G	208.776	163	Accident	20	35	34	41,600	1,000	42,600
16	4	14		Davey Hamilton	AJ Foyt Power Team Racing	G/A/G	212.398	141	Accident	19	226	2	40,500	0	40,500
17	7	21		Roberto Guerrero	Pennzoil/Pagan Racing Dallara	D/A/G	210.215	141	Accident	18	171	9	39,400	750	40,150
18	23	99	R	Sam Schmidt	HOPE Prepaid Fuel Card Racing Special	D/A/F	N/T	114	Engine	17	55	30	16,300	0	16,300
19	10	28		Mark Dismore	Bombardier Business Aircraft Grainger	D/A/G	209.237	97	Engine	16	104	18	37,200	0	37,200
20	12	22	R	Vincenzo Sospiri	Old Navy-Scandia-Royal Purple-Alta-Xcel	D/A/G	209.035	70	Engine	15	88	23	36,100	250	36,350
21	2	5		Arie Luyendyk	Treadway Racing WavePhore Sprint PCS	G/A/F	214.524	67	Handling	14	181	7	35,000	0	35,000
22	17	31	R	Greg Ray	Thomas Knapp Motorsports	D/A/F	207.262	30	Engine	13	68	27	13,000	0	13,000
23	19	40	R	Dr. Jack Miller	AMS/Crest Racing	D/I/F	206.162	13	Electrical	12	92	22	35,000	5,000	40,000
													$1,046,000	$121,000	$1,167,000

Time of Race: 1:55:29 **Average Speed:** 162.096 mph **Margin of Victory:** 3.301 sec.
Fastest Lap: #1 Billy Boat (Lap 9, 213.506 mph) **Fastest Leading Lap:** #91 Buddy Lazier (Lap 82, 212.089 mph)
PPG Pole Winner: Tony Stewart **True Value Pole Winning Chief Mechanic:** Bill Martin/Team Menard
MBNA America Lap Leader: #2 Tony Stewart **Coors Pit Performance Winner:** #51 Eddie Cheever/FirstPlus Team Cheever **IRL Points Bonus:** x - 2 points PPG Pole; y - 1 point most laps led
Legend: R - Indy Racing League Rookie **Chassis Legend:** D - Dallara; G - G Force **Engine Legend:** A - Oldsmobile Aurora; I - Nissan Infiniti **Tire Legend:** F - Firestone; G - Goodyear

Caution Flags:

Laps	Reason/Incident
74-76	Debris
99-106	Oil
145-154	#21 Guerrero & #14 Hamilton, Accident T2
165-170	#33 Kite, Accident Front Straight
	Total Caution Laps 27

Lap Leaders:

Lap-Lap		Driver
1-47	#2	Tony Stewart
48	#6	Scott Goodyear
49-75	#2	Tony Stewart
76-92	#91	Buddy Lazier
93-100	#1	Billy Boat
101-126	#21	Roberto Guerrero
127-139	#1	Billy Boat
140-145	#33	Jimmy Kite
146	#1	Billy Boat
147-151	#33	Jimmy Kite
152-166	#1	Billy Boat
167-195	#91	Buddy Lazier
196	#1	Billy Boat
197-208	#91	Buddy Lazier

Lap Leader Summary:

Driver	Times	Total
Tony Stewart	2	74
Buddy Lazier	3	58
Billy Boat	5	38
Roberto Guerrero	1	26
Jimmy Kite	2	11
Scott Goodyear	1	1

1997 Official Box Score Indy Racing League Pennzoil 200 at New Hampshire International Speedway
August 17, 1997

FP	SP	CAR	DRIVER	CAR NAME	C/E/T	QUAL. SPEED	LAPS COMP.	RUNNING/ REASON OUT	IRL PTS.	TOTAL IRL PTS.	IRL STANDINGS	IRL AWARDS	DESIGNATED AWARDS	TOTAL AWARDS
1	7	3	Robbie Buhl	Quaker State/Menards/Special	G/A/F	156.728	200	Running	35	138	16	$78,000	$45,500	$123,500
2	9	22 R	Vincenzo Sospiri	Old Navy-Scandia-Royal Purple-Alta-Xcel	D/A/G	155.151	200	Running	33	121	20	$82,000	$8,500	$90,500
3	8	5	Arie Luyendyk	Treadway Racing Wavephore Sprint PCS	G/A/F	156.618	200	Running	32	213	4	$69,000	$8,500	$77,500
4	7	7	Eliseo Salazar	Copec-Cristal-Scandia	D/A/G	159.511	200	Running	31	172	10	$57,000	$500	$57,500
5	3	4 R	Kenny Brack	Monsoon Galles Racing	G/A/G	160.296	200	Running	30	124	19	$52,000	$5,750	$57,750
6	10	21	Roberto Guerrero	Pennzoil/Pagan Racing Dallara	D/A/G	155.062	200	Running	29	200	7	$47,000	$4,000	$51,000
7	11	18	John Paul Jr.	Klipsch Overhead Door Earl's Performance V-Line	D/A/G	154.496	199	Running	28	140	14	$46,000	$2,250	$48,250
8	16	1 R	Billy Boat	Conseco AJ Foyt Racing	G/A/G	152.559	199	Running	27	137	17	$45,000	$2,750	$47,750
9	14	51	Eddie Cheever Jr.	FirstPlus Team Cheever	G/A/G	151.884	198	Gearbox	27 y	216	3	$44,000	$10,250	$54,250
10	19	30 R	Robbie Groff	Fast Rod/Team Losi/McCormack Motorsports	G/A/G	151.775	198	Running	25	118	22	$43,000	$2,250	$45,250
11	23	28	Mark Dismore	Bombardier Aircraft Mechanics Laundry	D/A/G	N/T	197	Running	24	128	18	$42,000	$2,000	$44,000
12	15	91	Buddy Lazier	Delta Faucet Cinergy Hemelgarn Racing	D/A/F	153.723	195	Running	23	205	5	$41,000	$0	$41,000
13	20	10	Johnny Unser	Jonathan Byrd's Cafeteria Bryant Heating & Cooling	G/A/F	151.498	189	Running	22	91	24	$40,000	$0	$40,000
14	14	2	Tony Stewart	Glidden/Menards/Special	G/A/F	153.860	174	Engine	21	254	1	$39,000	$0	$39,000
15	6	77	Stephan Gregoire	Chastain Motorsports	G/A/G	156.947	154	Electrical	20	166	12	$16,000	$0	$16,000
16	2	6	Scott Goodyear	Treadway Racing Nortel Quebecor	G/A/F	160.567	152	Engine	19	193	9	$37,000	$0	$37,000
17	12	14	Davey Hamilton	AJ Foyt Power Team Racing	G/A/G	154.377	121	Engine	18	244	2	$36,000	$0	$36,000
18	17	17 R	Affonso Giaffone	General Motors of Brazil Chitwood Dallara	D/A/G	152.242	93	Accident	17	139	15	$35,000	$0	$35,000
19	22	40	Dr. Jack Miller	AMS/Crest Racing	D/I/F	N/T	81	Handling	16	108	23	$34,000	$5,000	$39,000
20	1	70	Marco Greco	Monsoon Galles Racing	G/A/G	160.594	59	Oil Fitting	17 x	205	6	$11,000	$22,500	$33,500
21	13	12	Buzz Calkins	Bradley Food Marts	G/A/G	153.922	36	Electrical	14	197	8	$32,000	$0	$32,000
22	24	99 R	Sam Schmidt	HOPE Pre-paid Fuel Card Racing Special	D/A/F	N/T	30	Accident	13	68	27	$10,000	$0	$10,000
23	4	33 R	Jimmy Kite	Old Navy-Scandia-Royal Purple-Alta-Xcel	D/A/G	160.000	4	Accident	12	47	32	$32,000	$250	$32,250
24	21	27 R	Jim Guthrie	Jacuzzi Armour Golf Odyssey Golf ERTL Collectibles	D/A/F	145.518	0	Gearbox	11	155	13	$32,000	$0	$32,000
												$1,000,000	$120,000	$1,120,000

Time of Race: 1:46:50.574 **Average Speed:** 118.829 mph **Margin of Victory:** 0.064 sec.
Fastest Lap: #22 Vincenzo Sospiri (Lap 195, 153.315 mph) **Fastest Leading Lap:** #164 Eddie Cheever Jr. (Lap 164, 152.279 mph)
PPG Pole Winner: Marco Greco **True Value Pole Winning Chief Mechanic:** Darren Russell/Galles Racing International
MBNA America Lap Leader: #51 Eddie Cheever **Coors Pit Performance Winner:** #3 Robbie Buhl/Team Menard
Legend: R - Indy Racing League Rookie **Chassis Legend:** D - Dallara; G - G Force
Engine Legend: A - Oldsmobile Aurora; I - Nissan Infiniti **Tire Legend:** F - Firestone; G - Goodyear

Lap Leaders:

Lap-Lap	Driver	#
1-34	Marco Greco	#70
35-62	Scott Goodyear	#6
63-64	Eliseo Salazar	#7
65	John Paul Jr.	#4
66-95	Eliseo Salazar	#7
96-133	Eddie Cheever Jr.	#51
134-136	Scott Goodyear	#6

Lap-Lap	Driver	#
137-138	Arie Luyendyk	#5
139-145	Eliseo Salazar	#7
146-154	Kenny Brack	#4
155	Vincenzo Sospiri	#22
156-197	Eddie Cheever Jr.	#51
198-200	Robbie Buhl	#3

Caution Flags:

Laps	Reason/Incident
1-5	Spin #30 Groff, T4
7-10	Wall #33 Kite, S/F
34-39	Wall #99 Schmidt, T2
61-66	Spin #70 Greco, S/F
69-72	Spin #91 Lazier, S/F
95-102	Wall #17 Giaffone, T1
154-157	Tow-In #6 Goodyear

Total Caution Laps 37

Lap Leader Summary:

Driver	Times	Total
Eddie Cheever Jr.	2	80
Eliseo Salazar	3	39
Marco Greco	1	34
Scott Goodyear	2	31
Kenny Brack	1	9
Robbie Buhl	1	3
Arie Luyendyk	1	2
John Paul Jr.	1	1
Vincenzo Sospiri	1	1

1997 Official Box Score
Indy Racing League
Las Vegas Motor Speedway
October 11, 1997

FP	SP	CAR		DRIVER	CAR NAME	C/E/T	QUAL. SPEED	LAPS COMP	RUNNING/ REASON OUT	IRL PTS.	TOTAL IRL PTS.	IRL STANDINGS	IRL AWARDS	DESIGNATED AWARDS	TOTAL AWARDS
1	5	7		Eliseo Salazar	Copec/Cristal/Scandia	D/A/G	204.615	208	Running	36 y	208	9	$90,000	$43,500	$133,500
2	3	6		Scott Goodyear	Treadway Racing Nortel Quebecor Printing	G/A/F	203.489	208	Running	33	226	5	$75,000	$22,750	97,750
3	4	8		Robbie Buhl	Quaker State/Menards/Special	G/A/F	205.074	208	Running	32	170	13	$42,000	$6,250	48,250
4	19	27	R	Jim Guthrie	Jacuzzi/Keller Ladders/ERTL Collectibles	D/A/F	200.602	208	Running	31	186	12	$53,000	$11,750	64,750
5	9	28		Mark Dismore	Bombardier Aircraft Mechanics Laundry	D/A/G	203.443	208	Running	30	158	17	$49,000	$5,250	54,250
6	7	33	R	Jimmy Kite	Old Navy/Royal Purple/Scandia/Alta/Xcel	D/A/G	203.758	208	Running	29	76	27	$44,000	$250	44,250
7	2	14		Davey Hamilton	AJ Foyt Power Team Racing	G/A/G	205.300	207	Running	28	272	2	$43,000	$2,750	45,750
8	25	19	R	Stan Wattles	Metro Racing Systems / NCLD	R/A/G	197.542	206	Running	27	63	31	$20,000	$0	20,000
9	16	77		Stephan Gregoire	Chastain Motorsports	G/A/G	201.372	204	Running	26	192	11	$20,000	$2,250	22,250
10	10	70		Marco Greco	Monsoon Galles Racing	G/A/G	203.221	204	Running	25	230	3	$19,000	$2,250	21,250
11	3	2		Tony Stewart	Glidden/Menards/Special	G/A/F	205.113	204	Running	24	278	1	$40,000	$0	40,000
12	24	18		John Paul Jr.	Klipsch Overhead Door V-Line Earl's Perf Products	G/A/G	197.679	201	Running	23	163	15	$39,000	$1,000	40,000
13	26	21	R	Billy Roe	Roe Racing	D/A/F	196.951	198	Accident	22	55	34	$16,000	$250	16,250
14	18	24	R	Roberto Guerrero	Pennzoil/Pagan Racing Dallara-Aurora	D/A/G	200.714	197	Running	21	221	7	$37,000	$250	37,250
15	11	17	R	Affonso Giaffone	General Motors of Brazil Chitwood Dallara	D/A/G	202.916	193	Running	20	159	16	$36,000	$0	36,000
16	28	23	R	Mike Shank	Nienhouse Motorsports	R/A/G	191.918	191	Running	19	19	46	$13,000	$0	13,000
17	12	35		Jeff Ward	SRS/ISM Racing	D/A/G	202.680	168	Overheating	18	69	30	$12,000	$0	12,000
18	27	30	R	Robbie Groff	Fast Rod/Team Losi/McCormack Motorsports	G/A/G	195.893	168	Running	17	135	20	$34,000	$5,000	39,000
19	30	9		Johnny Unser	Delta Faucet Cinergy Hemelgarn Racing	D/I/F	NS	142	Engine	16	107	24	$11,000	$5,000	16,000
20	13	4	R	Kenny Brack	Monsoon Galles Racing	G/A/G	202.589	139	Suspension	15	139	19	$32,000	$0	32,000
21	29	51		Eddie Cheever Jr.	FirstPlus Team Cheever	G/A/G	NS	129	Engine	14	230	4	$31,000	$0	31,000
22	15	22		Vincenzo Sospiri	Old Navy/Royal Purple/Scandia/Alta/Xcel	D/A/G	201.568	114	Mechanical	13	134	21	$31,000	$0	31,000
23	1	1		Billy Boat	Conseco AJ Foyt Racing	D/A/G	207.413	97	Electrical	14 x	151	18	$31,000	$27,000	58,000
24	23	95		Tyce Carlson	IZ Racing/Keco Coatings	D/I/G	197.998	96	Ignition	11	84	25	$9,000	$0	9,000
25	6	5		Arie Luyendyk	WavePhore-Mi-Jack	G/A/F	204.460	72	Engine	10	223	6	$31,000	$0	31,000
26	31	10	R	Paul Durant	Jonathan Byrd's VisionAire Bryant Heating & Cooling	G/A/F	200.185	62	Mechanical	9	23	40	$31,000	$0	31,000
27	22	99	R	Sam Schmidt	BG Product/Keco Coatings Racing Special	D/A/F	198.231	60	Accident	8	76	28	$9,000	$0	9,000
28	21	12		Buzz Calkins	Bradley Food Marts	G/A/G	198.529	60	Accident	7	204	10	$31,000	$0	31,000
29	17	40		Dr. Jack Miller	AMS/Crest Racing	D/I/F	200.885	59	Accident	6	114	23	$31,000	$0	31,000
30	20	97		Greg Ray	TKM/Zali Racing	D/A/F	199.837	35	Accident	5	73	29	$9,000	$0	9,000
31	14	91	R	Buddy Lazier	Delta Faucet Xerox Hemelgarn Racing	D/A/F	202.240	4	Mechanical	4	209	8	$31,000	$0	31,000
													$1,000,000	$135,500	$1,135,500

Time of Race: 2:11:07 **Average Speed:** 142.757 mph **Margin of Victory:** 1.204 seconds
Fastest Lap: #1 Billy Boat (Lap 19, 204.360 mph) **Fastest Leading Lap:** #17 Affonso Giaffone (Lap 108, 201.801 mph)
PPG Pole Winner: Billy Boat **True Value Pole Winning Chief Mechanic:** Craig Baranouski/AJ Foyt Enterprises
MBNA America Lap Leader: #7 Eliseo Salazar **Coors Pit Performance Winner:** #6 Goodyear/Treadway Racing
Chassis Legend: D - Dallara; G - G Force **Engine Legend:** A - Oldsmobile Aurora; I - Nissan Infiniti **Tire Legend:** F - Firestone; G - Goodyear

Legend: R - Indy Racing League Rookie

Lap-Lap	Driver		Lap-Lap	Driver		Laps	Reason/Incident		Driver	Times	Total
1-3	#1 Billy Boat		121-122	#28 Mark Dismore		1-3	Cold & Wind		Eliseo Salazar	2	70
4	#14 Davey Hamilton		123-131	#27 Jim Guthrie		9-12	Tow-in #91 Lazier		Mark Dismore	2	45
5-45	#35 Jeff Ward		132-137	#4 Kenny Brack		38-43	Accident T2 #97 Ray		Jeff Ward	1	41
46-51	#3 Robbie Buhl		138-158	#7 Eliseo Salazar		64-71	Accident BS #99 Schmidt, #40 Miller, #12 Calkins		Affonso Giaffone	1	16
52-94	#28 Mark Dismore		159	#3 Robbie Buhl		118-125	Lost Wheel T2 #17 Giaffone		Robbie Buhl	1	12
95-99	#3 Robbie Buhl		160-208	#7 Eliseo Salazar		131-135	Mechanical #51 Cheever		Jim Guthrie	1	9
100-116	#17 Affonso Giaffone					158-163	Tow-in #9 Unser		Kenny Brack	1	6
116-120	#6 Scott Goodyear					201-204	Accident BS #21 Guerrero		Scott Goodyear	1	5
							44 - Total Caution Laps		Billy Boat	1	3
									Davey Hamilton	1	1

148

1996-97 IRL Season Statistics Recap
Indy Racing League

EVENT	RACE WINNER (SP)	MARGIN OF VICTORY	SECOND	LAP LEADERS DRIVERS	CHANGES	ON LEAD LAP	CAUTION FLAGS	LAPS	SIZE FIELD	CARS RAF	PPG POLE WINNER	QUAL. SPEED	FP
TRUE VALUE 200 (NHIS)	Scott Sharp (12)	20.4	Calkins	4	5	3	4	25	23	13	Richie Hearn	175.367	14
LAS VEGAS 500 (LVMS)	Richie Hearn (8)	1.693	Jourdain Jr.	5	10	2	9	83	28	13	Arie Luyendyk	226.491	20
INDY 200 (WDWS)	Eddie Cheever Jr. (5)	UC	M. Groff	3	3	5	3	12	19	9	Tony Stewart	166.013	10
PHOENIX 200 (PIR)	Jim Guthrie (2)	0.854	Stewart	5	10	3	9	86	22	9	Tony Stewart	170.012	2
INDY 500 (IMS)	Arie Luyendyk (1)	0.57	Goodyear	7	17	5	15	62	35	13	Arie Luyendyk	218.827	1
TRUE VALUE 500 (TMS)	Arie Luyendyk (11)	UC	Boat	9	14	1	8	59	26	13	Tony Stewart	167.133*	5
SAMSONITE 200 (PPIR)	Tony Stewart (2)	0.222	Gregoire	4	6	7	9	82	22	12	Scott Sharp	176.117*	22
VISIONAIRE 500 (CMS)	Buddy Lazier (5)	3.301	Boat	6	13	2	4	27	23	13	Tony Stewart	217.164*	7
PENZOIL 200 (NHIS)	Robbie Buhl (7)	0.064	Sospiri	9	12	6	7	37	24	12	Marco Greco	160.594	20
LAS VEGAS 500 (LVMS)	Eliseo Salazar (5)	1.204	Goodyear	10	13	6	8	44	31	15	Billy Boat	207.413	23

* New track record

1996-97 Top 10 Leading Driver Money*

	Driver	Money
1	Arie Luyendyk	$2,079,150
2	Tony Stewart	1,090,450
3	Scott Goodyear	953,350
4	Davey Hamilton	785,950
5	Buddy Lazier	736,550
6	Eddie Cheever Jr.	725,400
7	Jim Guthrie	627,200
8	Billy Boat	604,150
9	Roberto Guerrero	601,000
10	Buzz Calkins	599,750

*Does not include Championship Prize Money

Indy Racing League Awards

Pole Awards

Driver	Pole Wins
Tony Stewart	4
Arie Luyendyk	2
Scott Sharp	1
Marco Greco	1
Billy Boat	1
Richie Hearn	1

TrueValue. Pole Winning Chief Mechanics

Team	Pole Wins
Team Menard, Inc.	4
Treadway Racing	2
AJ Foyt Enterprises	2
Galles Racing International	1
Della Penna Motorsports	1

Lap Leaders

Top 5 Drivers		Total Laps Led
1	Tony Stewart	812
2	Buddy Lazier	122
3	Arie Luyendyk	120
4	Eliseo Salazar	112
5	Richie Hearn	96

Pit Stop Challenge

Teams		
#5	Treadway Racing	TMS
#2	Team Menard	PPIR
#51	FirstPlus Team Cheever	CMS
#3	Team Menard	NHIS
#6	Treadway Racing	LVMS

Based on the performance after the 1997 Indianapolis 500 through 1998 Phoenix 200.

Teams will qualify to compete in the $70,000 Coors Pit Stop Competition in Indianapolis.

Total Laps Completed

Driver		Total Laps
1	Davey Hamilton	1,806
2	Tony Stewart	1,794
3	Marco Greco	1,554
4	Roberto Guerrero	1,493
5	Eddie Cheever Jr.	1,485

Total after 10 races - 1,973

Indy Racing League Awards

INDY RACING LEAGUE

Rookie Points

	Drivers	Points
1	Jim Guthrie	186
2	Affonso Giaffone	159
3	Billy Boat	151
4	Kenny Brack	139
5	Robbie Groff	135
6	Vincenzo Sospiri	134
7	Dr. Jack Miller	114
8	Tyce Carlson	84
9	Fermin Velez	82
10	Jimmy Kite	76
11	Sam Schmidt	76

Rookie Points

	Drivers	Points
12	Greg Ray	73
13	Jeff Ward	69
14	Stan Wattles	63
15	Billy Roe	55
16	Jeret Schroeder	37
17	Brad Murphey	25
18	Paul Durant	23
19	Steve Kinser	21
20	Mike Shank	19
21	J.C. Carbonell	16
22	Joe Gosek	14
23	Allen May	13

Engine Manufacturer

	Engine	Points
1	Oldsmobile Aurora	88
2	Nissan Infiniti	56
3	Ford Cosworth	22
4	Menard V6	11
5	Buick	11

Leading Driver Points

	Driver	Points
1	Tony Stewart	278
2	Davey Hamilton	272
3	Marco Greco	230
4	Eddie Cheever Jr.	230
5	Scott Goodyear	226

Leading Driver Money

	Driver	Money
1	Arie Luyendyk	$2,079,150
2	Tony Stewart	1,090,450
3	Scott Goodyear	953,350
4	Davey Hamilton	785,950
5	Buddy Lazier	736,550

1996-97 IRL Season Entrant Point Standings Indy Racing League

	CAR	ENTRANT	POINTS	MULT.	TOTAL PTS.
1	2	Team Menard, Inc.	278	10	2,780
2	14	AJ Foyt Enterprises	272	10	2,720
3	1	AJ Foyt Enterprises	240	10	2,400
4	10	Jonathan Byrd-Cunningham Racing	239	10	2,390
5	22	Team Scandia	236	10	2,360
6	51	FirstPlus Team Cheever	230	10	2,300
7	6	Treadway Racing, LLC	249	9	2,241
8	5	Treadway Racing, LLC	223	10	2,230
9	21	Pagan Racing	221	10	2,210
10	33	Team Scandia	220	10	2,200
11	18	PDM Racing, Inc.	216	10	2,160
12	91	Hemelgarn Racing, Inc.	209	10	2,090
13	30	McCormack Motorsports	208	10	2,080
14	12	Bradley Motorsports	204	9	1,836
15	40	Arizona Motorsports	168	10	1,680
16	27	Blueprint Racing, Inc.	186	9	1,674
17	7	Team Scandia	208	8	1,664
18	28	PDM Racing, Inc.	161	8	1,288
19	4	Galles Racing International	158	8	1,264
20	17	Chitwood Motorsports, Inc.	156	8	1,248
21	3	Team Menard, Inc.	163	7	1,141
22	77	Chastain Motorsports	156	7	1,092
23	97	Thomas Knapp Motorsports	73	5	365
24	70	Galles Racing International	90	4	360
25	9	Hemelgarn Racing, Inc.	58	4	232
26	16	Blueprint Racing, Inc.	45	4	180
27	54	Beck Motorsports	60	3	180
28	8	Team Scandia	53	3	159
29	44	Sinden Racing Service	52	23	156
30	34	Team Scandia	49	3	147
31	74	Della Penna Motorsports	59	2	118
32	99	LP Racing, Inc./PCI	38	3	114
33	15	Tempero/Giuffre Racing	34	2	68
34	50	Eurointernational Inc.	33	2	66
35	52	FirstPlus Team Cheever	32	1	32
36	11	AJ Foyt Enterprises	28	1	28
37	19	Metro Racing Systems, Inc.	27	1	27
38	90	LSJ Racing/Hemelgarn Racing, Inc.	22	1	22
39	24	Roe Racing	22	1	22
40	43	Walker Racing	21	1	21
41	23	Nienhouse Motorsports	19	1	19
42	96	ABF Motorsports, L.L.C.	14	1	14
43	64	Project Indy L.P.	13	1	13
44	95	IZ Racing, Inc.-Zali Racing Corporation	11	1	11
45	42	Team Sabco	6	1	6
46	72	Blueprint Racing, Inc.	5	1	5
47	35	SRS/ISM Racing	18	1	18

Statistically Speaking

Lap Prize Leaders

1	Emerson Fittipaldi**	.$227,250
2	Mario Andretti*	.199,350
3	Michael Andretti	.171,900
4	Rick Mears****	.144,450
5	Al Unser****	.123,200
6	A.J. Foyt Jr****	.97,716
7	Bobby Unser***	.82,597
8	Parnelli Jones*	.75,050
9	Danny Sullivan*	.72,900
10	Gordon Johncock**	.67,273

Lap Leaders

1	Al Unser****	.644
2	Ralph DePalma*	.612
3	Mario Andretti*	.556
4	A.J. Foyt Jr****	.555
5	Wilbur Shaw***	.508
6	Emerson Fittipaldi**	.505
7	Parnelli Jones*	.492
8	Bill Vukovich**	.485
9	Bobby Unser***	.440
10	Rick Mears****	.429

Total Money Winners

1	Arie Luyendyk**	.$5,027,329
2	Rick Mears****	.4,299,392
3	Al Unser Jr**	.4,262,690
4	Emerson Fittipaldi**	.4,042,767
5	Al Unser****	.3,378,018
6	Bobby Rahal*	.2,789,596
7	Mario Andretti*	.2,766,931
8	A.J. Foyt Jr****	.2,637,963
9	Roberto Guerrero	.2,338,763
10	Michael Andretti	.2,287,921

Mileage Leaders

1	A.J. Foyt Jr****	.12,272.5
2	Al Unser****	.10,890.0
3	Gordon Johncock**	.7,895.0
4	Mario Andretti*	.7,625.0
5	Johnny Rutherford***	.6,980.0
6	Bobby Unser***	.6,527.5
7	Cliff Bergere	.6,145.0
8	Lloyd Ruby	.6,097.5
9	Mauri Rose***	.6,040.0
10	Rick Mears****	.5,855.0

Number of Races

1	A.J. Foyt Jr****	.35
2	Mario Andretti*	.29
3	Al Unser****	.27
4	Johnny Rutherford***	.24
5	Gordon Johncock**	.24
6	George Snider	.22
7	Gary Bettenhausen	.21
8	Bobby Unser***	.19
9	Lloyd Ruby	.18
10	Roger McCluskey	.18
11	Tom Sneva*	.18

500 AAA/USAC Point Leaders

1	Al Unser****	.11,000
2	A.J. Foyt Jr****	.10,190
3	Rick Mears****	.7,375
4	Gordon Johncock**	.6,910
5	Wilbur Shaw***	.6,370
6	Bobby Unser***	.6,170
7	Ted Horn	.6,000
8	Louis Meyer***	.5,784
9	Mauri Rose***	.5,581
10	Al Unser Jr**	.5,550

Each * = One Indy 500 Win

153

1996-97 IRL Season Driver Performance Indy Racing League

DRIVER	EVENT	NHIS SP/FP	LVMS SP/FP	WDW SP/FP	PIR SP/FP	IMS SP/FP	TMS SP/FP	PPIR SP/FP	CMS SP/FP	NHIS SP/FP	LVMS SP/FP
Alboreto, Michele		2/ 3	18/ 5	—/—	—/—	—/—	—/—	—/—	—/—	—/—	—/—
Boat, Billy		—/—	—/—	—/—	—/—	22/ 7	21/ 2	15/19	3/ 2	16/ 8	1/23
Bourbonnais, Claude		—/—	—/—	—/—	—/—	32/30	—/—	—/—	—/—	—/—	—/—
Brack, Kenny		—/—	—/—	—/—	9/11	15/33	3/18	6/14	18/ 5	3/ 5	13/20
Buhl, Robbie		13/22	15/ 8	—/—	5/18	4/ 8	2/16	—/—	—/—	7/ 1	4/ 3
Calkins, Buzz		10/ 2	16/ 6	3/11	22/ 8	16/11	10/19	7/ 5	—/—	13/21	21/28
Carbonnell, J.C.		—/—	28/19	—/—	—/—	—/—	—/—	—/—	—/—	—/—	—/—
Carlson, Tyce		16/11	14/23	—/—	—/—	26/19	25/14	—/—	—/—	—/—	23/24
Cheever Jr., Eddie		8/15	27/25	5/ 1	7/12	11/23	7/ 6	13/ 4	15/ 6	18/ 9	29/21
Dismore, Mark		5/20	10/17	—/—	—/—	25/28	14/11	21/11	10/19	23/11	9/ 5
Durant, Paul		—/—	—/—	—/—	—/—	33/21	—/—	—/—	—/—	—/—	31/26
Giaffone, Affonso		—/—	23/10	—/—	21/13	14/32	16/20	10/ 9	16/ 4	17/18	11/15
Goodyear, Scott		—/—	—/—	6/ 3	3/17	5/ 2	5/ 4	3/ 7	8/ 3	2/16	8/ 2
Gordon, Robby		—/—	3/14	—/—	—/—	12/29	—/—	—/—	—/—	—/—	—/—
Gosek, Joe		21/21	—/—	—/—	—/—	—/—	—/—	—/—	—/—	—/—	—/—
Greco, Marco		15/ 7	24/ 9	12/ 8	8/ 4	27/16	12/26	22/13	11/ 9	1/20	10/10
Gregoire, Stephan		14/ 8	25/26	19/19	19/ 5	13/31	—/—	11/ 2	9/ 8	6/15	16/ 9
Groff, Mike		9/ 4	6/ 3	14/ 2	16/ 6	18/12	—/—	—/—	22/14	—/—	—/—
Groff, Robbie		—/—	—/—	—/—	—/—	21/ 9	13/15	16/10	20/13	19/10	27/18
Guerrero, Roberto		18/ 6	9/ 4	17/17	10/ 7	19/27	15/13	5/18	7/17	10/ 6	18/14
Guthrie, Jim		19/23	19/13	9/ 6	2/ 1	6/26	8/21	—/—	6/12	21/24	19/ 4
Hamilton, Davey		17/ 5	5/11	7/ 7	14/ 3	8/ 6	9/ 3	4/ 3	4/16	12/17	2/ 7
Harrington, Scott		—/—	—/—	—/—	—/—	—/—	—/—	—/—	—/—	—/—	—/—
Hearn, Richie		1/14	8/ 1	—/—	—/—	—/—	—/—	—/—	—/—	—/—	—/—
Jourdain Jr., Michel		—/—	22/ 2	—/—	—/—	—/—	—/—	—/—	—/—	—/—	—/—
Kinser, Steve		—/—	—/—	—/—	—/—	20/14	—/—	—/—	—/—	—/—	—/—
Kite, Jimmy		—/—	—/—	—/—	—/—	—/—	—/—	9/20	13/15	4/23	7/ 6
Kudrave, David		22/17	—/—	—/—	—/—	—/—	—/—	—/—	—/—	—/—	—/—
Lazier, Buddy		4/19	4/24	11/ 5	13/21	10/ 4	4/17	12/ 8	5/ 1	15/12	14/31
Luyendyk, Arie		3/13	1/20	2/12	4/22	1/ 1	11/ 1	8/15	2/21	8/ 3	6/25
May, Allen		—/—	—/—	—/—	—/—	—/—	18/22	—/—	—/—	—/—	—/—
Miller, Dr. Jack		—/—	—/—	18/15	18/20	17/20	19/24	20/16	19/23	22/19	17/29
Murphey, Brad		23/18	26/27	—/—	—/—	—/—	—/—	—/—	—/—	—/—	—/—
O'Connell, Johnny		—/—	11/12	—/—	—/—	—/—	—/—	—/—	—/—	—/—	—/—
Ongais, Danny		—/—	—/—	16/13	—/—	—/—	—/—	—/—	—/—	—/—	—/—
Parsons, Johnny		—/—	17/28	—/—	—/—	—/—	—/—	—/—	—/—	—/—	—/—
Paul Jr., John		11/10	12/15	13/18	11/ 9	—/—	—/—	—/—	21/11	11/ 7	24/12
Ray, Greg		—/—	—/—	—/—	—/—	30/25	6/ 8	17/17	17/22	—/—	20/30
Roe, Billy		—/—	—/—	—/—	17/15	24/22	—/—	—/—	—/—	—/—	26/13
Salazar, Eliseo		6/ 9	13/ 7	—/—	—/—	9/24	22/ 7	14/12	14/10	5/ 4	5/ 1
Schmidt, Sam		—/—	—/—	—/—	6/10	23/34	20/23	—/—	23/18	24/22	22/27
Schroeder, Jeret		—/—	—/—	15/14	12/19	—/—	—/—	—/—	—/—	—/—	—/—
Shank, Mike		—/—	—/—	—/—	—/—	—/—	—/—	—/—	—/—	—/—	28/16
Sharp, Scott		12/ 1	7/16	4/ 4	20/16	—/—	—/—	1/22	—/—	—/—	—/—
Sospiri, Vincenzo		—/—	—/—	—/—	—/—	3/17	17/ 9	18/ 6	12/20	9/ 2	15/22
St. James, Lyn		—/—	—/—	—/—	—/—	34/13	—/—	—/—	—/—	—/—	—/—
Stewart, Tony		7/12	2/21	1/10	1/ 2	2/ 5	1/ 5	2/ 1	1/ 7	14/14	3/11
Unser, Johnny		—/—	20/22	—/—	—/—	35/18	23/10	19/21	—/—	20/13	30/19
Velez, Fermin		—/—	—/—	10/ 9	15/14	29/10	24/25	—/—	—/—	—/—	—/—
Vitolo, Dennis		—/—	—/—	—/—	—/—	28/15	—/—	—/—	—/—	—/—	—/—
Ward, Jeff		—/—	—/—	8/16	—/—	7/ 3	—/—	—/—	—/—	—/—	12/17
Wattles, Stan		20/16	21/18	—/—	—/—	—/—	—/—	—/—	—/—	—/—	25/ 8
Zampedri, Alessandro		—/—	—/—	—/—	—/—	31/35	26/12	—/—	—/—	—/—	—/—

1996-97 IRL Season Driver Point Standings Indy Racing League

	DRIVER		NO. OF STARTS	RUNNING AT FINISH	HIGHEST FINISH	LAPS LED	LAPS COMPLETED	TOTAL POINTS	TOTAL AWARDS*
1	Tony Stewart		10	5	1	812	1,794	278	$1,090,450
2	Davey Hamilton		10	8	3	5	1,806	272	785,950
3	Marco Greco		10	7	4	34	1,554	230	554,850
4	Eddie Cheever Jr.		10	5	1	89	1,485	230	725,400
5	Scott Goodyear		8	6	2	40	1,375	226	953,350
6	Arie Luyendyk		10	4	1	120	1,294	223	2,079,150
7	Roberto Guerrero		10	5	4	26	1,493	221	601,000
8	Buddy Lazier		10	5	1	122	1,243	209	736,550
9	Eliseo Salazar		8	7	1	112	1,459	208	586,650
10	Buzz Calkins		9	4	2	14	1,310	204	599,750
11	Stephan Gregoire		9	5	2	5	1,180	192	410,550
12	Jim Guthrie	(R)	9	5	1	89	1,060	186	627,200
13	Robbie Buhl		7	4	1	31	1,020	170	528,400
14	Mike Groff		6	6	2	0	1,106	169	562,850
15	John Paul Jr.		7	6	7	23	1,183	163	346,850
16	Affonso Giaffone	(R)	8	4	4	29	1,074	159	397,500
17	Mark Dismore		8	4	5	45	1,113	158	433,300
18	Billy Boat	(R)	6	4	2	51	993	151	604,150
19	Kenny Brack	(R)	7	2	5	33	987	139	419,200
20	Robbie Groff	(R)	6	3	9	3	1,118	135	441,450
21	Vincenzo Sospiri	(R)	6	4	2	1	951	134	432,100
22	Scott Sharp		5	2	1	22	582	119	324,150
23	Dr. Jack Miller	(R)	8	0	15	0	567	114	439,100
24	Johnny Unser		6	2	10	0	782	107	318,150
25	Tyce Carlson	(R)	5	2	11	0	676	84	315,050
26	Fermin Velez	(R)	4	2	9	0	437	82	345,150
27	Jimmy Kite	(R)	4	1	6	11	414	76	155,000
28	Sam Schmidt	(R)	6	0	10	0	416	76	224,700
29	Greg Ray	(R)	5	1	8	0	425	73	238,300
30	Jeff Ward	(R)	3	1	3	90	431	69	449,150
31	Stan Wattles	(R)	3	1	8	0	488	63	92,000
32	Michele Alboreto		2	2	3	0	397	62	137,250
33	Richie Hearn		2	1	1	96	366	59	181,000
34	Billy Roe	(R)	3	1	13	0	390	55	185,700
35	Jeret Schroeder	(R)	2	0	14	0	144	37	81,500
36	Michel Jourdain Jr.		1	1	2	0	200	33	95,250
37	Robby Gordon		2	0	14	60	198	27	156,500
38	Brad Murphey	(R)	2	0	18	0	105	25	47,000
39	Alessandro Zampedri		2	1	12	0	201	24	167,150
40	Paul Durant	(R)	2	0	21	0	173	23	209,000
41	Johnny O'Connell		1	0	12	3	183	23	22,000
42	Lyn St. James		1	0	13	0	186	22	188,000
43	Danny Ongais		1	0	13	0	94	22	24,500
44	Steve Kinser	(R)	1	0	14	0	185	21	193,250
45	Dennis Vitolo		1	1	15	0	173	20	200,000
46	Mike Shank	(R)	1	1	0	0	191	19	13,000
47	David Kudrave		1	0	17	0	118	18	14,000
48	J.C. Carbonell	(R)	1	0	19	0	112	16	34,000
49	Joe Gosek	(R)	1	0	21	0	30	14	10,000
50	Allen May	(R)	1	0	22	0	36	13	13,700
51	Johnny Parsons		1	0	28	0	7	7	10,000
52	Claude Bourbonnais	(R)	1	0	30	0	9	5	152,250
									$18,952,450

*Doesn't include Championship Prize Money

1996-97 IRL Championship

By Jan Shaffer

INDY RACING LEAGUE

The Indy Racing League's second season is now history. At this writing, only an awards banquet remains to close the book before attention turns to Walt Disney World and the dawn of another campaign.

So, what did we see during the 1996–97 season? Nine different winners in 10 races. The successful development of a brand new car/engine package. Arie Luyendyk extending his reputation as an "ovalmeister" by winning his second Indianapolis 500. A championship battle between close friends Tony Stewart and Davey Hamilton going down to the wire in the desert of Las Vegas.

But there were many, many, other facets and people who played roles in the continuing growth process of the world's newest premier racing series.

Each victory had its own unique story. Take Eddie Cheever Jr., in his first race as an owner/driver, claiming victory at Walt Disney World, spouting spirited one-liners about his dual role. At Phoenix, after Jim Guthrie had "maxed out" his credit cards to field a car, he went the final 82 laps without a pit stop and outfought Stewart for the win in Cinderella fashion. And at the close of the season, Eliseo Salazar got his first IRL triumph and the first for Team Scandia and veteran owner/driver engineer Dick Simon.

There were other, less known elements that made up the season and formed the character of the series, the undeniable qualities of human chemistry that have become the soul of the IRL.

It started on a chilly week in Phoenix, when Treadway Racing and Arie Luyendyk put the first G Force with an Oldsmobile Aurora engine on the track for the first time. It continued in Orlando, where Leo Mehl traveled to meet with the troops he would lead throughout 1997. During race week, he gathered up all the teams in uniform and parked their cars on the front straightaway for a group photo—the cast which would shape the IRL's second season.

The magic of the "500" was alive and well at 16th and Georgetown. The day before the "500" word traveled to those attending FanFest that some cars might actually get on the track. As the

157

The sessions reached full force at Charlotte, when countless fans poured out of the stands on the front straightaway for autographs and a close look at the IRL cars during a break in an open test. Crewmen said later that they knew these were real race fans by the questions they asked. The belief that stock car fans wouldn't warm up to anything without fenders disappeared forever.

Another myth was dispelled previously at Charlotte's sister track in Texas. Indy-style cars had not run on 1 1/2-mile, high-banked stock car tracks since the early 1980s. It was thought that they couldn't. And when stock-car drivers complained about the new track in Texas, it raised eyebrows further.

But the IRL cars ran three-wide at times in Texas. Buddy Lazier and Stewart ran side-by-side for two and a half laps in a furious battle for the lead. Fans stood throughout the race watching the faster, more maneuverable Indy machines putting on a different kind of show than their stock car brethren.

There were other memorable moments, including Steve Kinser coming to Indianapolis and Paul Durant qualifying a Foyt car for the "500" just 52 minutes after sitting down in it. Few will forget

Pole sitter Tony Stewart (#2) and Arie Luyendyk (#5) set to pace the Indy 200 at Walt Disney World, sporting new engines and chassis.

Above: Brothers Robbie (left) and Mike Groff wish each other good luck before the 81st Indy 500.

Right: Rookie Billy Roe signs a few autographs for some young Indy fans.

rumor spread, people started drifting into the Tower Terrace stands. A few hours later, there were thousands waiting. A handful of drivers and teams were allowed a few laps each for a systems check after major changes. When the engines were fired, the crowd cheered mightily because cars were on the track at Indy.

One emotional moment was when John Paul Jr. received the first Scott Brayton Driver's Trophy but was not able to make the show because of injuries.

At autograph sessions IRL drivers reached out to the public in a way that hadn't been seen in the sport for many years. Incidentally, it had been veteran drivers like Luyendyk and Roberto Guerrero who had suggested the sessions in January of 1996 at Walt Disney World as a way to help build the series.

Chastain crewman Mike Smith holding the pit board high at Pikes Peak with "P1" on it, when Stephan Gregoire took the lead for a team that operated out of the garage beside the owner's home, or Mark Dismore qualifying with a Riley & Scott chassis at Loudon, and Stan Wattles completing the first racing lap for the American-built car at Las Vegas.

Fans will remember rookie Jeff Ward nearly winning the "500" and Vincenzo Sospiri coming from Formula One to the front row at Indy, the boundless enthusiasm of Jimmy Kite, and Robbie Buhl winning on his home turf. Let's not forget Billy Boat getting his chance, finishing seventh at Indy, second twice, and getting the pole at Vegas, or the professionalism and class of Scott Goodyear, Scott Sharp, Lyn St. James, and Buzz Calkins, the ever-present smile of Kenny Brack and his "record" of the longest tow-in in Indianapolis history when he didn't drop the tow line at his pit; or impressive newcomers like Greg Ray and Affonso Giaffone; and the competitive desire of Mike Groff.

Then there was Dr. Jack Miller working with the Infiniti, Robbie Groff and the McCormack team forging a solid bond with a low budget, and Johnny Unser as everyone's relief pitcher—Tyce Carlson, too. And Marco Greco getting a pole, Alessandro Zampedri coming back, his team-mates applauding as he walked unaided to pit road from Gasoline Alley on a cold March day at Indy, and Sam Schmidt and Larry Nash forming a team.

Let's switch to McGilvery's West, a westside Indianapolis watering hole. It is three days after the season closing at Las Vegas. It is the night that Autosport '97, hosted by Don Kay and Rodger Ward Jr. is broadcast on WQFE radio in nearby Brownsburg.

On this night, IRL executives and officials Fred Nation, Brian Barnhart, and Phil Casey are the

Al Unser, Davey Hamilton and Tony Stewart relaxed during a down time at the track.

Dr. Jack Miller (#40), Scott Goodyear (#6) and Jimmy Kite (#33) race under the light at Charlotte Motor Speedway.

guests on the radio show recapping the season.

Nearby, other discussions are taking place. A regular named Forry is talking about sitting next to Tony Stewart's mother in the stands at Vegas. Another talks about meeting a fan named Clarence, who attended his 50th straight Indianapolis 500 this year and has been to every IRL race. And Mark McClanahan, who served on the press crew at Vegas, talks about interviewing Roberto Guerrero.

Luke Wethington, team manager for Team Scandia, is there. So is chassis man Jackie Howerton, Dick Simon, Mike Devin, and others. It's a gathering of racing personalities.

Dick Jordan, USAC's news bureau director, walks up and introduces Todd Thomas, a young USAC midget regular.

"I'm really looking forward to being with you guys someday," Todd said.

Someday, in our new family called the Indy Racing League, he probably will.

Marco Greco (#70) won his first career pole at the Pennzoil 200 at New Hampshire Int'l Speedway.

159

Photo Credits

Autographs